W9-BZJ-209

THE SPANISH CIVIL WAR

DAVID MITCHELL

THE SPANISH CIVIL WAR

BASED ON THE TELEVISION SERIES

GRANADA
London Toronto Sydney New York

Granada Publishing Limited
Frogmore, St Albans, Herts AL2 2NF
and
36 Golden Square, London W1R 4AH
515 Madison Avenue, New York, NY 10022, USA
117 York Street, Sydney, NSW 2000, Australia
100 Skyway Avenue, Rexdale, Ontario M9W 3A6, Canada
61 Beach Road, Auckland, New Zealand

Published by Granada Publishing 1982

Picture research by Annabel Davies

British Library Cataloguing in Publication Data

Mitchell, David
The Spanish Civil War.
1. Spain—History—Civil War, 1936–1939
I. Title
946.081 DP269

ISBN 0-246-11916-0

Printed in Great Britain by
William Clowes (Beccles) Limited,
Beccles and London

Granada ®
Granada Publishing ®

CONTENTS

FOREWORD

As a young journalist in 1936 Mario Neves was an eye-witness to one of the Spanish Civil War's most horrific massacres, which took place at Badajoz. He was so disturbed by what he saw that he swore never to return to the town.

In May 1982, however, he stood on the walls above Badajoz and told the Granada TV film crew: 'In my whole life as a journalist the events at Badajoz were the most traumatic, and I would like to have forgotten them forever. I have agreed to come here because I feel it is my duty, as a witness to those facts, to disclose them. We meet young people in Badajoz who knew that terrible things had happened, their families had disappeared, but they did not know why. Here is your television and here I am to tell what happened then. That tragic memory should not be erased.'

The value of this book's contribution to popular understanding of the human conflict in Spain's Civil War lies in its extensive use of eye-witness accounts of mainly Spanish people who lived through it. For these stories, it draws on nearly a hundred interviews filmed for the Granada TV series 'The Spanish Civil War'.

In spite of television's appetite for human drama and historical documentary there has never been, until now, a major television series devoted to the Spanish Civil War. In view of the war's place in the twentieth century, this seems surprising. After all, it is a key landmark in modern history. It was one of Europe's greatest social and political upheavals; indeed, it precipitated the most profound (albeit unsuccessful) revolution since the Russian Revolution of 1917. A tremendous amount of literature – political, historical, intellectual, poetic – flowed from the conflict. The passions of the war inspired a generation of writers, and yet the story has never found full expression on television, in Britain or elsewhere.

Such partial treatments as have appeared have tended to focus on the brave motivations of the International Brigade or to represent the war as pivotal in the profound disillusionment of a generation who had thought that communism represented a liberating alternative to the epidemic of fascism in the Europe of the 1930s. Other treatments have served to maintain romantic myths of Spain as 'the cause'. Whatever their merits, none of them has looked at the war in its overall context as above all a Spanish issue, with essentially Spanish origins, fought mainly by Spaniards who, on both sides, actually resisted the foreign influences which threatened to project the conflict beyond Spain's borders, and perhaps into premature World War II.

There is a practical explanation for this tunnel vision of TV documentary makers. Until the death of General Franco and the restoration of democracy in 1975 many Spaniards had been too frightened to recall the trauma of those years themselves or to recount their own experiences on camera. Much unique and fascinating contemporary film was locked up in government-controlled archives, so TV documentary-makers were restricted to 'official' history or used recycled archive footage from propaganda films. Only over the last few years has the veil of silence and suppression lifted, and therefore only recently have Spaniards on all sides been able to tell their story, their way.

Granada Television's series of six one-hour programmes seized the opportunity to capture that momentous period of European history, while the eye-witnesses were still alive and the archive film became available. The series, and hence this book, owes its existence to those witnesses. Even now, when the threat of imprisonment has faded away, opponents of Franco can be privately persecuted in their own towns and villages for their views. Even if they are now legally free to recount the part they played in Spain's upheaval, it has taken a great deal of courage to speak. On both sides, the memories must be unbearably painful; the war was intensely bitter and unremittingly brutal. Almost without exception our witnesses lost parents, husbands, wives, daughters and sons. Many have had to live the last forty years in exile, some in the knowledge that the ideals they had fought for were lost and betrayed. Those who remained in Spain, even if they were 'Franquistas', have lived their lives under a regime of physical and cultural repression that did so much to obscure the truth of those years. Their frankness now, in spite of the past, is remarkable. Granada would like to take this opportunity to recognize their contribution with deepest respect.

John Blake and David Hart,
producers of 'The Spanish Civil War'

PICTURE CREDITS

The publishers would like to thank the following for providing the illustrations on the pages listed below; *black and white:* Alfonso, Madrid: Title page, p. 5 right, p. 29, p. 45, p. 49, p. 52, p. 81 bottom, p. 122, p. 158, p. 160, p. 191; Ampliaciones y Reproducciones Mas, Barcelona: p. 58, p. 91, p. 110, p. 116 left; Associated Press, London: p. 44, p. 60, p. 83, p. 121, p. 124; Ignacio de Azaola Reyes, Bilbao: p. 66 top, p. 66 middle, p. 66 bottom; Bill Bailey, San Francisco: p. 167; Brandeis University, Boston: p. 75 left, p. 78, p. 166 top; Centelles, Barcelona: p. 25, p. 39, p. 40 top, p. 40 bottom, p. 43, p. 50 top right, p. 50 bottom, p. 51, p. 64, p. 127, p. 129 left, p. 129 right, p. 134, p. 137, p. 141, p. 144, p. 146, p. 148, p. 154 top, p. 154 bottom, p. 155, p. 173, p. 174, p. 187, p. 188; René Dazy, Paris: p. 71 left; Enimedia, Paris: p. 116 right; Fox Photos, London: p. 183, p. 184 bottom, p. 194; Granada Television, Manchester: p. 3; Illustrated London News, London: p. 36, p. 37, p. 99, p. 171 right; Imperial War Museum, London: p. 75 right, p. 156; Instituto Municipal de Historia, Barcelona: p. 8, p. 14, p. 50 top left, p.81 top left, p. 81 top right, p. 126, p. 139, p. 149, p. 150; Keystone Press, London: p. 53, p. 162; Jesús Lozano, Madrid: p. 87, p. 94, p. 100, p. 102, p. 106, p. 112, p. 113, p. 114 left, p. 114 right, p. 166 bottom; Medios de Comunicación Social del Estado, Madrid: Facing page 1, p. 13, p. 20 left, p. 20 right, p. 24, p. 27, p. 103, p. 125, p. 165; Gonzalo Menéndez Pidal, Madrid: p. 18; Juan Manuel Molina, Barcelona: p. 9; Teresa Pamies, Barcelona: p. 175; Popperfoto, London: p. 5 left, p. 11 top, p. 22, p. 38, p. 180, p. 186; Salmer, Barcelona: p. 107, p. 133; Josep Taradellas, Barcelona: p. 42; Carlos Saenz de Tejada, Madrid: p. 119 left, p. 119 right; Ediciones Urbión, Madrid: p. 62; Eugenio Vegas Latapie, Madrid: p. 11 bottom; Roger Viollet, Paris: p. 73, p. 184 top; *colour:* Ediciones Urbión, Madrid: opposite pages 48, 81 right, 144 top right, 145, 176, 177 bottom; Salmer, Barcelona: opposite page 49; Fundación Figueras, Centre d'Estudis d' Història Contemporània, Barcelona: opposite pages 80, 81 top left and bottom, 144 bottom, 177 top; Oronoz, Barcelona: opposite page 144 top left.

POLITICAL GLOSSARY

CEDA (Confederación Española de Derechas Autónomas) – composite right-wing Catholic party, founded 1933.

CNT (Confederación Nacional de Trabajo) – anarcho-syndicalist trades union, founded 1911 in Barcelona.

ERC (Esquerra Republicana de Catalunya) – Catalan Left Republican nationalist party, founded 1931.

FAI (Federación Anarquista Ibérica) – federation of militant anarchist groups, a kind of ideological vanguard to the CNT, founded 1927.

FIJL (Federación Ibérica de Juventudes Libertarias) – Libertarian or Anarchist Youth movement.

Izquierda Republicana – Left Republican Party, formed 1934 from four earlier social-democratic groups.

JONS (Juntas de Ofensiva Nacional-Sindicalista) – fascist group, founded 1931, merged with the Falange 1934.

JSU (Juventudes Socialistas Unificadas) – Unified Socialist Youth, formed 1936 from separate socialist and Communist youth movements.

PCE (Partido Comunista de España) – official Communist party, founded 1921.

POUM (Partido Obrero de Unificación Marxista) – revolutionary, anti-Stalinist Communist party, formed 1935 with fusion of two splinter groups, the BOC (Workers and Peasants Bloc) led by Joaquin Maurin and the Izquierda Comunista (Left Communist party) led by Andrés Nin.

PNV (Partido Nacionalista Vasco) – main Basque Nationalist party, founded 1895.

PSOE (Partido Socialista Obrero Español) – Spanish Socialist party, founded 1879.

PSUC (Partido Socialista Unificado de Cataluña) – United Catalan Socialist party, formed 1936 from several socialist and Communist groups, affiliated to the Comintern, and in effect the Communist party in Catalonia.

UGT (Unión General de Trabajadores) – Socialist trade union.

UME (Unión Militar Española) – right-wing army officers' group.

UMRA (Unión Militar Republicana Antifascista) – Republican army officers' group.

CHRONOLOGY OF EVENTS

	SPAIN	ELSEWHERE
1808	*Dos de Mayo* rising in Madrid (2 May) against French occupation: start of people's resistance, aided by British forces under Duke of Wellington	
1814	Ferdinand VII returns to throne, abolishes constitution	
1820	First *pronunciamiento* brings Spanish army into politics	
1823	French troops help Ferdinand VII to restore absolute rule	
1833–39	First Carlist War. British and French volunteers fight on liberal side	
1872–75	Second Carlist War	
1873–74	First Spanish Republic	
1874	Bourbon restoration under Alfonso XII	
1898	Spanish-American War: loss of Cuba, Puerto Rico, Philippines – end of Spanish empire	
1912	Spanish protectorate established over north-west Morocco	
		1914–18 First World War: Spain neutral
1920	Spanish Foreign Legion formed. Commanded by Franco 1923–27	
1917–23	Street war between CNT (anarcho-syndicalist) and employers' *pistoleros* (gunmen) in Barcelona. About 700 dead	
1923–30	Dictatorship of General Primo de Rivera	May 1926: UK General Strike 1928: Salazar assumes direction of Portuguese 'New State' 1929: Wall Street Crash heralds Great Depression

	SPAIN	ELSEWHERE
1931		
14 April	Second Republic proclaimed. Alfonso XIII into exile	August: Ramsay MacDonald heads National Government in Britain
October	Manuel Azaña Prime Minister	September: Britain abandons gold standard
1932		
January	Dissolution of Jesuits. CNT general strikes	July: Salazar premier in Portugal. Nazis gain 230 seats in Reichstag election. Second Five-Year Plan in USSR
August	General Sanjurjo's military rising flops	
September	Agrarian reform law and statute of Catalan autonomy approved by Cortes (parliament)	
October	CEDA founded with Gil Robles as leader	
1933		
January	Peasant unrest. Casas Viejas 'massacre'. Government crisis	March: F. D. Roosevelt President in USA. New Deal begins. Dollfuss dictator in Austria
October	Foundation of Falange Española led by José Antonio Primo de Rivera	October: Germany quits League of Nations. Massive unemployment in USA, UK, Germany
November	Right-wing victory in elections	
1934		
February	Falange-JONS unification	February: Socialist insurrection in Vienna crushed. Mussolini agrees to train Carlist militiamen (*requetés*)
April	Sanjurjo and fellow-conspirators amnestied. Left Republican party formed	June: First meeting of Hitler and Mussolini
October	CEDA ministers in government. United workers' rising in Asturias crushed by Army of Africa units summoned by General Franco. Risings in Madrid and Barcelona fail. Severe repression	July: Attempted Nazi *putsch* in Austria. Dollfuss murdered August: Death of Hindenburg. Hitler now Führer
1935		
September	POUM formed from two dissident Communist parties	July: Comintern 7th Congress approves Popular Front tactics

	SPAIN	ELSEWHERE
December	Preparation for general election after government crisis	October: Italy invades Abyssinia November: League of Nations proposes economic sanctions against Italy
1936		
16 February	Popular Front electoral victory. 1934 rebellion prisoners freed	
March	Falange banned. Peasant land seizures. Right-Left street fighting	Germany occupies Rhineland
April	Socialist/Communist youth movements merge in JSU	
May	Azaña President of Republic, Casares Quiroga Prime Minister	Italian conquest of Abyssinia completed June: Socialist Léon Blum heads Popular Front government in France
12 July	Lt José Castillo assassinated	
13 July	Monarchist leader Calvo Sotelo assassinated	
17–20 July	Military risings in Morocco and in Spain	
18 July	Insurgents successful in Morocco and in Seville.	
19–20 July	Military rising defeated in Barcelona and Madrid. General Sanjurjo killed in air crash. Anti-Fascist Militias Committee formed in Barcelona	Hitler agrees to aid insurgents (later known as Nationalists)
30 July	Airlift of Army of Africa begins	
14 August	Insurgents capture Badajoz. Massacre of 'Reds'. Terror and counter-terror	Blum closes French border to arms consignments for Republic
4 September	Largo Caballero forms Socialist/Communist/Left Republican government	Stalin's Purge Trials begin. Recruiting for International Brigades approved
5 September	Insurgents close Basque/French border at western end of Pyrenees	
27 September	Insurgents take Toledo, end siege of Alcázar	First meeting of Non-Intervention Committee in London
29 September	Franco appointed Commander-in-Chief and Head of State	

	SPAIN	ELSEWHERE
30 September	Republican government creates Popular Army	
1 October	Republican government approves grant of Basque autonomy	British Labour party rejects Communist party's application to affiliate. Sir Oswald Mosley leads anti-Semitic march through East End of London
12 October	In Salamanca, Miguel de Unamuno criticizes insurgent policy in celebrated speech. First Soviet aid to Republic arrives	
4 November	Republican government moves from Madrid to Valencia	F. D. Roosevelt re-elected as US President
7/8 November	Madrid threatened. People's defence, helped by International Brigades, halts insurgent offensive	
15–17 November	German Condor Legion in action	18 November: Germany and Italy recognize Burgos junta (Franco)
23 November	Madrid battle ends in stalemate	
17 December	POUM ousted from Generalitat (Catalan government) at Communist insistence	Mrs Simpson 'crisis'. Edward VIII abdicates
22–23 December	Italian 'volunteers' land in Cadiz to aid insurgents. CNT-dominated Council of Aragon recognized by Republican government	
1937		
7–8 February	Málaga captured by Italian-aided insurgents (Nationalists)	
5–24 February	Jarama battle: renewed Nationalist assault on Madrid foiled	
8–18 March	Battle of Guadalajara. Popular Army, with International Brigades, routs blackshirt Italian Corps. Madrid stalemate for next two years	
31 March	Nationalist offensive in Basque province of Vizcaya opens under command of General Mola	

	SPAIN	ELSEWHERE
19 April	Unification of Falange and Carlist-monarchist movements	Non-Intervention Committee establishes short-lived land/sea patrol
26 April	Condor Legion's saturation bombing of Guernica	
3–8 May	Barcelona: long-mounting tension between CNT/POUM and Communists/Generalitat explodes in street battle	Neville Chamberlain succeeds Baldwin as British Prime Minister
17 May	After Largo Caballero's resignation, Dr Juan Negrín heads new, Communist government	
16 June	POUM outlawed. Five days later, Andrés Nin murdered by Soviet agents	Soviet Purge Trials continue
19 June	Bilbao falls to Nationalists	
6–26 July	Battle of Brunete: failure of Republican offensive on Madrid front	Sino-Japanese War. Japanese occupy Peking
10 August	Council of Aragon dissolved. Some rural collectives disbanded	
15 August	Formation of Servicio de Investigación Militar (SIM). Intensification of political police terror in Republican Spain	
24 August	Popular Army offensive in Aragon (Belchite) frustrated	
19 October	Nationalists complete conquest of northern Spain	
31 November	Republican government moves from Valencia to Barcelona	
14 December	Start of Republican offensive at Teruel, Aragon	
1938		
22 February	Battle of Teruel ends with recapture of town by Nationalists	
10 March	Nationalists launch offensive in Aragon	
16–18 March	Round-the-clock bombing of Barcelona by Italian planes based in Majorca	The *Anschluss* – Germany occupies Austria. Blum, again premier, reopens French frontier, but government falls a month later

	SPAIN	ELSEWHERE
14 April	Nationalist forces reach Mediterranean coast above Valencia. Catalan offensive postponed	
1 May	Negrín tries 13-point 'peace offensive'. Franco continues to demand unconditional surrender	June: Daladier closes French frontier
24 July	Popular Army offensive along river Ebro	July: Non-Intervention Committee's plan to withdraw volunteers from Spain
28 October	Trial of POUM leaders in Barcelona. Two acquitted, four imprisoned	30 September: Munich Pact ends hopes that Republican Spain might become ally of western democracies in European war against Fascism
15 November	Ebro battle ends with retreat of Popular Army. Farewell parade of International Brigades	
23 December	Nationalist offensive in Catalonia opens, meets with only sporadic resistance	
1939		
26 January	Barcelona falls. Mass flight of refugees to French frontier	
1 February	In Figueras, Negrín presides over last meeting of rump Cortes in Spain	27 February: Britain, France recognize Franco regime
4–12 March	Negrín's seeming attempt at Communist dictatorship to ensure continued resistance provokes second Republican civil-war-within-civil-war. Heavy fighting in Madrid. Communist forces defeated. Negrín, his cabinet, and Soviet advisers fly out. Defence Council in Madrid, headed by Colonel Casado, attempts negotiations with Franco	15 March: German troops enter Prague
27 March	Nationalists enter Madrid. Refugees trapped in Alicante, Valencia	
1 April	Franco announces war is over	
		23 August: Nazi-Soviet Pact signed

	SPAIN	ELSEWHERE
1939–43	Repression at full blast. Estimated 150–200,000 'Red' victims	1939–45 World War II. Spain neutral, but 47,000-strong Blue Division of Spanish volunteers fights on Russian front (1942)
		1945 At Potsdam Conference, 'Fascist' Spain declared unfit for membership of United Nations
1947	Franco declares Spain a kingdom, with himself as regent	
1953	Franco signs agreement with USA: economic aid in return for NATO defence bases	
		1955 Spain admitted to membership of UN
1956	Moroccan independence ends Spanish protectorate	
1969	Franco nominates Juan Carlos de Borbón, grandson of Alfonso XIII, as heir to the throne	
1975	20 November: death of Franco	
June 1977	First general election since February 1936	

Note on Spanish nomenclature: a Spaniard's full title consists of Christian name(s), father's surname, and mother's surname, in that order. The mother's surname is often omitted; but if the father's surname is commonplace it will not be used alone and the mother's might be used instead: e.g. Federico García Lorca is referred to as 'Lorca' not 'García'.

CHAPTER ONE

COLLISION COURSES

During two weeks of savage fighting in August 1937 the town of Belchite in northern Aragon was reduced to ruins: and to this day it has been left in ruins, a bleak reminder of the havoc caused by the Spanish civil war.

Bill Bailey, from Hoboken, New Jersey, one of the volunteers from more than fifty countries who fought against Franco in the International Brigades, was involved in the house-to-house, room-to-room fighting. 'We would knock a hole through a wall with a pickaxe, throw in a few hand-grenades, make the hole bigger, climb through into the next house, and clear it from cellar to attic. And by God we did this, hour after hour. The dead were piled in the street, almost a storey high, and burnt. The engineers kept pouring on gasoline until the remains sank down. Then they came with big trucks and swept up the ashes. The whole town stank of burning flesh.'

When on 18 July 1936 the insurgents, later to be led by General Franco, rose against the Republican government in the name of law and order, they hoped that their coup would succeed in a matter of days. The government thought that the revolt would be swiftly defeated. But there followed a war which lasted for nearly three years.

The proclamation of the Second Republic in April 1931 – after seven years of dictatorship – had raised high, almost millennial, hopes in millions of Spaniards. Democracy, they expected, would bring freedom of thought, freedom of the press, better education for the masses, an end to grinding poverty and glaring social inequality. Eight years later, when the civil war ended, their dreams lay buried in the rubble of death and destruction. Half a million houses had been wrecked, the same number of Spaniards driven into exile. More than 170 towns had been so battered that decades would pass before they were adequately restored. Psychological scars took longer to heal; memories of the bitter divisions that split the nation are still a factor in Spain's stormy transition to democracy today.

First estimates of one million dead in the civil war have been scaled down to an approximate half million, of whom perhaps 100,000 were killed in pogroms during the first few months when personal, class and ideological fury ran riot. More than half the total deaths occurred behind the fronts, for in both

OPPOSITE *Madrid, 14 April 1931: crowds in the Plaza de Oriente hail the proclamation of the Second Republic.*

REPUBLICAN AND NATIONALIST SPAIN AT THE START OF THE CIVIL WAR

The ruins of Belchite, northern Aragon, stand today as a monument to the horrors of civil war. A new town has since been built nearby.

Nationalist and Republican camps spontaneous terrorism was followed by scientific terror.

Foreign intervention – German, Italian, Russian – transformed the conflict into a grinding prelude to World War II. Yet beyond the calculations of Hitler, Mussolini and Stalin, beyond the use of the Spanish War to test weapons, military tactics and the elasticity of the Western democracies' collective conscience, lay the original confrontations, which were shuffled out of sight in the world press even before they were ruthlessly suppressed in Spain. Anarcho-syndicalism, a mass movement with, at its height in the early 1930s, a membership of nearly two million industrial workers and peasants; its rival, the increasingly militant socialist movement; the anti-Stalinist POUM (Partido Obrero de Unificación Marxista); the Comintern-manipulated Communist party; conservative-minded Basque nationalists; and Left Republican social democrats – all were misleadingly lumped together as 'Reds'. Falangists, Carlists, orthodox monarchists and Catholic conservatives all figured as 'fascists'. Yet they were as likely to quarrel with each other as to combine against the common enemy.

The story of Spain in the long-gathering upheaval of 1936–39 is one of apocalyptic excitement followed by disillusion and exhaustion: a sequence that since the Napoleonic invasion of 1808 had been so frequently repeated as to have become almost traditional. Scored across by sierras, cut off from the rest of Europe by the Pyrenees, Spain had never been more than minimally unified. Primitive communications made for rural isolation. Aragon, Catalonia, the Basque provinces, Andalusia, Extremadura, Asturias, Galicia, Valencia, were all acutely conscious of cultural and linguistic differences and resentful of Castilian rule.

Basque and Catalan nationalists looked down on immigrant workers from the impoverished rural areas of Andalusia, Extremadura and Murcia who took low-paid jobs in the factories of Bilbao and Barcelona. Basque nationalists, proud of their region's racial homogeneity, regarded Spaniards as foreigners and southern Spain, with its Moorish architecture, customs and physical characteristics, as virtually African. Ideologues condemned mixed (Basque-Spanish) marriages and clung to the impenetrably different Basque tongue as a guarantee of cultural independence. In the 1930s a few fanatics even went so far as to suggest that autonomy might best be achieved if the three provinces of a Basque Republic (Euzkadi) applied for membership of the British Commonwealth of Nations.

Strategically placed between Europe and Africa, between the Mediterranean and the Atlantic, Spain had been invaded by Phoenicians, Greeks, Carthaginians, Romans, Goths, Byzantines, Arabs, French, Portuguese and English, each intruder playing off one group of Spaniards against another. Much blood had been shed in the resistance to liberal ideas, associated with the Napoleonic invasion of 1808. Based on the conservative peasantry of Navarre and fired by the ultra-clerical creed of their Society of the Exterminating Angels, the Carlists, who supported the claims to the throne of Don Carlos de Borbón and his descendants, had fought two wars (in 1833–39 and 1872–76) to restore an absolute monarchy in the manner of the sixteenth century when the Inquisition reigned supreme and Spain flashed into its short period of imperial splendour. Interviewed in 1981, Eugenio Vegas Latapié, a veteran monarchist intellectual, could remark that 'in 1936 we were really fighting against the influence of French Revolutionary ideas.'

During the first Carlist war British and French volunteers, forerunners of the International Brigades of 1936, had fought on the liberal side. So had most of the Army, led by officers who at that stage saw themselves as champions of a bourgeois-progressive revolution which, under a limited monarchy, might conceivably edge Spain out of an impoverished, anachronistic isolation and nearer to Europe. But from the 1870s, when the Anarchist 'Idea' of a society of loosely-federated, self-governing urban and rural collectives began to spread, the Army, holding the balance of power, had to contend with visionary fanatics on the Left as well as on the Right.

Identified with the capital, Madrid, and with a Cortes (Parliament) struggling for authority, the officer corps was firmly opposed to federalism. That the state was likely to disintegrate into a collection of mutually hostile 'nations' was alarmingly demonstrated during the short-lived First Republic (1873–74) when a liberal Cortes attempted a federal solution, only to see Catalonia declaring itself independent and most provinces behaving as though Madrid had ceased, governmentally, to exist. 'We embrace the entire heaven of thought and stumble over the first hole in the road,' lamented one liberal politician; and a *pronunciamiento* (army coup) ended the chaos by restoring the Bourbons to the throne in the person of Alfonso XII.

Between 1820 and 1923 there were forty-three *pronunciamientos*, the last of

which, with the connivance of Alfonso XIII, thrust General Primo de Rivera to power as 'the King's Mussolini'. This shrewd, genial, dissipated Andalusian aristocrat was a very different character from the abstemious, unflamboyant Franco. Though he created no mass movement along fascist lines, nevertheless during his seven-year dictatorship (1923–30) the 'farce' of party politics was stifled and unofficial union activity driven underground.

After the loss of its possessions – Cuba, Puerto Rico and the Philippines – to the USA in the war of 1898, post-imperial Spain was saddled with the problem of an under-employed, over-officered Army which sought to preserve some remnants of 'imperial' prestige in campaigns of pacification against restless tribes in the Moroccan Protectorate. The drafting of conscripts to Morocco caused a bloodily-suppressed revolt in Barcelona in 1909, and military incompetence reached a climax in 1921 with the disaster of Annual when Rif tribesmen led by Abd el Krim destroyed a Spanish force 20,000 strong. Frederic Escofet, then a young career officer, became disenchanted with the Army in Morocco. Money, he says, rated higher than brains, corruption was rampant, rich playboy officers dabbled in politics, to relieve the crushing boredom of colonial garrison life. 'Being brave, or reckless, was what really counted. If you took a position without losing a lot of men it didn't signify. If there was heavy mortality you would be promoted and decorated.' Such was the atmosphere in which Francisco Franco served his political and military apprenticeship.

Later Escofet was to play a leading role as chief of police in Barcelona, which, partly because of a massive influx of unemployed peasants bringing

LEFT *General Miguel Primo de Rivera, dictator in 1923–30, with his sister and children: back row (from left) – Miguel, José Antonio, who founded the quasi-fascist Falange in 1933, and Fernando; front row – Carmen and Pilar.*

RIGHT *Lt-Col. Francisco Franco, who commanded the Spanish Foreign Legion in 1923–27, with a Moorish chieftain during the campaign against the Rif tribes in Morocco.*

the anarchist gospel with them, had earned a reputation as Europe's most turbulent city. Despite frequent setbacks Catalan nationalism was very much alive and based in Barcelona, the centre of a flourishing textile industry. Josep Tarradellas, prominent in Catalan politics in the 1930s, explains that the Catalans were 'far more European in outlook than other Spaniards'. With the exception of the Basque provinces, 'the rest of Spain was still in the pre-industrial stage. Catalonia had undergone an industrial revolution which created an enlightened bourgeoisie lacking elsewhere, far closer to the French or British middle classes than to the Castilian or Andalusian ruling class and willing to negotiate at least some social reforms.' Like their Basque equivalents, Catalan bankers, businessmen and industrialists chafed under heavy taxation by the central government.

To travel from the bustling regions of Catalonia and the Basque provinces to Aragon, New Castile, Extremadura or Andalusia was to move from the 20th into the 18th century. The peasants lived in barrack-like agro-townships on harsh, sometimes infertile terrain dominated by the huge estates (latifundia) of aristocrats or rich bourgeois – the all-powerful *caciques* (political bosses). In Andalusia nearly three-quarters of a million landless day labourers struggled for bare existence. Single men drifted away to the industrial centres of the north. For those who stayed, life was a matter of poorly paid seasonal employment for about half the year and semi-starvation for the other months.

Since the 1840s the hated paramilitary civil guards had patrolled the countryside like an army of occupation, alert for trouble. Rural anarchists dreamed of the Great Day when *comunismo libertario* would take over and each village would achieve independence under a regime of spartan self-sufficiency – killing the *cacique*, the lawyer, and probably the priest if they could not be converted; banning money, alcohol, tobacco and coffee; and cutting free from the towns, those warrens of vice and corruption.

Felix Moreno de la Cova, of Palma del Rio, the son of one of Andalusia's wealthiest landowners in the 1930s, explains that 'some estates were under-exploited. Why? Because Spain's standard of living was so low, roughly the same as Morocco or an African nation nowadays . . . More than half the working population was in farming. That meant that if you grew wheat the market was very limited, you produced meat and couldn't sell it. What was the answer? To run the estates with the smallest possible expenditure. It's true that the workers were paid very little, but profits were small too.'

Régulo Martínez, the son of a village doctor in the province of Toledo, was sent to a seminary 'since it was the only way I could get a proper education.' In the 1920s, when he was a priest in a village near Guadalajara, his parishioners were mostly tenant farmers paying steep rents and always in debt to the local *cacique*, Don Agapito, who charged heavy interest rates so that 'often they had to pay back with their entire harvest, even with their mules.' Don Agapito was eventually murdered, but before that Father Martínez had 'told him not to come to Mass since his sins could not be forgiven until he returned what he had stolen. He just laughed. "You are too young," he said. "I own the land in this village and I represent Count Romanones."'

Caciques delivered the vote to wealthy politicians like Romanones and so had political pull. When Father Martínez formed a farmers' union to get cheaper credit he was denounced as a socialist. 'The Archbishop summoned me. When I told him I wanted to sell some valuable paintings in the church to help the union he said I must be mad. I replied: "If loving people who work hard all year and barely survive is to be mad or a socialist, then I am both."' Under pressure, Father Martínez left the parish to teach in an orphanage in Madrid. 'Eventually I went to Cardinal Segura and said I wanted to leave the Church. He argued with me and finally said: "I'll starve you to death." I said: "That's very Christian of you." He wrote to my school indicating that I should be dismissed as an atheist and therefore a bad influence on my pupils.'

Some of the poorly-paid rural clergy felt sympathy for the peasants, but few were as outspoken as Father Martínez; and the devotion of individual priests was nullified by the militant obscurantism of the hierarchy. The 1927 edition of the Church Catechism classed liberalism as 'a most grievous sin against the faith' and warned that it was 'generally a mortal sin' to vote for a liberal candidate.

Though at least two-thirds of the population were in no sense practising Catholics, the Church kept a strong, reactionary grip on education with little competition from an inadequate state system. Libertarian schools offered an alternative to some children. In the late 1920s Eduardo Pons Prades, the son of an anarchist wood-worker in Barcelona, attended one directed by 'a teacher called Germinal. He would always use persuasion instead of punishment and his lessons were based on the principles of liberty, equality and fraternity. We were raised to be pacifists. Little did we know that we would soon be fighting in the trenches to defend these principles.'

Illiteracy was rife. Largo Caballero, the socialist leader, did not learn to read until he was 24. As late as 1905 only about five cities in the whole of Spain had a public library. In Madrid alone 80,000 children received no schooling at all. In the countryside, even if schools existed, children were taken out early to work. Timoteo Ruiz, the son of a peasant smallholder in Toledo province, started ploughing at the age of nine in 1927 'because we needed the money. Even those not completely illiterate could hardly read or write, the standard of teaching was so low. Young labourers stood every morning in the village square hoping that the foremen would hire them for the day. I used to get up at midnight to milk the cows and again at sunrise to distribute the milk.'

Manuel Vázquez Guillén, one of nine children of peasant parents in Lora del Rio, a large village in Andalusia, went to work as a shepherd at the age of nine. 'I had to work virtually 24 hours a day. I was with the sheep in the fold and slept in a hut made of rushes, so I was there all the time. I used to have some soup in the morning and carried a bit of bread in my pocket. In the evening I ate stewed chickpeas. Every eight days I would go home for a change of clothes.' In 1927, after finishing his military service, Manuel joined the Socialist party in Seville and became an organizer for the UGT. 'It seemed to me that the Socialist programme was best for the workers. It didn't want to persecute anyone for their ideas: religious people could stay with the Church. It was a question of direction, not compulsion.'

Enrique Líster, who became a divisional commander during the civil war, never went to school and did not learn to read or write until he was fourteen. Born in a peasant family in Galicia, not far from El Ferrol, Franco's home town, Líster emigrated to Cuba with his father in 1916, aged nine. Eleven years later, when working as a quarryman in Cuba, he joined the Communist Party, returning soon afterwards as a trade union organizer to Galicia, a wet, verdant region where peasant holdings, known as minifundia, were too tiny to yield much more than bare subsistence.

Jailed several times during Primo de Rivera's regime, Líster was involved in a gun-fight with *caciques* in March 1932. 'The bosses were trying to create an opposing union. I took a group of our members along to one of their meetings. We were greeted with shots and replied in kind. One of the bosses died and five had to go to hospital. Then began the hunt for me as president of our union. The Party got me out to Madrid, then from Madrid to Paris, from Paris to Berlin, and finally to Moscow, where I stayed for three years. I was sentenced to thirty years' imprisonment in my absence.' In Moscow, with

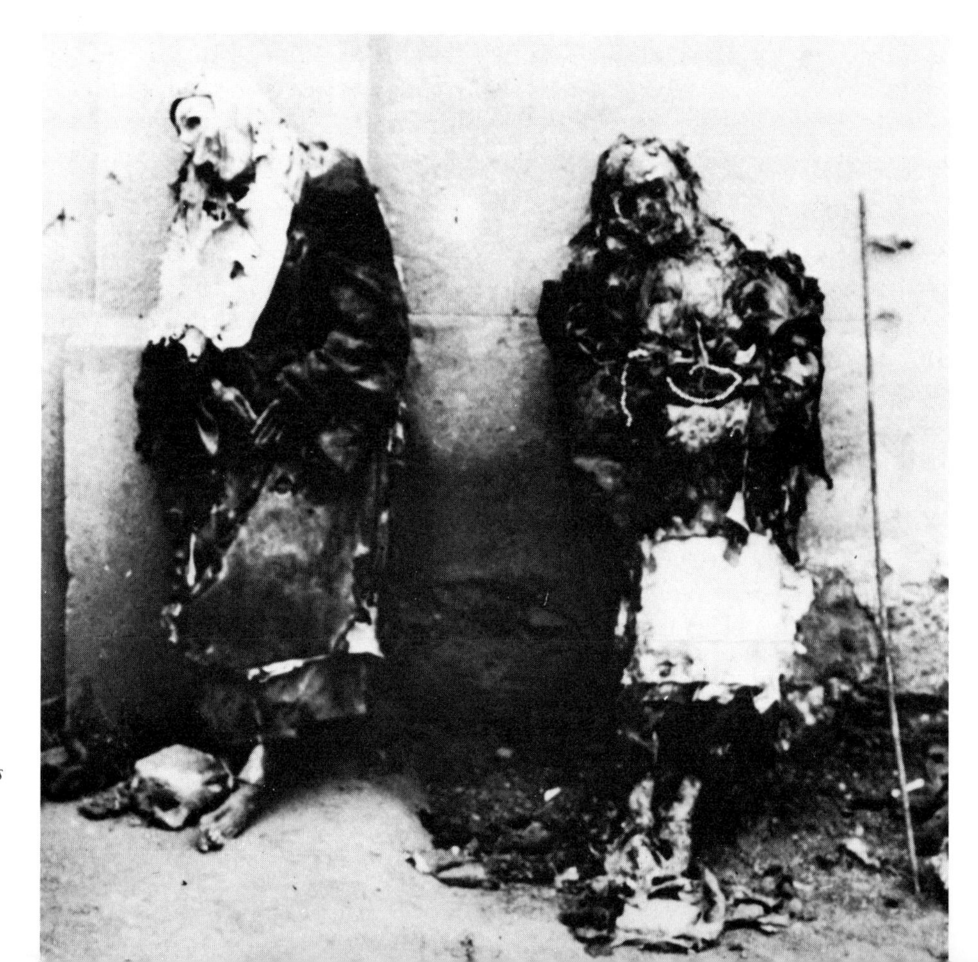

Anti-clerical fury in Barcelona, 1909. During the 'Tragic Week' of riots, churches and convents were burned and the corpses of nuns disinterred.

Anarchist leaders Buenaventura Durruti (left) and Francisco Ascaso in exile, c.1927. In 1924 they had tried to assassinate King Alfonso XIII in Paris.

other picked cadres, including Juan Modesto, an ex-woodcutter from Andalusia who became a general during the last months of the civil war, he studied in a Comintern training centre. After discussions with José Diaz, secretary-general of the Spanish Communist Party, it was decided that he should come back to Spain. 'I lived in Madrid under an assumed name. My mission was to be responsible for organizing the anti-military work of the party. I had about fifty helpers, many of them women, because they could make contacts with the soldiers more easily. We formed communist cells and published a clandestine magazine, the *Red Soldier*.'

While Líster travelled to Moscow, the anarcho-syndicalist movement in Spain was stirred by fierce debates about revolutionary tactics. Formed after the street battles of the 'Tragic Week' of 1909 in Barcelona, when about 200 socialist and anarchist workers had been killed, the anarcho-syndicalist union, the CNT (Confederación Nacional del Trabajo), whose members were known as *cenetistas*, aimed to combine the spontaneity of 'pure' anarchism with a degree of overall control and planning. *Sindicatos Unicos*, bringing together the workers of all crafts in a factory or town, were loosely linked in a regional and finally a national federation. Determined to avoid any hint of a permanent bureaucracy, the CNT employed only one paid official, and since there were no strike funds industrial action tended to be short and violent. Momentum was sustained by the ever-renewed belief that the abhorrent state would soon disintegrate under the impact of repeated blows.

A decision to affiliate to the Communist Third International (Comintern) was reversed when one of the delegates returned from Russia in 1921 with news of the Bolsheviks' persecution of anarchists and their brutal suppression of the Kronstadt sailors' revolt. The CNT was then in the thick of a four-year battle with employers in Barcelona during which *pistoleros* on both sides ran up a total of more than 700 killings. In 1921 an anarchist assassinated the Prime Minister Eduardo Dato and two years later Buenaventura Durruti shot the Archbishop of Saragossa in revenge for the murder by the police of Salvador Segui, a CNT leader.

A hero to some *cenetistas*, a thug to others, Durruti, a railwayman from León, and his equally fanatical and daring companion Francisco Ascaso gloried in their 'criminality', for were not all criminals victims of a distorted society? When the CNT was outlawed in 1923, Durruti, Ascaso and other *solidarios*, as they called themselves, went into exile; and the CNT's contempt for the rival, socialist Unión General de Trabajadores (UGT), organized on the English model with a cluster of paid officials, strike-fund levies, and tight central control, was sharpened when its leader Largo Caballero agreed to collaborate with the dictator Primo de Rivera as a councillor of state with responsibility for labour policy.

In 1927 at a secret meeting in Valencia a group of *solidarios* founded the Federación Anarquista Ibérica (FAI), an inner circle of all-or-nothing revolutionists who sought to leaven what they saw as the increasingly reformist lump of the CNT. Juan Manuel Molina and his *compañera* Lola Iturbe vividly remember those days. 'We at the FAI were ideologues,' Molina recalls, 'but the CNT was purely a trade union movement. We were not a political party, we despised governments and politicians. Our goal was to redeem the exploited workers. Our Ateneos Libertarios [workers' clubs with free lending libraries and lectures] educated people for better lives, dignified the workers. The FAI was clandestine. Not even my comrades knew my real name. Once the civil guards came to our house. Lola shouted and I escaped. The organization sent me to Brussels, where I was joined by Durruti and Ascaso. With the money from their bank raids in South America we opened a libertarian bookshop in Paris and financed an anarchist encyclopaedia.'

Lola Iturbe's mother 'came from a very good Basque family'; forced to leave home because she was pregnant, she worked as a domestic servant in Barcelona. Lola remembers: 'I always felt an outcast, the illegitimate child of a servant. But when I met libertarians I was accepted as a human being. It was like a religious conversion.' Since the turn of the century women had taken an active part in spreading the Idea, which included women's emancipation with its corollaries of 'free love', contraception, abortion and divorce. 'At the same time there was a strong puritan streak in anarchist philosophy. We didn't smoke or drink. Many of us were vegetarians. Wearing make-up was frowned upon. We didn't get married in churches, we just went to live with a comrade. Strangely enough our relationships seemed to be happier and to last longer than most of the bourgeois marriages I knew. We were always faithful to each other.'

While the FAI laboured to galvanize the CNT, the victory of fascism in

Alfonso XIII, the reactionary, pleasure-loving king who fought a losing battle with the forces of democracy and regional separatism.

15 April 1931. After the King's abdication, English-born Queen Victoria Eugenia leaves for exile.

Italy and Germany inspired the first sketches of a revolutionary ideology of the Right in Spain. In March 1931 Ramiro Ledesma launched a periodical, *La Conquista del Estado*, in which, using phrases not unlike those of the *solidarios*, he expressed contempt for vote-catching democracy and wrote of the need for 'military-style commandos'. With Onésimo Redondo, who was demanding 'a disciplined renaissance of the spirit of old Castile', Ledesma formed the Juntas de Ofensiva Nacional-Sindicalista (JONS), a title designed to appeal to the kind of impatient activists drawn to the FAI.

In January 1930 Primo de Rivera's dictatorship had ended. It was only a matter of time before King Alfonso XIII, universally distrusted, followed him into exile. In August 1930 representatives of most shades of Republicanism met at San Sebastian to plan concerted action to overthrow the monarchy. In December the customary high-flown manifesto that accompanied every *pronunciamiento* spoke of 'a passionate desire for justice surging upwards from the bowels of the people . . . Placing their hopes in a Republic, the people are already in the streets. . .' The garrison at Jaca in Aragon, acting prematurely, rose but was halted en route to Saragossa, where General Franco was Director of the Military Academy. Amid general execration, the two officers who had led the rising were executed and the signatories of the San Sebastian Pact imprisoned – a move which greatly boosted their popularity. Franco's democratically-minded brother Ramón, a well-known aviator, took off intending to bomb the royal palace in Madrid, but on second thoughts dropped only leaflets.

The King and his advisers now decided to hold municipal elections to test the public mood. The polls of 12 April 1931 resulted in an anti-monarchical landslide. Madrid, Barcelona, and 46 out of 50 provincial capitals voted Republican. Fearing a Red massacre if the King did not go, the middle classes had turned their backs on Alfonso XIII. Country districts, outnumbering the towns, voted monarchist, but their votes were controlled by the *caciques* and without the towns any government was doomed. When General Sanjurjo, commanding the Civil Guard, informed the King that the Army would not defend the monarchy, Alfonso finally accepted defeat.

On the same day, 14 April, the Republic was proclaimed amid scenes of wild rejoicing. There were exceptions. At Saragossa, Ramón Serrano Suñer was with his brother-in-law Franco on 13 April as the election results came in. 'We were standing staring out of the balcony windows. Franco was extremely anxious and suddenly said to me: "Things can't go on like this. I'm going to take the cadets to Madrid in lorries and coaches to restore order."' Next day, Franco reasoned that 'one had to be realistic, that the important thing was to see how the Republic behaved. If it respected everyone's rights then one should serve it. In fact, though a convinced monarchist, he immediately wrote a letter of allegiance to the Republic.'

OPPOSITE *Valencia, 14 April 1931. Crowds rejoice in the fall of the monarchy. The red-and-yellow royal flag was replaced by a tricolour of red, yellow and purple.*

In Madrid, Vegas Latapié, the monarchist intellectual, 'felt overcome by anguish. I could see that everything would be handed over to the masses who could commit any barbarity whatsoever. Images from the French Revolution

were very much in my mind. It was not that the King was going and an elected assembly taking over, but that disorder and anarchy seemed to be inevitable.' He went to his tailor to cancel an order for a dress uniform to be worn at a palace reception in honour of the King's birthday.

Socrates Gómez, a socialist, was one of those who, escorted by civil guards, entered the palace, partly out of curiosity and partly to guarantee the safety of the royal family. There was a special sympathy for the English-born queen and her children. Gómez saw them leaving by the back, where a car was waiting.

Alvaro Delgado, aged nine on that day, remembers it as a gala occasion, warm and bright with sunshine. Trams, lorries and private cars were crammed with citizens, Republican flags were flying, parents were proudly parading with their daughters 'dressed up as the Republic in a sort of tunic and wearing the Phrygian bonnet of the French Revolution. People were singing Mexican revolutionary songs like "La Cucaracha", with the words changed to refer to priests and the Church. Crowds were shouting, climbing lamp-posts, hugging each other, crying.'

In Barcelona Juan Manuel Molina and other CNT leaders opened the prisons to free their comrades 'and of course all the common criminals as well. We were caught in a whirlpool of enthusiasm.' Despite misgivings, Molina could not help feeling that the spectacle was 'some compensation for the battles we had fought for twenty years.' Josep Tarradellas, elected to the Cortes as a deputy for a newly-formed nationalist party, the Esquerra Republicana de Catalunya (ERC) led by Colonel Macià, recalls how in the

Barcelona, 14 April 1931. Colonel Francesc Macià proclaims 'the Republic in Catalonia'.

excitement of the moment Luis Companys, another ERC leader, proclaimed the *Catalan* Republic from the balcony of the Generalitat (Town Hall), only to have Macià hasten to proclaim 'the Republic in Catalonia as part of the Spanish state. He was making it clear that Catalonia was not asking for independence, only for its own elected representative to replace the Madrid-appointed Civil Governor and the form of colonial domination he represented.'

Would the government of the Second Republic prove more acceptable and adroit than that of the First? The anarchist Molina was not alone in doubting it. The monarchist Pedro Sáinz Rodríguez, one of only about 50 right-wing deputies (out of a total of 425) in the new Cortes, remarks that 'half of Spain wasn't represented. The victory had been too easy, so the violence came later.' The father of Régulo Martínez, a lifelong Republican, had turned to him amid the hubbub of the Puerta del Sol plaza in Madrid and said, with tears in his eyes, 'My son, will the people be able to keep something as wonderful as this or will they throw it all away?' But Martínez was impressed when he heard Manuel Azaña, the Republican leader and new Minister of War, speak at a rally in the bullring. 'He rejected extremism on both wings and said that we didn't need foreign ideologies because Spain could fashion her own form of democracy. The Republic would be democratic or nothing at all. I thought: "That's my man!"'

The outlook for the Republican regime was far from bright. A worldwide economic recession compounded its problems. Army leaders were watchful; and indeed General Sanjurjo led an abortive coup in August 1932. A fascistic ideology was beginning to emerge on the far Right. On the Left the CNT, though shaken by arguments between reformists and FAI firebrands, was set on the collision course with the state demanded by the *solidarios*. The socialist movement was hampered by open rivalry between Indalecio Prieto, the Finance Minister, a subtle and experienced politician who appealed to middle-class progressives, and the Minister of Labour, Largo Caballero, a union man par excellence who was ill at ease in Parliament but the idol of socialist workers. The two were united only in hatred for the 'wreckers' of the FAI. Alejandro Lerroux, the ageing, corrupt and wily leader of the so-called Radical party, with his lieutenant Diego Martinez Barrio, had to be included in a coalition government. Miguel Maura, a devout Catholic, was appointed Minister of the Interior, a post from which he later resigned in protest against the anti-clerical legislation that was to plunge the country into bitter controversy.

Using a system which tried to minimize the influence of the *caciques*, the general election of 28 June 1931 returned 117 socialists, 89 old-fashioned radicals led by Lerroux, 59 Republican radical socialists led by the Catalan Marcelino Domingo, 27 members of the Republican Action party led by Azaña, the same number of Right Republicans led by Alcalá Zamora, 33 Catalan nationalists of the Esquerra, and 16 Galician nationalists. The Right was, temporarily, in such disarray that it returned only 57 members. The

CNT was, on principle, unrepresented in a Cortes which faced the formidable task of making and implementing a new constitution. Only the socialists had any significant mass following, and they were not united. The Republicans, groups of like-minded friends rather than disciplined parties, did not achieve any cohesion until 1934 when the Left Republican party was formed.

The Republic's first Prime Minister, Alcalá Zamora, a lawyer from Andalusia, had had some experience in office, as, briefly, had Largo Caballero as a protégé of Primo de Rivera. Lerroux, however, was one of the few seasoned politicians on what might be loosely described as the Left. Fernando de los Rios, Minister of Justice, who described himself as a socialist, was a professor at Granada University. Casares Quiroga, Minister of Marine, was a wealthy liberal lawyer from Galicia preoccupied with gaining home rule for that region. They, Marcelino Domingo, the Minister of Education, and Azaña were all influenced by the liberal idealism of the 'Generation of '98' led by Miguel de Unamuno, a professor of classics at Salamanca University, and the political philosopher José Ortega y Gasset, both of whom were elected to the constituent Cortes as independents. Their reaction to the disaster of the Hispano-American war and the loss of empire had been to proclaim the need to combat intellectual sloth masquerading as patriotic pride. Teachers and writers of brilliance, theirs was the long-term aim of educating leaders of the future in sufficient numbers to advance the bourgeois-progressive revolution that for over a century had failed to make any real headway.

Now the first scattered products of this campaign were thrust from Republican clubs and debating societies into a thunderous political apprenticeship. Their contact with, and knowledge of, the masses, and especially the peasant masses, was minimal; and in the case of Azaña, a civil servant acknowledged as one of the most eloquent and intelligent of these progressive paladins, almost non-existent. Yet, with his intellectual detachment and coldly logical approach, it was he who, replacing Alcalá Zamora as Prime Minister in October 1931, emerged as the strong man of the government, and the key to the question: Can the Centre hold? A fat, ugly, chain-smoking middle-class savant with literary ambitions (the translator of Voltaire, Dickens, G. K. Chesterton and Bertrand Russell), he was a declared foe of militarism and the Church. By concentrating on these two issues and making only timid efforts to come to grips with the most urgent problem – land reform – the ill-assorted coalition succeeded over the next two years mainly in exasperating almost every faction. Perhaps only the Catalan nationalists, given autonomy in September 1932, were satisfied with its performance.

After a series of peasant risings and industrial strikes a frightened government was forced to call on the Army, the Civil Guard, and a newly-created Republican paramilitary force, the Assault Guards, to maintain a semblance of order. Ironically, Spain became more of a police-ridden state than it had been under Primo de Rivera. When peasant rebels were unceremoniously shot down while military rebels like Sanjurjo were merely exiled or comfortably imprisoned, the worst suspicions of the FAI were confirmed; and, under pressure from his supporters, Largo Caballero began to swing the socialist party and the UGT from a moderate reformism to a more revolutionary stance.

Azaña's legislation to reduce the officer corps and to purge it of disaffected personnel backfired. Some right-wingers took advantage of an offer of retirement on full pay (which gave them more time to meddle in politics); but the unintended effect was that most of those who left were young, better-educated, pro-Republican officers with reasonably good prospects in civilian life. The grant of Catalan autonomy antagonized the Basques and convinced conservative centralists that this was the beginning of a process of separatist erosion. Cardinal Segura predictably cursed the 'atheist' Republic in an apoplectic pastoral letter. Vegas Latapié saw crowds whipped to frenzy by a rumour that the Marques Luca de Tena had shot his chauffeur. 'The car I was travelling in belonged to a count and had a coat of arms painted on the doors. We covered it with mud to drive through Madrid.' A provocative gathering of monarchists in Madrid on 10 May 1931 was followed by an outburst of church and convent burning, a time-honoured gesture of proletarian defiance.

Anti-Republicans gleefully seized upon Azaña's rash, well-publicized remark that all the convents in Madrid were not worth one Republican life. Father Alejandro Martínez Gil, a priest of right-wing views, considers that 'on that day the Republic virtually signed its death warrant. People on the Right knew from then on what to expect. Everything that came afterwards, the laws on secularism, separation of Church and State, the expulsion of the Jesuits, civil marriage and burial, divorce, didn't come as a surprise.'

Cristina de Arteaga, a young upper-class woman who was soon to become a nun, remembers that 'on the first day of the burnings I was in the country and saw the columns of smoke over Madrid. The mob attacked the Salesians, people who are totally committed to the poor. There was a rumour that the nuns were giving poisoned sweets to children. Some nuns were grabbed by the hair in the streets. One had her hair pulled out – Mother Jaime, who is still alive in Seville. I know her, she is a saint.' For Pilar Primo de Rivera, daughter of the dictator (who had died in exile), 'our feelings were aggravated by the knowledge that these actions were being condoned, nothing was being done to stop them.'

The government publicly blamed the monarchists for provoking the riots, and there was a widespread belief that the arson had been deliberately organized. Régulo Martínez spoke to 'two youths who had been caught setting fire to a church. They told us that some elegantly-dressed gentlemen had paid them to do it.' But for him the real issue was the folly of a dogmatic anti-clericalism that made no distinction between prelates and underlings and by abolishing state stipends punished poor priests most. 'I agreed with the dissolution of the Jesuits – they were the bitterest enemies of the Republic. One, I remember, preached a sermon saying that any woman who applied for

The Republican government appointed the poet-playwright Federico García Lorca (second from left on stage) director of La Barraca, a travelling theatre company.

a divorce was no better than a whore. But in my opinion the Republic could have won over about 90 per cent of the priests by retaining them as teachers and paying them a decent salary.'

Anti-clerical legislation not only united the various elements of reaction but had a devastating effect on education. Half the secondary and primary schools were threatened with closure. Yet within twelve months nearly 10,000 schools were built – a remarkable contrast to the average of 500 a year in the previous 25 years. There were other heartening developments. Literacy teams and cultural missionaries spread their wares before the peasant masses of Spain. In 1931 the Ministry of Education appointed Granada-born Federico García Lorca director of a travelling theatre company, La Barraca, which took classical drama to small towns and villages. Aged 33, Lorca was the most famous living Spanish poet and playwright.

The actress Maria del Carmen Lasgoite, who at 19 was one of the founding members of La Barraca, remembers how surrealistic costumes designed by Lorca's artist friends made a startling impact; as did a production of *Fuenteovejuna*, Lope de Vega's 16th-century drama about the killing of a village tyrant. Like members of the 'teaching missions' with their basic libraries and didactic playlets, the personnel of the troupe received only living expenses.

Films like Luis Bunuel's *Land without Bread* demonstrated the extremes of rural poverty. But the government shrank from its complexity and explosiveness; and the times were not favourable. As throughout Europe and in the USA, the economic slump caused a sharp fall in agricultural prices. Land was taken out of cultivation. Unemployment rose. Legislation did not, as hoped, expropriate all large estates but only those owned by grandees, though rich bourgeois owned about 90 per cent of the latifundia. Nothing was proposed to relieve the lot of families working minifundia at excessive rents.

Agrarian reform, in fact, bristled with problems. Many peasants wanted to own the land, and the government favoured the creation of a peasant 'middle class' through land distribution, hoping that this might restrain the revolutionary impetus of landless labourers. Both socialists and anarchists wanted the land to be communalized. But whereas the UGT thought that this should be done by peasant *cooperatives*, the CNT favoured a more radically egalitarian policy of *collectivization*. Furthermore, the FAI was determined to harass a 'bourgeois' government in which Largo Caballero, as Labour Minister, seemed well placed to influence the CNT's peasant membership.

Apart from all this, lack of funds to provide tools, seed or credit made such land redistribution as was achieved largely meaningless. The peasants were in a state of almost constant agitation. *Guardias* were kept busy foiling attempted land seizures. Timoteo Ruiz's father was evicted after a few hours of occupation and badly beaten for his temerity. His family of four children continued to live on vegetable soup and chickpeas. Day labourers continued to assemble every morning in the village square in the hope of being selected for casual work. Five men still practically owned the village. After reading dramatic accounts of the peasants' revolt in the early stages of the Russian revolution, Timoteo and his friends began to scrawl 'Long Live Russia!' on walls.

In Lora del Rio, Manuel Vázquez was equally disappointed. 'The trouble was that the government were not just socialists, and there was a lot of squabbling. The socialist party was not able to develop its programme because of strong reactionary opposition. That was the reason for the failure of the agrarian reform. It was not a true government of the people; there was a capitalist majority the same as there is today.'

Shocked by the violence of some socialist propaganda, Ernesto Castaño, a lawyer in Salamanca, founded the Agrarian Bloc, which, while preparing to resist reform, appealed for a greater sense of responsibility among landowners. He himself was jailed in 1932 for advising landowners not to sow wheat except on really fertile soil since the price the government offered was so low. The government's cautious legislation was seen as the thin end of a revolutionary wedge. Felix Moreno de la Cova comments that 'it was the Republic that brought the slogan "Neither God nor Property nor Bosses," and that's semi-anarchist language. It's natural that landowners would resist any such attempt.'

José Vergara, one of the agricultural experts sent out to supervise administration of the agrarian reform, found himself on a battlefield. 'In Jaén, Andalusia, landowners refused to allow peasants to weed uncultivated land for re-sowing. Elsewhere peasants had cut the water supply to the *caciques*' properties.' In the province of Ciudad Real a peasant's wife, suckling her baby, told Vergara, 'Look, this child is being fed with hatred.' Politically neutral but with liberal sympathies, he concluded that reform by legislation would not work. It had to be accompanied or preceded by 'a revolution to dismantle the existing political or social structures. When the land is owned by a small group of politically powerful people, you have to fight for it. It will not be given away voluntarily.'

On 31 December 1931, in the Extremaduran hill village of Castilblanco, four civil guards breaking up an assembly of disgruntled peasants were beaten to death and mutilated in a sudden spasm of collective rage. In January 1933 a confused anarchist rising at Casas Viejas, a village near Jerez, ended in a siege by assault guards and troops, with aeroplanes flying overhead. Twenty-five rebels were killed when the houses in which they had barricaded themselves were fired. This panic operation, the result of Azaña's determination to smash the CNT's campaign of disruption, achieved the CNT's objective of utterly discrediting the government – and by implication Largo Caballero, the socialist Minister of Labour.

Was this how Azaña's 'even-handed justice' worked out in practice? The prisons were full of political offenders, including thousands of *cenetistas*. Unemployment was soaring. In September 1933, with its policies and its reputation in tatters, the government resigned. Eduardo de Guzmán, whose disenchantment led him to join the CNT after reporting the Casas Viejas

LEFT *January 1933. In Casas Viejas, Andalusia, a prisoner is led away by civil guards after one of many peasant insurrections in the poverty-stricken villages of southern Spain.*

RIGHT *José Antonio Primo de Rivera, leader of the extreme right-wing Falange Española, founded in 1933.*

massacre, remarks that 'after 1932 people were tired of waiting for a revolution that didn't come.'

What did come, after the November 1933 elections, was reactionary rule during what the Left christened the *Bienio Negro* (Two Black Years). The decisive factors were the mass abstention of CNT voters and the refusal of the socialists to cooperate with the Republicans. The electoral system favoured alliances or 'united fronts', and the Right, which had cobbled together a patchwork middle-class Catholic party, the CEDA (Confederación Española de Derechas Autónomas), secured twice as many seats though it got fewer votes than a fractured Left.

The CEDA was led by José Maria Gil Robles, a professor of law turned political journalist. Impressed by visits to Hitler and to Dollfuss, whose Catholic Corporative State in Austria was the model for what he hoped to achieve in Spain, he had made an electoral alliance with other right-wing groups – the monarchist Renovación Española, the Basque nationalists (seeking autonomy), and the Agrarian Bloc. But whatever minimally democratic notions Gil Robles may have cherished, he was the prisoner of the landowners and financiers who had contributed heavily to party funds. Timoteo Ruiz witnessed the bribing of peasant voters, known as *morcilleros* because they were rewarded with a *morcilla* (sausage) and perhaps some blankets.

Though the largest party in the Cortes, the CEDA did not have an absolute majority. But under pressure from its deputies the government, headed by Alejandro Lerroux, either repealed or ignored the 'subversive' legislation of its predecessor. Grandees' estates were restored, peasants evicted, wages cut. All those involved in Sanjurjo's rising were amnestied. By February 1934 Largo Caballero was saying that 'the only hope of the masses now is in social revolution. It alone can save Spain from fascism.' At this point the Spanish Communist party (PCE) had a membership of around 10,000 and one deputy. Abrasively anti-bourgeois, it was soon to change its tune in line with Comintern orchestration and was already in conflict with anti-Stalinist splinter groups – Left Communists led by Andrés Nin, the Workers' and Peasants' party led by Joaquin Maurin – which in 1935 merged to form the POUM with headquarters in Barcelona.

The CNT continued its campaign of perpetual opposition with risings in Aragon, strikes in Andalusia, and a four-week industrial stoppage in Saragossa (a truly heroic achievement without strike funds). At the same time, authoritarian groups were shaping up for what most Spaniards now accepted as the inevitable major confrontation. In March 1934 a delegation of monarchists and Carlists went to Rome to negotiate with Mussolini for money and arms. Later several hundred *requetés* (Carlist militiamen) underwent military training in Italy. Jaime del Burgo, then president of the Carlist Student Association in Pamplona, recalls that they posed as Peruvians and emphasizes that they were *not* fascists – 'we thought the whole fascist atmosphere in Italy was hilarious.' The *requetés* trained at an airfield near

Rome, and the monarchist envoy Sáinz Rodríguez watched them 'receiving military instruction right under the nose of the ambassador of the Spanish Republic, because he entered and left the country from that airfield.'

In October 1933 the Falange Español, led by the 30-year-old lawyer José Antonio Primo de Rivera (usually known as José Antonio), had been founded. Influenced as much by devotion to his father as by admiration for Mussolini, it merged in February 1934 with the JONS, using the latter's yoke-and-arrows emblem and Ledesma's slogan '*Arriba! España, Una, Grande, Libre!*' ('Arise! Spain, One, Great, Free'). Elected as a deputy for Cadiz, José Antonio was a rich, charming Andalusian playboy with something of a social conscience, a rapport with the anarchists, a distaste for bone-headed reactionaries, and a sophistication which made him uneasy in a sloganeering, Roman-saluting ambience.

His flowery speeches, spiced with violence, appealed mainly to university students. But the Falange's revolutionary rhetoric did not commend it to old-fashioned conservatives. José Antonio talked of socializing the banks and the railways and promised a radical land reform. The Catholic hierarchy was not attracted to an ideology that treated the Church as a symbol of Spain's past glory which was itself in need of drastic purging to measure up to the 'destiny' of a national renaissance. Calling for 'service to a united nation', José Antonio characterized fascism as 'a new way of understanding our epoch' and, in a phrase which echoed the fears of the Left, observed that 'Fascism has already triumphed in some countries and in some, as in Germany, by the most irreproachably democratic means.'

Was the Falange really fascist? The Conde de Montarco, a founding

Barcelona, October 1934. Strikers arrested after an abortive separatist rebellion, timed to coincide with the rising in Asturias.

member, has no doubts. 'I had known José Antonio well since 1930, we used to play golf together . . . I find it quite ludicrous for Falangists to deny that they were fascists. Of course they were. But being a fascist then was not degrading. I was a fascist because I was a revolutionary. Our aim was to overthrow the existing system and create a new one.' Narciso Perales, who joined the JONS when he was 19, had read 'all the revolutionary authors – Proudhon, Bakunin, Marx, Lenin'; but being a Catholic could never be a communist, and as a fervent nationalist did not hold with the class struggle. Fascism offered a revolutionary alternative which he could accept, though realizing that it would have to be adapted to Spanish conditions. He and other young falangists did not want yet another right-wing military dictatorship. They envisaged a new Spain based on 'organic democracy' as opposed to 'the corrupt kind of parliamentary democracy with which the Republic was destroying Spain'. Raimundo Fernández Cuesta, deputy leader of the Falange, maintains that the blue-shirt uniform was chosen 'because it was the workers' colour' (the same applied to the Italian fascists' black shirt), that José Antonio tried to prevent violence, and that, 'because of its refusal to make common cause with the non-revolutionary Right the Falange was starved of funds.' Nevertheless the Falange did receive some small financial aid from Mussolini.

In 1934 the Falange was an insignificant mini-faction. The CEDA, with Gil Robles boosted as the 'Jefe' or Duce, seemed to be the real fascist threat. When on 4 October three CEDA ministers were included in the government this was treated as the signal for a concerted attack which was in effect the first campaign of the civil war.

Insurrections in Madrid and Barcelona, timed for 5 October to coincide with a formidable miners' rising in the northern province of Asturias, failed dismally. Except in Asturias, where the CNT, UGT, and PCE temporarily cooperated in an anti-fascist front with the rallying cry 'Unite, Proletarian Brothers!', there was little sign of unity. The Left Republicans led by Azaña were, as the former priest Régulo Martínez points out, against the rising. 'True, a right-wing government was in power, but it was still Republican. Why give the reactionaries the perfect excuse to take over?' In Madrid, says Lorenzo Iñigo, CNT participation was half-hearted. 'We supported it so that people couldn't say that it failed because we hadn't.' But since a promised arms consignment did not arrive, 'all we did was walk around the streets'.

In Catalonia the CNT played no part in an opportunist putsch led by right-wing nationalists. Against the advice of other members of the Generalitat (Catalan parliament), President Companys proclaimed Catalonia independent. Josep Tarradellas was present when troops surrounded the building. 'One of the ministers hid under a table when the shooting began. I was arrested with Companys and others. We stayed in prison until the Popular Front election victory of February 1936.'

In Asturias the rising, well-prepared and comparatively well-armed, was a far more serious, indeed epic, affair. Manuel Montequín, a miner, remembers

The Asturias rising, October 1934. Working-class insurrectionists are taken prisoner. Nearly 2,000 were shot after the defeat of the rising.

'the tremendous excitement. We had dynamite ready to blow everything up. The whole village was ready to go – men, women and children, everybody.' By 8 October much of the province was being administered by all-party revolutionary committees. Within three days a 'Red Army' of 30,000 workers had been mobilized. Fighting was heaviest in the capital, Oviedo, and around Gijón, a large industrial centre. There was even talk of a march on Madrid. Prime Minister Lerroux asked Generals Franco and Goded, as joint chiefs of staff, to suppress the rebellion. Knowing that the Foreign Legion and the Moorish *regulares* (mercenary troops) were the only units capable of dealing with such a challenge, Franco decided to use them. Commanded by Colonel Juan Yagüe, the legionaries (mostly Spanish but with some Germans and Frenchmen) did their job with extreme ferocity.

Of about 2,000 killed or wounded before surrender on 19 October, all but ten per cent were rebels: almost as many rebels were killed in the merciless repression that followed. Manuel Montequín remembers that 'in some places Moors, legionaries and civil guards didn't spare even dogs, cats, pigs or calves. They slaughtered everything in sight. I saw it with my own eyes when I was fighting in the village of Villafria. They even cut off the heads of children's dolls.' Defeat was 'as if we had had a leg or an arm amputated. After fighting for freedom we were forced to slink back to our homes like beaten animals and wait for another round of revenge.'

The 'October Revolution' ended with some 30,000 political prisoners, including Azaña and Largo Caballero. Eduardo de Guzmán's despatches were suppressed. Though the rebels' atrocities had been mild compared with those of the licensed military killers, the right-wing press unleashed a barrage of atrocity tales – nuns raped, the eyes of policemen's children gouged out, priests burnt alive or skewered on meat hooks.

The use of Moroccan troops and the horrors of the repression forced the bickering Left towards solidarity as nothing else could have done. As so often in Spain, a courageous failure was hailed as a moral victory. The Communists, who had advocated continuing the hopeless struggle (among them Dolores Ibarruri, an Asturian miner's wife later known as La Pasionaria), reaped the reward in a surge of popularity and membership. In prison, 67-year-old Largo Caballero read Marx and Lenin for the first time. Azaña's imprisonment and trial (unmerited since he had opposed the rising) did much to atone for the guilt of Casas Viejas. In summer 1935 a financial scandal involving Lerroux finally discredited the creaking Radicals. Gil Robles, in danger of being classified as a paper tiger, expected the President, Alcalá Zamora, to ask him to form a government. Instead, a caretaker administration was installed in the hope that a new Centre party would emerge during the elections set for 16 February 1936.

The CEDA-Monarchist National Front had no real programme to offer. Left Republicans, Socialists and Communists grouped in the Popular Front promised amnesty for all political prisoners, a return to the policies of 1931, and a more radical land reform. With the help of the CNT vote, used largely in order to release the thousands of *cenetistas* in jail, the Popular Front gained a slender majority of votes and, again thanks to the workings of the electoral system, an absolute majority of seats in the Cortes.

The victory would have been greater but for widespread intimidation of peasant voters. In Granada, for instance, where anyone without a collar was barred from the polling booths, this was so blatant that a new election was held in May. Preceded by the burning of the offices of the Falange and the

Barcelona, 19 February 1936. Joy for political prisoners amnestied by the newly elected Popular Front government.

wrecking of bourgeois cafés, a theatre, two churches and the local tennis club, this predictably resulted in a sweeping Popular Front win.

Peasants seized land on a much larger scale. On one day, 25 March, about 60,000 peasants took over 3,000 farms in Extremadura. 'After February 1936 the situation in Andalusia became impossible,' says Felix Moreno de la Cova. 'Workers wrecked my father's farms, breaking the legs of sheep, burning tractors.'

There were more church burnings, more street battles. Falangist gunmen toured the streets of Madrid and Seville in cars like gentlemen gangsters. Fernández Cuesta reckons that 'during February we had 66 dead. After the amnesty the tension grew red hot.' The Conde de Montarco remembers that José Antonio, foreseeing the result of the elections and predicting that a Popular Front victory would 'mean the destruction of Spanish unity', had decided on a policy of confrontation. When the Left fought back, every casualty brought immediate retaliation. 'If someone was killed,' says the Conde de Montarco, 'there had to be a revenge killing in less than 24 hours. We had to show that we would not allow them to wipe us out.'

Anxious to conciliate the Western democracies as possible allies against the Nazi menace, the Comintern had instructed its satellites to 'form a People's Front for joint action with Social Democratic parties', a 'Trojan horse' tactic which envisaged a long phase of collaboration with petty bourgeois reformism. During the elections the socialists had joked: 'Vote Communist to save Spain from Marxism.' But the myth of a Communist plot financed by Moscow gold, as dear to the Right as that of a fascist conspiracy financed by Hitler and Mussolini was to the Left, remained a standard ingredient of Nationalist propaganda.

Though reluctantly agreeing to support the government, Largo Caballero, remembering his 1931–33 experience, refused to be part of it – and prevented his more level-headed rival, Indalecio Prieto, from accepting the post of Prime Minister. A feeble cabinet of Left Republicans was headed by Casares Quiroga, an excitable Galician whose powers of judgement were impaired by bad health. Over this unpromising scene Azaña equally reluctantly acted as President. The Centre had been given the kiss of life, but survived only as a target for abuse from movements which, like the CNT, despised the Cortes as a futile charade.

With the collapse of the CEDA which, though still the largest single party, was written off as a spent force, the real beneficiaries of the do-or-die mood were the well-organized PCE and the Falange. By May 1936 PCE (Partido Comunista de España) membership had increased to about 100,000 and the socialist and Communist youth movements, now merged as the JSU (Unified Socialist Youth), filled city streets with huge, noisy, taunting demos. The Falange, though outlawed by the government, was swamped by frustrated ex-CEDA supporters, its original members vastly outnumbered by recruits looking for action and idolizing José Antonio, who had been jailed by the 'Reds'. His sister Pilar, a trained nurse, founded a Women's Section of the

General Franco (centre, second row) at a meeting of garrison officers at Tenerife, 17 June 1936.

Falange 'to visit our prisoners and to look after their families and the families of those who had been shot in the streets. We went to see José Antonio almost daily, keeping him informed and acting as a link with the outside world.' Many young CEDA militants, encouraged by the ambitious lawyer and CEDA deputy Serrano Suñer, joined the Falange. Both movements began courses of military training.

In Madrid on 16 April the funeral of Lt Anastasio de los Reyes, a civil guard who had been shot by 'Red' assault guards (picked for loyalty to the Republic), developed into a gun-fight between slogan-chanting Falangists and Internationale-bellowing JSU militants. 'A Falangist next to me was hit,' says the Conde de Montarco, 'and I decided to take him to a friendly chemist. On the way I was arrested at a police road block.' Enrique Miret Magdalena, a scrupulous Catholic university student, asked his father confessor if it was morally permissible to kill before one had been attacked. 'He got out an old text which said that when you can foresee an attack it is legitimate self-defence to kill first.'

By June 1936 preparations for a military-monarchist coup were well advanced. The Army itself was divided. A 'patriotic' Unión Militar Española (UME) provided a network of right-wing junior officers. Pro-Republican officers were grouped in the Unión Militar Republicana Anti-Fascista (UMRA). With Franco banished to the Canary Islands – supposedly out of harm's way – and General Goded in Minorca, overall direction was in the capable hands of General Emilio Mola, who had been transferred from Morocco to Pamplona, the capital of Navarre and headquarters of the Carlist movement. There he wrestled with the problem of contriving some kind of unity among Carlists, Alfonsine monarchists and Falangists. Each demanded a price for participation. Royalists of both varieties wanted assurances that the new regime would be authoritarian – and monarchist. José Antonio, from prison, instructed Falange units to operate independently as far as possible.

Mola, says Serrano Suñer, was 'an incredible conspirator. He had tremendous difficulties. Franco wouldn't have been able to do his job. And it was Mola, as Director, who assigned tasks.' Franco's vacillation was exasperating, and there was a contingency plan to fly General Sanjurjo from Lisbon to Morocco to take his place. But by 9 July Franco had at last agreed to Mola's plan that he should assume command of the Army of Africa after flying to Tetuán in an aeroplane that would, somehow, be provided.

On 11 July a de Havilland Dragon Rapide, flown by a 26-year-old ex-RAF pilot, Captain Cecil Bebb, took off from Croydon airport, near London, en route to Las Palmas to collect Franco. The enterprise had an amateur daring worthy of a Dornford Yates thriller. Chartered by Luis Bolín, the London correspondent of *ABC*, a monarchist journal, the plane had been selected because no reliable civil aircraft could be located in Spain. Told that his mission was 'to get a Rif leader from the Canary Islands to start an insurrection in Spanish Morocco', Bebb considered it 'a lovely challenge'. The affair seemed like an expensive frolic of the idle rich, especially when a Major Hugh Pollard (retired), with his daughter Diana and her friend Dorothy Watson – 'two beautiful blondes' – also in ignorance of the true purpose of the flight, boarded the plane. Bolín calculated that 'it would look like a party, two couples having a good time'. The vital English extras had been recruited by Douglas Jerrold, a Catholic writer who was soon to refer to Franco as 'a hero . . . possibly a saint'.

The start of the rising was hastened by two assassinations in Madrid. On 12 July Lieutenant José Castillo, who had commanded the assault guards at the funeral of Lieutenant de los Reyes and was helping to train JSU militia units, was shot dead by four Falangists as he left home. In the early hours of 13 July a group of assault guards seeking revenge arrived at the apartment of Calvo Sotelo, a militant monarchist politician who had virtually replaced Gil Robles as leader of the parliamentary opposition. In a typically hard-hitting speech in the Cortes he had said that 'against the sterile state I am proposing the integrated state, which will bring economic justice . . . National production will be for the benefit of all classes, all parties, all interests. This state many may call fascist. If so, then I, who believe in it, proudly declare myself a fascist.'

On being arrested, Calvo Sotelo promised to telephone his family 'if these gentlemen do not blow my brains out.' One of them, becoming trigger-happy as the car drove fast through the streets, did just that. The body, dumped at the gate of a cemetery, was identified in the morgue next day. One of the first examples of the *paseo* (taking for a ride), this murder of a political leader gave the rising wider popular support and a moral urgency hitherto lacking. Casares Quiroga groaned when he heard the news. Mola set a definite date in a telegram ('On the 15th last at 4 a.m. Helen gave birth to a beautiful child') which, decoded, meant that the rising would begin in Morocco on 18 July and on the mainland the following day.

In Lisbon, where the Dragon Rapide landed on 12 July, Luis Bolín met Sanjurjo. In Las Palmas on 16 July Bebb was contacted by General Luis

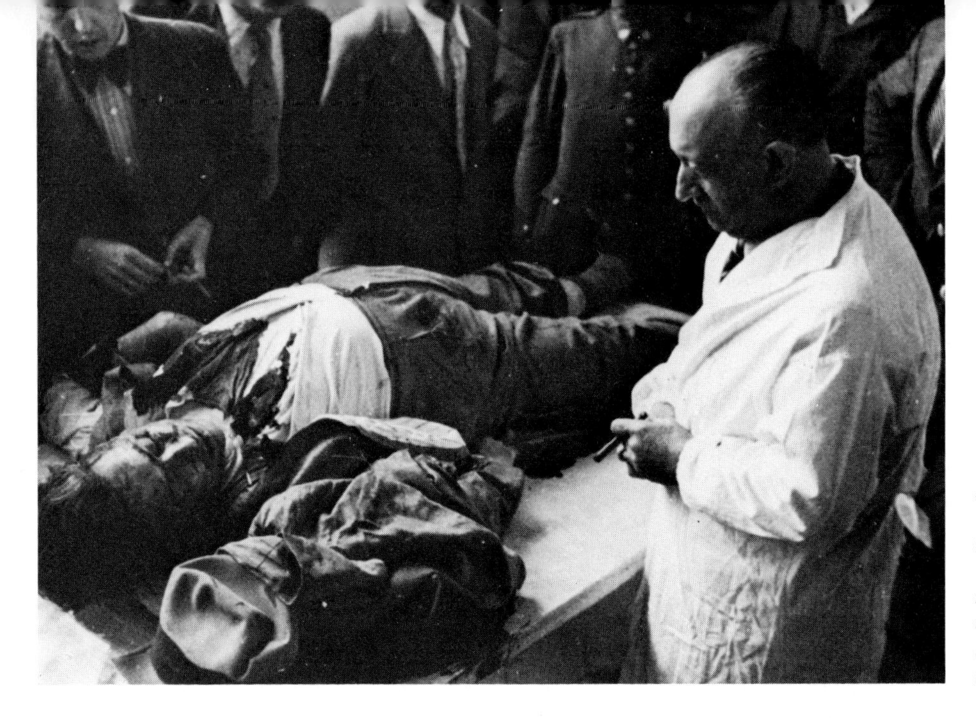

Madrid, 13 July 1936. The assassination of right-wing politician Calvo Sotelo climaxed months of mounting violence. Four days later the military rising began in Morocco.

Orgaz, a close friend of Franco. Major Pollard, who with the two girls had gone on to Tenerife by boat, gave the agreed password – 'Galicia saluda a Francia' – and told Bolín's contact that the plane was waiting on Grand Canary. 'Dear April,' wrote Diana Pollard in a letter to a friend, 'I am having a mild flirtation with the pilot who is a redhead . . . At midnight we had to sail from Las Palmas to Tenerife since Pop has business there! Thank God for Angela's sea-sick remedy, though it cost us 30 shillings! There is a strike of private chauffeurs. This is Spanish territory and they are very unsettled in Spain at the moment.'

On 17 July news reached Madrid of a coup in Melilla, Spanish Morocco. The conspirators, who had been forced to jump the gun because of an unexpected night tour of inspection, quickly overcame scattered resistance. Hurrying from Barcelona, where rumours were flying, Josep Tarradellas was astounded by the government's apparent refusal to face uncomfortable facts. Casares Quiroga, who a week earlier had flippantly dismissed urgent warnings, was still maddeningly impervious. 'My old friend Casares, who perhaps was not as confident as he pretended to be, said: "Look, General Batet came to see me the other day, very agitated . . . He asked for authority to arrest General Mola and I told him to calm down because nothing is going to happen."'

Luck favoured Franco, now as in the years to come. Seeking an excuse to leave his post in Tenerife without arousing suspicion, he cabled the War Ministry for permission to attend the funeral of General Amadeo Balmes, Military Governor of Las Palmas. Permission was granted and at midnight on 16 July he left Tenerife on the island ferry. Diana Pollard, also on board, noticed 'grim-faced civil guards patrolling the deck and armed men in the corridors.' At 2.30 p.m. on 17 July Bebb, waiting anxiously at the airstrip, saw 'a scruffy tugboat come into view around the headland. Soldiers waded out to carry passengers in military uniform ashore . . . I couldn't see any Rif leader

. . . One of them wore a red sash and turned out to be Franco.' At last he was let into the secret.

Stopping at Agadir, then at Casablanca to collect Bolín, Bebb flew to Tetuán in Morocco early on the morning of 19 July. Franco, who had changed from military uniform into civilian clothes during the flight from Las Palmas to Agadir, changed back into uniform as the Dragon Rapide approached Tetuán. A smoke signal gave the all-clear to land. 'We taxied across to where soldiers of the Foreign Legion were drawn up on parade to welcome my very important passenger,' says Bebb. 'The funny part was that a Republican Dakota came over and dropped some bombs. Luckily they landed on the native quarter. Bolín said that Franco wanted me to load up with bombs and drop them on Madrid. I told him that I might get there but wouldn't be able to get back.' So after taking Bolín to Biarritz, Bebb returned to Croydon, honouring his promise to keep quiet about his mission 'until Franco captures Madrid'. He had the impression that this would happen in a matter of days.

By midnight on 18 July the main centres in Spanish Morocco – Melilla, Ceuta, Tetuán, Larache – had been secured with little resistance. On the mainland an audacious coup by General Queipo de Llano won Seville for the rebels. Yet everywhere the Republican authorities hesitated to supply arms to the union and party militias which clamoured for them. Backed by Azaña, Casares Quiroga continued his forlorn attempt to rule by the book. Decrees dismissing Franco and other rebel commanders were issued. Radio bulletins announced that the rising had been totally quelled. 'Eventually,' says Eduardo de Guzmán, 'an artillery officer's decision to hand out some 5,000 rifles to UGT workers saved the day in Madrid.' Lorenzo Iñigo remembers that during a CNT meeting 'a boy arrived and said that a lorry-load of rifles was being distributed to the socialists. We joined the queue and got two armfuls.' Régulo Martínez, a Left Republican, was 'not sure that arms should have been given to the people. There was a lot of hatred and many wanted to kill their oppressors. This is what happened.' Like Azaña and Casares Quiroga he clutched at the hope that 'initially the generals had risen against Communism, not against the Republic as such.' But he admits that 'even our own party members were angered by such reasoning. I saw many tear up their party cards that day.'

In Barcelona Colonel Escofet, who had been sentenced to life imprisonment for his part in the 1934 rebellion, was on duty as the newly-appointed Police Commissioner. Through informers in army barracks and by tapping telephone conversations between officers and their girl-friends he had proof that the rising was timed for 5 a.m. on 19 July; but he met with vacillation at the Generalitat, evasive replies from General Llano de la Encomienda, and disbelief in Madrid. 'All they did was to dismiss three disloyal officers from a list of 60 I had compiled.' The best he could do was to 'post lookouts near all the barracks to warn us when the troops came out.'

This did not mean that there was any intention to arm the masses. 'As soon as they heard about the Moroccan revolt,' says Molina, 'our members poured into the streets. We kept pressing the Generalitat to give us arms, but they were afraid of our power. On 18 July Durruti and I went to police headquarters but were fobbed off.' Escofet admits that he was reluctant to arm the anarchists. 'They tried to deceive me with stories that such-and-such a regiment had left the barracks, and they managed to steal some rifles from a ship in the harbour. But we recovered most of them. When the CNT leaders returned on the night of the 18th I lied, saying they could go home since the rising had been postponed.' He, President Companys, and Tarradellas were gambling on the loyalty of the civil guards and the assault guards to prevent the dreaded alternative of power passing to the streets.

In a village near Toledo, 17-year-old Timoteo Ruiz broke into a landowner's empty mansion with some friends, seeking suitable weapons. 'We must have looked like something out of a circus because what we found were Moorish daggers, antique swords, and hunting knives. I was one of the last to enter and all I could get was a lance. Can you imagine going off to war with a lance? That's how it started.'

Everywhere there was confusion and improvisation. Wanting to set up defence units in Agrarian Bloc villages around Salamanca, Ernesto Castaño travelled to San Sebastian, where an arms shipment from Belgium was due to arrive. The town was controlled by the Republicans and he had to go into hiding. In Salamanca, university student Juan Crespo, who had been viciously assaulted by May Day demonstrators and had seen a retired army officer killed for shouting 'Long live Spain!', found that on 18 July radio bulletins about the crisis aroused little serious interest in the bars. 'People went on drinking. They thought it was just another false alarm, like the Sanjurjo fiasco of 1932.'

During the night of 18–19 July Prime Minister Casares Quiroga resigned and Azaña asked Martínez Barrio, an adept in the art of political compromise, to form a studiously moderate government to negotiate with the rebel leaders. As menacing crowds in the hot streets roared their demand for weapons and Largo Caballero threatened to 'unleash the social revolution', Martínez Barrio and General Miaja, the newly-appointed War Minister, telephoned General Mola, offering him a post in the government. He replied: 'Pamplona is full of Carlists. Everyone is ready for battle. If I tell these men now that I have made an arrangement with you, the first head to roll will be mine. The same would happen to you in Madrid. Neither of us can control our masses.'

Realizing that the crisis was not phoney, Crespo dreaded to think what might happen in his own family. His father had died when he was young, but of his uncles one, in León, was a fanatical Carlist, while another was president of the Left Republicans in Salamanca. Juan considered himself 'a liberal monarchist'. Yet for him, as for many Spaniards, the war came as a relief, a psychological necessity. 'We couldn't go on living like that. It was like a storm on one of those days when you can't breathe and you're just waiting for the first clap of thunder and for the downpour to start – because that's the only way you'll be able to breathe again.'

CHAPTER TWO

REVOLUTION, COUNTER-REVOLUTION AND TERROR

SOON after the rising began, Régulo Martínez, now president of the Left Republican party in Madrid, visited the royal palace where Manuel Azaña, as President of the Republic, was installed. 'He was looking out of the window and there were tears in his eyes. He said: "To think that Spaniards are killing each other in that beautiful sierra where I have taken so many pleasant walks. Why?" He had heard that many people were being murdered on the other side simply because they had voted for left-wing parties or belonged to the local *casa del pueblo* [socialist club].' Martínez tried to comfort the President. '"Don't worry, Don Manuel, we are different. We won't murder our enemies. We'll have them tried."' But both knew that the killing had begun on their side too; both regretted that the masses had been armed. Martínez offered another crumb of comfort. '"Look, Don Manuel, it is they who have risen against the legitimate government and our people are defending it." Azaña replied: "Yes, but they are using the weapons for different purposes," and mournfully added: "This will tarnish our image abroad."'

The former priest and the intellectual-turned-politician were to find their ideal of even-handed justice becoming more utopian still in the turbulence of a civil war that refused to be fought with kid gloves to impress the Western democracies. A clear warning of the likely outcome of civil war had been given by the repression that followed the Asturias rebellion, which made the 'massacre' in the Andalusian village of Casas Viejas seem insignificant.

The fate of Lora del Rio at the beginning of August 1936 was just one example of the carnage of revenge and reprisal, or (more formally) of revolution and counter-revolution, which in those opening weeks fully justified Azaña's apprehension. Ninety-five dead are listed on the Nationalist war memorial erected in the middle of the village's cemetery. Not until 1979 was another memorial put up to mark the mass grave of the losers. More than 400 relatives and friends of the dead contributed donations, and according to Lora del Rio socialists the grave contains the bones of around 1,000 men and women killed in Lora and some neighbouring villages during the terror that drastically punished a short-lived peasant revolution. Some villagers threatened that if the reference to murders by 'Marxist hordes' was not erased

OPPOSITE
A militiawoman in Madrid symbolizes the spontaneous people's resistance to the generals' rising.

from the Nationalist inscription they would mention 'murders by fascist hordes' in theirs. Finally, says Manuel Vázquez Guillén, who survived the Nationalist slaughter, 'we decided to rise above the level of right-wing vindictiveness and content ourselves with a generalized reference to the struggle for freedom.'

On 18 July 1936 all this was in the future. For the moment the government was paralysed by indecision. Resisting calls to arm the people, it sought compromise. The CEDA deputy Serrano Suñer, now edging towards the Falange, found himself involved in the desperate last-hour scramble for a negotiated settlement. 'Azaña asked: "What can we do?" And Indalecio Prieto [the moderate Socialist leader] replied: "Nothing at all; just wait until the first shell comes through the window."' With the army garrisons in Madrid known to be pro-insurgent the position seemed hopeless. Josep Tarradellas, from Barcelona, was shattered to find a complete power vacuum with Azaña 'the most frightened man I'd ever seen', terrified that the legionaries and the Moors might already be at the gates.

An announcement that the government had resigned to make way for an 'emergency' administration headed by the utility politician Martínez Barrio brought howls of 'Treason!' from the crowds in the streets. The 'peace' government collapsed, to be succeeded by a reshuffled version of the one that had resigned 24 hours before. After further hesitations the new Prime Minister, José Giral, authorized the arming of the unions as the only hope of effective resistance to 'fascism's declaration of war on the Spanish people.' At dawn on 19 July lorries loaded with rifles rattled through the streets to the headquarters of the UGT and the CNT. Most of the rifles, it was discovered, lacked bolts and so were useless. The bolts were in the armoury of the Montaña Barracks and the commanding officer refused to hand them over, thus providing the first target for the fury of the masses.

So at last, reluctantly and inefficiently, the deed was done. Frantic phone calls to civil governors in provincial towns often came too late, since the insurgents had already struck. In Madrid the troops – still hoping for a bloodless coup or waiting for a definite order – had made no move. Pilar Primo de Rivera, who was forced into hiding, remembers that 'we never thought the rising would turn into civil war. The change could have taken place without bloodshed as with my father's dictatorship – it was not really a dictatorship, it was an excellent government. But from the moment that they armed the people violent confrontations began.' Sensing the enemy's indecision Prieto shed his fatalism sufficiently to remark that 'these people don't know which way to go. Now perhaps we can try something.'

Fernández Cuesta, who with other Falangists was in the Modelo Prison where he was soon to be joined by right-wing politicians, among them Serrano Suñer, was amused by the warders' reactions to events. 'At first they were sure that the rising would succeed and told us that if we were well-behaved they would open our cell doors. They even gave us a radio. But when the situation changed they took away the radio and became very strict. Hopes for a more or less bloodless *pronunciamiento* came to nothing because the regiments which were supposed to come out of their barracks didn't do so.' Attempts to organize a concerted sally 'failed, as they failed in Barcelona, in Valencia, and in almost all the major cities. But the government also failed, because it didn't have sufficient military strength to quell the rising completely and had to arm the people.' This double failure spelt disaster. 'Had the military risings been simultaneous throughout Spain,' says Eduardo de Guzmán, 'the rebels would probably have triumphed quickly. Had the government been more decisive the rising might have been crushed. Instead we got a divided nation and a long war.'

Before leaving Las Palmas on 18 July General Franco had broadcast a manifesto 'to whomsoever feels a sacred love for Spain . . . The situation is becoming more critical every day.' After referring to 'glorification of the Asturian and Catalan revolutions which violated the Constitution,' he mentioned 'the unheeding spirit of the masses, exploited by Soviet agents who veil the bloody reality of a regime which has sacrificed 25 million people in order to survive', and asked: 'Can we consent one day longer to the shameful spectacle we are presenting to the world?' Yet, like the politicians in Madrid, he had hesitated until the last moment before committing himself. The Army had already taken control in Spanish Morocco before he arrived there; and as a precaution he had sent his wife and daughter to Le Havre on a German passenger boat.

Now he faced the problem of transporting the Army of Africa to Spain. The sea between north Africa and the Spanish mainland was seemingly controlled by the Republic. The crews of two destroyers, the *Sánchez Barcaiztegui* and the *Almirante Valdes*, ordered to Melilla to bombard the town, had mutinied when their officers, after hearing Franco's broadcast, urged them to join the rebels. Similar mutinies occurred on most of the major ships of a small and none too effective fleet. It became rather less effective when, after a wholesale massacre of officers, command passed to the chief engineers closely watched by sailor soviets. One destroyer, the *Churruca*, went over to Franco and was able to carry several hundred Moorish *regulares* across the Straits of Gibraltar to play a vital part in Nationalist successes in Andalusia.

There the most daring coup was carried out by General Queipo de Llano, who had been implicated in Republican plots in 1926 and 1930, prospered under Republican governments, and was generally regarded as something of a 'Red'. Arriving in Seville with only three other officers on an inspection tour of frontier police, he had bamboozled and bullied the army garrison into surrender and, despite hastily contrived opposition from union militants and some assault guards, had gained control of the city centre: including the radio station from which, in the hoarse, bibulous voice that was to entertain – and terrify – listeners for many months to come, he uttered his first blood-curdling threats to the 'rabble' who, if they resisted the rising, would be 'shot like dogs'.

Airlifted from North Africa, Moorish troops hastened the insurgents' advance from Seville to Badajoz.

Helped by *regulares* the insurgents also captured Cadiz, Algeciras and Jeréz. On 20 July the first units of the Foreign Legion – which was, in fact, predominantly Spanish – arrived in Seville, having been flown from Morocco. There ensued a frightful butchery in the Triana, the working-class district, which was then flattened by artillery fire. The initial Nationalist gains were consolidated and a rapid advance made possible by the airlift of 1,500 Army of Africa troops to Seville by German planes. By the end of September 1936 more than 12,000 had been so transported. For once Hitler did not exaggerate when he said that 'Franco ought to erect a monument to the glory of the Junkers 52.' On 6 August Franco, until then mainly concerned with negotiations for German and Italian help, flew to Seville to direct the campaign.

Neither side could hope for a swift, decisive outcome. The air force, though largely in Republican hands, was too rudimentary to be of much account. About half the Army of Africa had to stay in Morocco to keep order. Perhaps seventy per cent of the regular army in Spain was nominally Nationalist, including the great majority of officers; but the rank and file were illiterate, undisciplined conscripts used mainly for garrison duty, and the NCOs were overwhelmingly Republican in sympathy. The rebels could count on support from at least two-thirds of the 30,000 civil guards, but the 18,000 assault guards were almost solidly Republican. Carlist militiamen – perhaps about 12,000 in July 1936 and a force to be reckoned with in Andalusia as well as Navarre – provided a useful Nationalist stiffening, as did the Falangists, who were about 50,000 strong.

At Burgos, the capital of Old Castile where, as one aristocrat said, 'the very stones are Nationalist', the insurgents met with no resistance and scored successes in some Aragonese towns, notably Saragossa, Huesca and Jaca,

After killing their officers, sailors on the cruiser MIGUEL DE CERVANTES *fly the Republican flag and give the socialist salute.*

where the garrisons made their move before the unions could mobilize. From Pamplona, where 6,000 fanatical *requetés*, baying their battle cry 'Viva Cristo Rey!' (Long Live Christ the King), were straining at the leash, General Mola, commanding the Army of the North, controlled Navarre and prepared to invade the other Basque provinces – which, though predominantly conservative and Catholic, had declared for the Republic in return for a promise of self-government.

In Salamanca, also safely Nationalist, Juan Crespo, the 19-year-old student, asked his mother to buy him some mechanic's overalls (the usual militia uniform on both sides) and discovered that 'the Spanish army was an army in name only. The Republican government had reduced its numbers, and summer leave was granted to enable conscripts to help on the land; so that in July 1936 the army was at no more than half strength.' There had been no time to form proper militias, so he and his friends regarded themselves vaguely as volunteers. 'We bought the overalls, went to the barracks and were issued with ammunition belts and rifles, did guard duty or went out on patrol in lorries, came back whenever we liked, handed in our rifles, and went home.'

By the end of July the insurgents had occupied about one-third of Spain, including the meat-rearing provinces of Extremadura and Castile and more than half the cereal-growing regions. The Republic held the fertile fruit- , rice- and vegetable-growing areas along the Mediterranean coast and the industrial trump cards of Catalonia and the Basque provinces, together with the coal and the explosives factories of Asturias. Militarily, the rebels were more plentifully officered and in the Army of Africa possessed the only effective fighting units. Financially, the Republic had the advantage of holding the substantial gold reserves of the Bank of Spain and seven of the most populous cities, including Madrid and Barcelona. But the insurgent grip

Seville, 20 July 1936. Foreign Legionnaires and civil guards end resistance in the working-class district.

on the Canaries and all but one (Minorca) of the Balearic islands, together with their domination of most of the territory near the border of Portugal – which was to play an important role as a channel for foreign aid – gave them a long-term strategic advantage.

The situation was far from clear-cut, being liable to sudden shifts according to the fortunes of war. 'Geographical loyalty' – the feigning of Republican or Nationalist sympathies in the interests of personal survival – was inevitably common. Families were painfully divided. Two brothers of Buenaventura Durruti, the anarchist leader, were Falangists. A brother of General Pozas, the Republican Minister of the Interior, was one of General Mola's ADCs. Frederic Escofet, Police Commissioner in Barcelona, smuggled some of his wealthy factory-owning family to safety in Italy and saw one brother join the Nationalists 'because of the barbarities committed by our side. If he'd been in Nationalist territory he'd probably have come over to us for the same reason. That's the way it was.' Escofet also found it 'heart-breaking' when in the resistance to the rebellion in Barcelona 'we destroyed the Santiago Cavalry Regiment, the regiment I'd been in when I was a young lieutenant.' While Juan Crespo was having his first experience of the war as a happy-go-lucky volunteer, his Left Republican uncle, a lecturer in the Faculty of Medicine at Salamanca University, was arrested, imprisoned and executed together with a socialist politician. 'They drove the bodies out into the country and threw them into a ditch. In the morning a shepherd discovered them.'

On neither side was there much unity. Barcelona had not lost its contempt for Madrid and vice versa. The Basques were solely interested in fighting for their independence. At this point Nationalist Spain seemed almost as potentially fissiparous. Franco was not yet installed as Generalissimo. Some favoured Mola as Caudillo (Leader); others, including Vegas Latapié and Sáinz Rodríguez, felt that General Sanjurjo had a better grasp of political reality and were shocked by the news that on 20 July he had been killed when the plane flying him from Lisbon to Burgos crashed shortly after take-off. Queipo de Llano's dash and flamboyance seemed to make him a strong candidate in some quarters.

With the scales so evenly balanced, both sides sought to tip them with aid from abroad. Meanwhile the Republic's most important achievement, and the crucial blow to insurgent hopes for a rapid coup, was to have foiled the rising in Barcelona and Madrid.

Colonel Escofet remembers Sunday 19 July as 'the longest day of my life', preoccupied as he was with two problems in Barcelona: would the civil guards declare for the Republic, and would they, with the assault guards, be able to cope with the 5,000 troops in the barracks, thus averting the danger of power passing to the streets, with the prospect of an uncontrollable revolutionary free-for-all?

From early in the morning, as the troops left their barracks and converged on the Plaza de Catalunya, factory and ships' sirens began to wail. Escofet's alarm, shared by President Companys and Josep Tarradellas, was not unqualified. 'I knew it was a call from the CNT-FAI to their people. Lacking weapons and any exact knowledge of the tactical situation, they were unlikely to be very effective. But for a short time at least my reaction was one of relief,

Barcelona, 19 July 1936. Assault guards and armed workers in a truck adorned with the female symbol of the Republic.

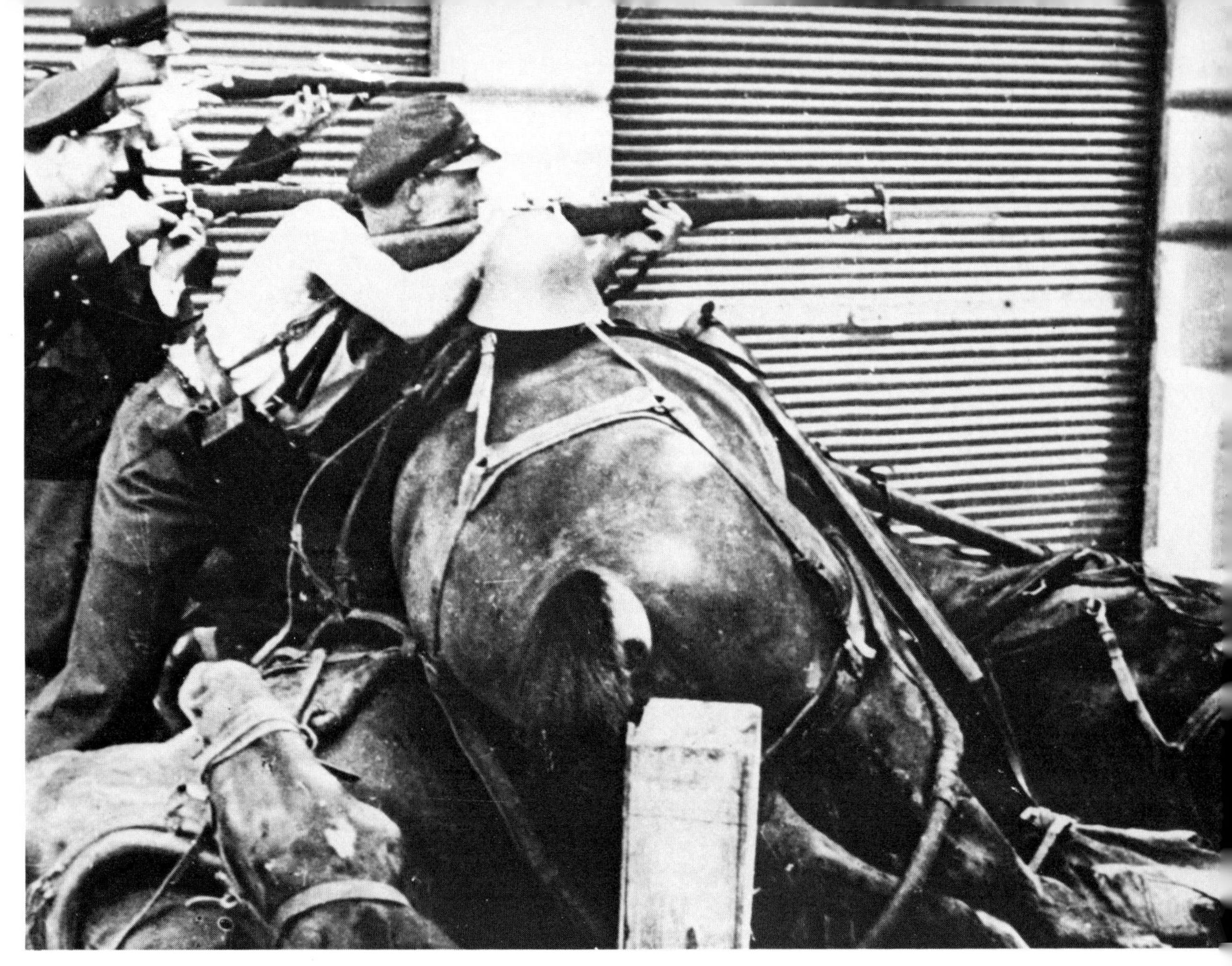

ABOVE

Barcelona, 19 July 1936. Assault guards fire at insurgent troops from behind a barricade of dead horses.

Barcelona, 20 July 1936. In the two-day street battle it is estimated that more than 500 people were killed and some 3,000 wounded.

knowing that I had their support.' The civil guards had not yet shown their hand, the assault guards were therefore still on their own.

Enric Adroer, a schoolteacher, had been in the main street, the wide, tree-shaded Rambla, from 7 a.m. with about fifty other POUM militants. 'We met some *asaltos* [assault guards]. At first they were suspicious, but when they realized we were friendly they changed their attitude. They stripped off their military tunics and threw them on the ground as if to show solidarity with the workers.' Raiding gun-shops and arsenals into which they were admitted by sympathetic NCOs, even persuading assault guards to hand over their rifles, the CNT swarmed into the streets. Paving-stones were torn up and 'suddenly,' says Eduardo Pons Prades, 'there were barricades at the end of every street and most people were wearing red-and-black anarchist neckerchiefs. I suppose these must have been made by women of the textile workers' union toiling at home with their sewing machines, preparing for the moment when the revolution at last arrived. Those scarves had a remarkable effect. Years later a Falangist officer who had taken refuge in the Hotel Colon told me that when he peered through the blinds and saw all those scarves at the barricades around the Plaza de Catalunya he said to his fellow rebels: "This time the CNT are out in force. We're done for."'

Not all the activity was focused on the military threat. Lola Iturbe was distressed to see a mob burning and looting the church of San Jaime. The looting especially offended her libertarian ideals. 'I found that hard to take. It seemed to me that they were acting barbarously.'

One troop column was defeated without a shot when armed workers, holding rifles above their heads, successfully urged their rank-and-file brothers to disobey their officers. Elsewhere the fighting, though confused, was fierce. 'All that day was an explosion,' says Juan Molina; 'even if we had died then we should have lived through something extraordinary.' Cut off and forced to surrender by rebel units, he and other *cenetistas* were imprisoned in a classroom of the University after several of their comrades had been killed.

As the battle raged on, the Plaza was littered with corpses. Lola Iturbe 'saw women snatch the rifles from wounded comrades and join in the fighting.' The recklessness of these amateur combatants seemed appalling to a professional soldier like Escofet. 'They showed plenty of guts but had no idea of caution or discipline. Often they were wearing white shirts and were perfect targets. That's why so many were killed and wounded.'

Not until mid-day did the civil guards enter the fray. On the balcony at police headquarters, Escofet, Companys and Tarradellas nervously watched them as they marched along the Vía Layetana. Tarradellas remembers it as 'one of the few moments in my life when I've been really scared. The street was utterly silent. I kept thinking "they could shoot us."' 'You could hear the click, click, click of their footsteps,' says Escofet. 'Then, when they got really close, the colonel shouted "Halt!", turned towards the balcony, saluted, and said: "At your orders, Mr President."' Tarradellas now felt '90 per cent certain that the coup would fail'.

Barcelona, 20 July 1936. The left-wing Catalan nationalist Josep Tarradellas (in double-breasted suit and black tie) with members of the Anti-Fascist Militias Committee. Andrés Nin, a leader of the anti-Stalinist POUM and one-time secretary to Leon Trotsky, is next to Tarradellas (wearing glasses).

In his improvised jail Juan Molina was 'waiting for the final blow. Suddenly the doors opened and the *guardias* [civil guards] came in. My first reaction was: "They'll be worse than the army." But no, they embraced us and set us free. I got hold of one of the machine-guns the fascists had been using on us, and we marched along the Rambla, a column on each side, in a rather showy way, clearing up some pockets of resistance.' The action had now switched to the harbour district where troops in the Atarazanas barracks were holding out. While Molina and some of the union and party militias assaulted the barracks, others stormed the military headquarters, where General Goded, arriving by hydroplane from Majorca to take command of the rebellion at the very moment when the *guardias* were declaring for the Republic, had set up headquarters.

Captured and taken to the Generalitat, Goded, another possible rival to Franco, was ordered by President Companys to broadcast an appeal to surrender, as he himself had been forced to do when the October 1934 rebellion collapsed. After some argument, Goded did as he was told: 'Destiny has been adverse and I have been taken prisoner. I release from their obligations all those who have followed me.' A few weeks later he was tried and executed.

The siege of the Atarazanas barracks continued, nevertheless, until the morning of 20 July. Molina was there during the final assault. 'We covered a lorry with mattresses, mounted a machine-gun on it, drove out into the open

Bujaraloz, Aragon, August 1936. Grenade-throwers of the Durruti Column from Barcelona.

and at last silenced the machine-guns on the upper gallery.' When a white flag of surrender was flown 'a huge mass surged into the barracks, tearing it apart'.

The battle had been won, thanks to the initiative of the CNT and the POUM and the loyalty of the security forces. 'The victory was shared', says Molina. It was also partly due to a certain half-heartedness on the part of the rebels. Soldiers had left the barracks under the impression that they were to crush an anarchist revolt. They had been given a large ration of brandy, and when the effects of this began to wear off they began to suspect the truth.

Though able to announce to a disbelieving Azaña that the rising was over and General Goded a prisoner, triumph was tinged with anxiety for President Companys. The combined operation, though unplanned and fundamentally undesired, had been a success. But would the CNT, and the disorderly elements surrounding it, back down now that they were in full, excitable cry – and lavishly armed? For not only had weapons been taken from captured troops but Commissioner Escofet's attempt to prevent the sacking of the Sant Andreu arsenal, containing 30,000 rifles, many machine-guns, and other war material, had failed. Commandeered vehicles with CNT-FAI scrawled on them dashed hooting through the streets. Even the *guardias* and *asaltos*, tunics discarded, saluting with clenched fists, seemed to be affected by the atmosphere of half-menacing jamboree. 'From that moment,' says Escofet, 'the rabble took over and started murdering indiscriminately. The police were

Madrid, 20 July 1936. Officers from the Montaña Barracks guarded by an armed civilian after surrendering.

powerless. President Companys asked me: "What can we do now?" I replied: "There's nothing I can do. You must seek some political solution."'

Amazingly a political solution, though temporary and fragile, was found, thanks largely to the CNT's refusal to take full power. That, as Juan Molina points out, 'would have meant establishing a dictatorship, which would have been a betrayal of everything we stood for. So when Companys suggested handing over everything to us – not that he had anything to hand over, it was all in our hands – we said no.' A compromise was proposed, a kind of dual authority. The Generalitat still nominally ruled but the real power was centred in an Anti-Fascist Militias Committee with five CNT members, five from the various Republican parties, three from the UGT, one from the POUM, and one from the newly-formed PSUC (a fusion of socialists and Communists which in effect became the Catalan Communist party).

Tarradellas, appointed as liaison between the Central Committee and the Generalitat, did not relish the job. 'We would arrive with our machine-guns and automatic rifles and pile them on the table,' says Enric Adroer, the POUM delegate, 'and the meeting would be held around this great heap of weapons. It lent a very special character, as you can imagine. But within a week the Committee became the true government of Catalonia. The Generalitat was just a symbol.'

More than 500 had been killed and 3,000 wounded in the two-day battle in Barcelona. The question now was: how many more would perish in the aftermath of vengeance?

In Madrid, where the military rising was even less co-ordinated than in Barcelona, a similar combination of enthusiastic workers backed by the security forces had achieved victory by 20 July – and with similar results: a

Insurgent dead in the courtyard of the Montaña Barracks, taken by storm after a five-hour siege.

paralysed government, nominally led by Azaña, and power in the streets where the dominant union, the UGT, maintained such order as existed.

During the night of 19/20 July fifty churches went up in flames. Huge, angry crowds assembled in front of the Montaña barracks, where some 2,000 troops, with about 500 monarchist and Falangist volunteers, prepared for a siege and waited for a relief column from the barracks at Carabanchel which never arrived. Enrique Líster, who since 1935 had been secretly organizing communist cells in the Army, had contacts in most of the barracks. With La Pasionaria, who in the first of many radio harangues had uttered the much-repeated slogan *No pasarán* (they shall not pass), he personally persuaded the troops at one infantry barracks to change their allegiance.

Only at the Montaña barracks did his system break down; and like Escofet in Barcelona he found the reckless behaviour of the besiegers exasperating. Two captured cannon were being fired 'practically at random, just to impress those inside. The real objective was to force an entry to seize weapons, and people were actually swarming to the attack unarmed.' Líster spoke to the gunners and their aim, he says, improved.

According to Eduardo de Guzmán the wildness of the earlier cannonade infuriated the mob, 'who thought that the artillerymen had betrayed them. Then the guns began to hit the target and people crept forward, climbing trees, approaching the corners of the building, firing if they had rifles. At about eleven o'clock on the Monday morning a white flag was shown. There was a general rush, but machine-guns opened fire and many were killed.' The flag-showing was probably not a dirty trick, simply a mistake as Líster's contacts or frightened conscripts acted on their own initiative: but it was regarded as black treachery. When a little later the gates were dynamited by

Asturian miners, the slaughter was terrible. Nearly all the officers were killed. 'The people were maddened by the deception,' says Guzmán, 'so when they saw an officer they would shoot him. Union and political leaders tried to restrain them, but it was a logical reaction, wasn't it?'

The anti-fascist terror in Madrid and Barcelona was a continuation of that kind of logical reaction; for the irony of the generals' failed coup was that in the name of restoring law, order and authority it had, notably in the two main cities, comprehensively destroyed them – thus strengthening the excuse for mounting a ruthless counter-terror in the name of law, order and authority.

Few people were more aware of this vicious circle than Police Commissioner Escofet. The ransacking of the Sant Andreu arsenal in Barcelona meant that the 5,000 *guardias* and *asaltos* were outnumbered by six to one; and the weapons were in the hands not just of the CNT and other 'official' organizations but of anyone who had chosen to help himself. 'I told President Companys: "Things are beyond control. Even the anarchists can't control their own people. How can I ask my men to start fighting workers with whom they have just shared a victory, apart from the fact that they're exhausted?"'

The revolution began with an orgy of killing and destruction. But inevitably, since the Nationalist zone was constantly expanding, and ultimately included the whole of Spain, the counter-revolutionary terror, being concerned mainly with the most numerous class – the rural and industrial proletariat – claimed more victims than the more limited and spontaneous assassinations in the Republican zone. Figures for the number of people murdered or executed by both sides during the war are still largely a matter of guesswork. For the Republican zone, estimates range from 17,000 to 55,000, with Nationalist killings at around 75,000.

In town or village a 'committee of control' acted as a local inquisition. But the new authorities were often ignored by unofficial avengers, common criminals or callow youth gangs. The anarchist leader Abad de Santillán reckoned that about 5,000 people perished in Catalonia, including more than 1,200 monks, nuns and priests in the province of Barcelona. Looting was uncommon. But the anti-clerical eruption in Catalonia – of 58 churches in Barcelona only the cathedral was spared and crowds flocked to see the corpses of some disinterred nuns – was paralleled by similar outbreaks almost everywhere in Republican Spain. This was regarded as an act of social hygiene. For, as a priest who had been helped to escape to France by President Companys admitted: 'The Reds have destroyed our churches, but we had already destroyed the Church.'

Caciques, civil guards, priests, lawyers and hated employers were prime targets, but 'reactionary' shopkeepers and workers were also at risk: and in Barcelona the renowned cellist Pablo Casals, whose name was on a death-list, came dangerously close to extinction. As early as 25 July the CNT-FAI strongly protested against 'illegal' violence. Juan Peiró, for instance, condemned those who 'killed for the sheer sake of killing, because they were able to do so with impunity. Many were shot for personal vengeance. A people in rebellion have been infiltrated by amoral elements who rob and murder by profession. Many of those who carry out expropriations have had no other interest than to seize other people's property for themselves.' A CNT proclamation issued in Barcelona warned: 'Comrades! The revolution must not be drowned in blood! Conscious justice, yes! Assassins, never!'

Federica Montseny, an anarchist intellectual who was one of the first to condemn the assassinations, compares the killings with those in France in the period immediately following liberation at the end of World War II. Juan Manuel Molina talks of the impossibility of controlling the explosion. 'Think of the years of unemployment, starving children, glaring inequality. All that helps to explain, but does not justify, what happened.' Enric Adroer argues that all revolutions have 'painful, unpleasant aspects' but that in a wider perspective 'the deaths which occurred at that time were of incidental importance. Social change was not the product of repression but of a drive for emancipation upon which it was difficult to impose any order. That was one of the biggest tasks for the Militias Committee. Gradually the situation improved.'

Escofet's strenuous efforts to impose order had already made him far from popular; and the use of his position to save members of his family and other potential victims of the repression made him a marked man. 'The Italian consul came to see me every day with a list of people that were to leave on Italian ships, and I authorized it. I didn't take into account whether they were leftists or rightists. My brother tried to save the Jesuit teachers at his son's school, but the anarchists found out and shot them all. They wanted to try me for treason. First I saved my brother, then, in September, I resigned and was sent abroad to buy arms for the Republic.'

In Madrid, too, influence was sometimes mercifully used. Azaña, who from his rooms in the National Palace could hear the nightly executions in the Casa de Campo, managed to save some of the monkish teachers at his old (and abhorred) school. La Pasionaria, though a vehement atheist, saved many nuns from being shot by the FAI, and set them to work making military uniforms. Dr Juan Negrín, Minister of Finance and later Prime Minister, was equally active. But the government as such made little attempt to control the many left-wing *checas* (named after the original Bolshevik security police). Assassinations and 'dawn patrols' kept the city in a sweaty ferment. The infrequent 'trials' of suspects by self-appointed 'courts' were occasions mainly for insult and abuse.

Willie Forrest, reporting for the London *Daily Express*, talked to the chief of a Communist *checa*, who admitted that Communists, anarchists and socialists were rivalling each other 'to see who could get the biggest score of assassinations' but saw the role of the *checas* as similar to that of an examining magistrate. It was, he said, their job to assess whether or not to send a suspect for trial by a Popular Tribunal. Turbulence was unavoidable. In the early stages of the civil war nearly all the assault guards and loyal civil guards were at the fronts. Cities were virtually unpoliced and common criminals had been let out of jail. 'When this man heard that I was born in Glasgow,' says Forrest, 'he asked: "Isn't that where razor gangs are active in some areas? Now supposing Glasgow was left without a police force and those gangs were free to go on the rampage – wouldn't there be plenty of assassinations, plenty of corpses in the parks and streets?"'

Cristina de Arteaga, who with the other nuns in her convent had for some months slept with civilian clothes by her bed, ready for flight, took refuge in a friend's flat. 'Three anarchists arrived wearing high-ranking officers' uniforms. They boasted that the uniforms had belonged to aristocratic victims who happened to be friends or relatives of mine. "Ah," they said, "by now grass must be growing over them", and used vile language which I don't wish to repeat.' José Vergara, trying to stay neutral in a conflict where neither side's aims or methods appealed to him, saw a friend killed – 'two men with a machine-gun were shooting at anyone who crossed the street.' Caretakers in apartment buildings now had powers of life or death. 'One of the things the search squads asked was which paper did the tenants buy. My caretaker said I took *El Sol*, a liberal daily, so I was not bothered. In the early days corpses were left in the streets, and twice I saw more than a hundred lying around. It was difficult to identify most of them because they had been shot in the face or head so that their features were completely distorted.'

As in Barcelona, clothes as well as newspaper-reading habits offered clues to killer gangs. It was common for well-to-do citizens to go about their business disguised as proletarians, perhaps in overalls, at any rate without collar, tie or hat. 35-year-old Francisco Poyatos, a public prosecutor, refused to conform: 'I decided to dress even more correctly than before – stiff collar, white tie, well-cut suit – when one day in August I saw this long convoy of lorries, the Mangada column [led by the eccentric Colonel Mangada, vegetarian and nudist], known as the Lions of Navalperal. The men were nearly naked, the women were stripped to the waist, a dreadful sight. Afraid that they would tear me to pieces, I hid in a doorway and took my shirt off so that I was a bit more bare-chested. Even magistrates and judges were trying to look as much like beggars as possible.'

As in the Nationalist zone the early-hours executions were public spectacles. Alvaro Delgado remembers hearing people say: '"We've just come from Manzanares or the Retiro, there were twenty stiffs today", or whatever the number might be. They went into details. "One must have been a priest, to judge from his clothes, another was a girl with lacy, embroidered underwear."' This period of anarchy, for which the anarchists were, often unjustly, held to be solely responsible, goes far to explain the success of the communists, especially among the middle classes, when they came out unequivocally as the party of law and order.

In those early days the Republic was trying to wage war without an army, relying on improvised, ill-armed, haphazardly uniformed union or party militias familiar perhaps with street-fighting but with no conception of campaigning outside the cities.

An allegorical portrayal of the proclamation of the Republic,
14 April 1931.

A Communist Party poster urges people to vote for the Popular Front in the February elections, 1936.

Madrid, 23 July 1936. Militiamen leave for the front in the Sierra de Guadarrama.

It was a war of columns with no fixed fronts. Mola's Carlists and Falangists had, by 22 July, reached the Somosierra Pass in the Guadarrama mountains north of Madrid. Three days later insurgent columns from Valladolid and Salamanca captured the Alto de León Pass to the north-west. From Madrid, says Alvaro Delgado, columns set out 'as though it was a great party, a party in honour of the revolution, you might say. Early in the morning you would hear men calling to each other, "Manolo, Paco, Antonio," the window would open – "I'm coming" – and a man would run downstairs doing up his overalls, fixing his cartridge belt. He would climb into the lorry and head for the hills to fight, then come back for the night. The women would say: "Paco's gone off to the front today and I made him a tortilla and he's taken a few bottles of wine." People went to the front as if to a picnic.'

On 22 July Enrique Líster, already recognized as a tough, resourceful leader, accompanied a column to the Alto de León as political commissar. 'It was a mixed column, workers from various districts and some regular troops who were said to be loyal to the Republic. For transport we requisitioned 50 Fiat lorries and cars from a firm I knew. At dawn we practically wiped out a company of Falangists from Valladolid, but when their reinforcements started using explosive bullets our men fled.' Sometimes, in those motley columns, the enemy of yesterday might be the man standing beside you. The writer Ramón Sender, also in action near the Alto de León, found 'plasterers, carpenters, metalworkers, alongside civil guards and assault guards. A young newspaper-seller said to me, pointing at a *guardia*: "That man broke my father's arm when he beat him up in October 1934."'

From Barcelona columns were setting out into Aragon with the main

ABOVE LEFT *'More Men, More Arms, More Munitions' – to fight fascism: a Catalan socialist poster.*

ABOVE RIGHT *Militiamen of the Red and Black Column head for the Aragon front.*

RIGHT *Barcelona, 28 July 1936. Family farewell for an anarchist (FAI) militiaman of the Red and Black Column led by García Oliver.*

objective of liberating Saragossa, a CNT stronghold which had been taken by the insurgents. The first column of 2,500 *cenetistas* was led by Durruti – 'The Free Man against the Fascist Hyena'. Enric Adroer had been given the job of finding transport for the columns. 'There were thousands of militants, no uniforms or equipment, just wearing ordinary working clothes. Women and children waved goodbye as the men climbed into the lorries wearing their red-and-black caps or scarves. No tears, it was a festive occasion.' The trouble was locating vehicles. 'We just had to requisition cars wherever we could find them,' and this was done on a class basis. 'My team visited the most suitable districts – the haunts of the rich – and when they saw cars parked in front of a brothel, say, or a night club, they would drive them to our garage and next day, at crack of dawn, those cars would be on their way to the front.'

Nationalist columns were almost as casual and naively optimistic. Mola's advance on Madrid was slowed by lack of ammunition as much as by Republican militias. Yet Juan Crespo, climbing into a lorry in Salamanca, was convinced that 'it would be a race to see which column would reach Madrid first – to have a cup of coffee in Madrid as the saying was. At dawn we left Avila en route to the Alto de León, but were routed in the village of Navalperal by Colonel Mangada's column. Except for some *guardias* with machine-guns we ran, I among the rest, all the way back to Avila, about 40 kilometres.'

When he got back to Salamanca, Crespo heard that a second uncle had been imprisoned, 'simply because he was a relative of the one who had been assassinated.'

While insurgent and Republican militias skirmished in the Guadarramas, legionaries and Moors, flown in to the Nationalist bridgehead at Seville, prepared to advance to Mérida and Badajoz, thence up the valley of the

Anarchist militiamen and militiawomen leave Barcelona for the front.

Republican troops and peasant volunteers skirmish with insurgent columns in the Alto de León, north of Madrid.

Tagus to Madrid. They advanced in columns of 500 to 1,000 under such seasoned commanders as Colonel Juan Yagüe, the 'butcher' of Asturias. The ferocious reputation of the Moors and the voice of Queipo de Llano, promising that for every 'patriot' killed ten of the 'Marxist rabble' would be shot, spread terror – and a determination to 'make the revolution' before it was too late.

In Lora del Rio Republican propaganda had perhaps helped to encourage the great experiment. Manuel Vázquez Guillén, then aged 26 and a UGT (socialist) official, helped form a revolutionary committee including *cenetistas* on 19 July. 'The civil guard captain ordered all weapons to be handed in, but we set pickets in every street leading to the barracks and confiscated the weapons. That way we accumulated about 4,000 shotguns and revolvers.' After a four-day siege the *guardias* surrendered when the committee threatened to cut the water supply. The captain was shot as he walked out, but 'the others were protected and put in jail. That night truckloads of militants, about 200 of them, arrived from other villages, out for blood after hearing about the killings by fascist columns from Seville. We couldn't stop them. The two priests were among those killed the first night.'

A rationing system was worked out, with food supplies stored in a barn. Fighting bulls belonging to the famous Miura family were slaughtered and 'many families in Lora ate steaks for the first time in their lives.' Distribution of clothes and footwear was also organized, but 'most of the peasants couldn't make use of the shoes because they had always worn sandals.' Warned of the approach of a Nationalist column, the committee supervised the construction of barricades but realized that resistance was useless when the village was shelled by light artillery. Women and children fled to the sierra. After hiding in a mountain farmhouse, Vazquez eventually reached the Republican lines. His mother-in-law was shot immediately after returning to Lora.

Carlos Aparicio, aged 19, stayed on when the Nationalists had occupied Lora, confident that his lack of political commitment would guarantee his safety. But he was arrested and early next morning, 8 August, marched to the cemetery and lined up against the wall with 17 other 'Reds.' He collapsed when the shooting started but was only grazed by a bullet. Covered in blood from the other victims but still conscious, he heard an officer going down the line administering the coup de grâce. The officer ran out of bullets after finishing off the seventeenth Red and did not bother to reload, apparently assuming that Carlos was dead. When the firing squad had gone, Carlos started out for the village to clear up what he still considered a misunderstanding, but was warned by a woman to go into hiding. He did so, but after three days, still obstinate, went back to Lora del Rio, presented himself to the commanding officer, swore that he had never been a Red, and said he was willing to fight for the Nationalists. Escorted home by *guardias*, he found his family in mourning for him.

Asunción Martínez, then a girl of 12, can remember the church being looted in 1931 and witnessing a gun-fight between peasants and *guardias* in

Insurgent troops capture an outpost at Somosierra, north of Madrid.

1934. 'The Republic didn't change my father's life. He still worked from dawn to dusk for 2.50 pesetas a day.' During the siege of the barracks she smuggled in food 'because my cousin was married to a *guardia*.' She estimates that about 130 'fascists' were held in the town hall, and executions in the cemetery, beginning on 25 July, continued for ten days. Asunción still remembers the three weeks of the revolution, of freedom, as the most exciting period of her childhood. She and her family went to a farm in the sierra when the shelling started, but two days later her mother returned to find out if it was safe for the men to return. She noticed piles of corpses outside the cemetery but was told that the villagers could return wearing a white armband. Many of the men who came back were immediately arrested, and executions, at first by column troops, later by Falangists and *requetés*, continued until the end of 1936. After that, says Asunción, most prisoners were taken to Seville.

Eighteen miles east of Lora, in Palma del Rio, 24-year-old Felix Moreno de la Cova had seen the increasing chaos caused by strikes and sabotage on his father's farms. 'I never voted for the Falange but I sympathized with José Antonio. I felt then as I feel now, that we need a strong, idealistic right-wing group to stand up to left extremism.'

When he heard of the coup in Seville he thought it meant a Republican victory, since 'Queipo was known as a Republican supporter'. Hearing that Queipo had come out against the Republic and that a column was leaving Cordoba to 'pacify' the *pueblos* (villages), he joined it on 19 July. In one *pueblo* after another the Lora del Rio sequence was repeated. A brief revolutionary spree, the shooting of 'fascist' prisoners in a gesture of defiance and despair as the enemy column approached, then summary retribution – justified by the proclamation of martial law and the necessity to secure the rear as the columns moved on, leaving a small garrison behind.

In Baena, a large hillside *pueblo*, the peasants had fought a gruelling nine-day battle with *guardias* and landowners' defence groups to gain temporary control on 28 July. That same day the column from Cordoba, mainly of legionaries and *regulares*, arrived on the scene. De la Cova considered Baena 'the worst example of Red atrocities. We shelled the place but there was stiff resistance. A Moor who walked beside me into the village kicked a door open and was shot dead. I killed his assailant. The Reds had taken about 80 hostages to the convent of San Francisco and tied many of them to the windows so that we could not shoot. They surrendered next morning and we went in. It was like a vision from Dante's Inferno. Nearly all the hostages had been killed. The stench was unbearable. I saw a little girl tied to a window who had been stabbed and left to bleed to death. In one room I found a father and son, friends of my family, who had been mutilated with axes. All the Reds were taken to the village square, where the *guardias* and the troops shot about sixty of them.'

Atrocity bred atrocity. In Cordoba province there were stories of Falangist *señoritos* (sons of the gentry) forcing peasants to dig their own graves and jeering at them as they did so.

'We left him in a ditch. I fired two bullets into his arse for being a queer,' claimed a Falangist executioner. He was talking of Federico García Lorca who, though he had signed some anti-fascist manifestos, was admired by Falangist writers and littérateurs (including José Antonio), had many right-wing friends, and described himself as 'like all true poets, a revolutionary, but a politician – never!'

Lorca was homosexual; but 'left' intellectuals were usually classified as sexual perverts by Nationalist killer squads. Lorca's real mistake was to decide, on 18 July, that he might be safer in the family house, the Huerta de San Vicente, in the countryside near Granada than in the sudden, frightening upheaval of Madrid. In view of his published attacks on the philistinism of the Granada bourgeoisie, this was a strange, almost suicidal, decision. By 23 July working-class resistance in Granada had been crushed, the Huerta de San Vicente was under observation, and there were rumours that Lorca himself was a spy sending radio messages to the Red monsters.

Frightened, he took refuge with the Falangist Rosales family in the centre of Granada – the son Luis, a writer, was a close friend. But on 16 August (the day his brother-in-law, the socialist mayor of Granada, was shot) Lorca was arrested by the civil governor – who, after a telephone conversation with Queipo de Llano, sentenced him to death. Three days later, with a batch of 'Reds' including a one-legged schoolteacher and two *banderilleros*, he was shot and, it seems, buried in a narrow trench in an olive grove, near a fountain-spring celebrated by the Moorish poets he had so admired.

Lorca was one of 572 victims executed in Granada in August 1936. Between 2,000 and 4,000 people from Granada and the surrounding villages were liquidated before the war ended. But because of his stature as a poet and dramatist Lorca's fate had a special significance. Trying to shift the blame, the Nationalist press reported that Lorca had been assassinated by 'Reds' in Barcelona (according to one version), in Madrid (according to another), not forgetting to add the slur that Lorcas was 'to be compared with Azaña in doubtful sexuality'. His death became a symbol of the barbarity of the Nationalist repression, with its pogrom of liberal intellectuals. As Ian Gibson comments in *The Death of Lorca*, 'the flower of Granada's intellectuals, lawyers, doctors and teachers died in the cemetery, among them all the most brilliant university professors . . . including Rafael García Duarte, Professor of Paediatrics, a much-loved man who treated his poor patients free of charge. His crime was to have been a freemason.'

This pattern of killings was repeated wherever the Nationalists held sway. Schoolteachers were shot and *casas del pueblo* (those proletarian temples) closed down, just as, in the Republican zone, priests were shot and churches sealed off or used for storage: a sight which offended W. H. Auden as much as did the liquidation of Lorca.

Five days before Lorca's squalid killing, early in the morning of 15 August, Mario Neves, a Portuguese journalist, visited the cemetery in Badajoz. 'The bodies,' he says, 'were arranged in piles, petrol poured over them, and burnt

. . . The smell was awful. A lorry full of corpses drove in . . . A priest, seeing how I was reacting, said: "They deserved it. The city is being cleansed."'

Badajoz, the capital of Extremadura, where revolutionary land seizures had been most extensive, was a strategically placed city near the Portuguese frontier. Since 18 July it had been firmly controlled by the army garrison which had declared for the Republic. Right-wingers had been jailed but very few killed. On 14 August, after a tough battle – the first serious opposition they had encountered – the legionaries and Moors of Yagüe's column had breached the defence. Reports of the ensuing shambles, though exaggerated by some reporters (the American Jay Allen wrote of 4,000 deaths in the bullring), shocked the Western world when it hit the headlines. Neves 'saw legionaries and Moors grabbing men by the shirt and tearing it to look at the right shoulder. If it was bruised by rifle recoil they would be shot. In the central square bodies were left lying to terrorize the populace. There were even corpses in the cathedral.'

Neves, who refused to revisit Spain during the war, reckons that 'certainly 2,000 is not an exaggeration, although it's an approximation.' Interviewed by Neves, Yagüe calmly agreed that the number of deaths was probably about right. Neves had seen refugees from the slaughter and the looting turned back at the Portuguese frontier on President Salazar's instructions. They too were penned in the bullring and then shot in the cemetery. The terror continued well into September. Teresa Villalobos' husband, a street photographer of mildly Republican sentiments, was arrested on 17 September 'for questioning'. Then she heard that he had been taken to the bullring. 'He was locked in a crowded bullpen . . . We could only hold hands through a small, high window. His face was like yellow wax and his eyes – they were big blue eyes – were fixed on me . . . I knew I would never see him again. Next day some relatives told me he had been shot.'

The capture of Badajoz meant that the Nationalists dominated the approaches to the Portuguese frontier. By 3 September, only a month after leaving Seville, Yagüe's troops had covered more than 300 miles and had occupied Talavera, the last centre of importance on the way to Madrid.

Political prisoners, placed in a special wing of the Modelo Prison in Madrid, had come to think of it as a haven of security in the surrounding welter of revenge killings. But on 17 August, following the first air raids on the city and news of the Badajoz massacre, there was an ominous visit of inspection by what Serrano Suñer describes as 'anarchists with machine-guns. The inspection consisted of robbing us of our valuables.'

Five days later the prison was assaulted. 'They rigged a fire in one of the blocks,' says Fernández Cuesta, 'and claimed that fascist prisoners were responsible. Then they stormed the place, machine-gunning prisoners from the roof of a garage which overlooked one of the yards.' At nightfall the 'politicians' were taken to a room remembered by Cuesta as 'like an engraving from the French Revolution. There was a tribunal of men and women dressed in overalls and wearing strange hats. Six or seven names were called out and the victims taken away to be executed in a cellar below.' Among them were Melquiades Alvarez, a former president of the Chamber of Deputies, and Fernando Primo de Rivera, a brother of José Antonio. 'We could hear the shots,' says Serrano Suñer. 'Even Prieto, arriving with bodyguards, was nearly lynched when – so I was told – he said: "Animals! We've lost the war thanks to what you've done tonight."'

Compared with Badajoz or Queipo de Llano's reprisals, twenty or thirty murders seemed trivial. But to Azaña and Prieto, concerned for the effect on public opinion abroad, they were a disaster. Eduardo de Guzmán and Régulo Martínez were among those who regretted that there had been so many random killings and so few 'legal' executions after open trial. Socrates Gómez, an official in the Security Department of the Ministry of the Interior, recalls how instructions to free certain prisoners were ignored. 'Once I personally supervised the release of thirty or so people, including Ricardo Zamora, a famous football player. He was so nervous that he hit his head against the door-frame and cut himself.' Visiting Valencia, Gómez had a permanent police escort 'because we ourselves were under constant threat by these hooligans'.

After the Modelo incident, which brought angry protests from foreign ambassadors, a system of popular tribunals was established; and in conjunction with a curfew and a network of street controls these had some effect in reducing the number of indiscriminate killings. But the poet Pablo Neruda, then Chilean consul in Madrid, narrowly escaped a *paseo* when a hit squad tried to seize him in a restaurant. Ramón Sender was on the brink of being shot by a patrol which, when he revealed his identity, accused him of impersonating himself. Crowded with the carts and livestock of peasant refugees bearing terrible tales of fascist atrocities, Madrid continued to react to the insurgent threat with the murderous defiance that had characterized the doomed *pueblos* of Andalusia and Extremadura.

By mid-September, thanks to a timely consignment of ammunition, Mola's plan to capture Irún and San Sebastian, thus blocking the French supply route to the Republic in the western Pyrenees, had been achieved; and he took possession of a large area of farm land and a number of Basque industrial centres. The campaign had been marked by disputes between Basque nationalists, disinclined to wreck their towns before retreating, and anarchist and communist militias favouring a more drastic policy. The CNT actually did set fire to Irún. Ironically, the decree approving Basque autonomy was approved just as the putative Basque Republic was beginning to disintegrate. The remaining province, Vizcaya, with its capital Bilbao, would almost certainly have been conquered but for Mola's decision to concentrate on the drive southward to Madrid. But with Nationalist columns poised to advance from Talavera, the Republican defence in almost total disarray, and expertly-piloted German and Italian aircraft dominating the sky, the fall of Madrid seemed temptingly inevitable.

This, however, was postponed – for 2½ years as it turned out – when Franco,

The ruins of the Alcázar after the fortress was dynamited by Asturian miners.

against the advice of Yagüe, ordered a diversion to relieve the Alcázar, a massive stone fortress, used as a military academy, perched on a crag over the river Tagus at Toledo. Here, after a savage three-day battle (19–22 July) in the narrow, winding streets of Toledo, Colonel José Moscardó had taken refuge with about 1,300 combatants – army officers, civil guards, some right-wing militiamen – and 700 non-combatants (including the civil governor and about 100 'Reds' as hostages), and was holding out in what became a heroic set-piece of Nationalist propaganda: a point which Franco shrewdly did not overlook.

The Nationalist press thrilled to the romantic tale of how the intrepid Moscardó, when informed by telephone that if he did not surrender forthwith his 24-year-old son Luis would be shot, told the latter: 'Commend your soul to God, shout *Viva España!* and die like a hero. The Alcázar will never surrender.' Luis Moscardó was, with other prisoners, shot some weeks later in reprisal for a Nationalist air raid: a move which was countered by the execution of hostages in the Alcázar. But in the absence of heavy artillery the siege did not prosper. Mere numbers were of little significance when desultory rifle fire, accompanied by loudspeaker taunts and appeals to surrender, were all that the Republican forces could contrive. Some of the besiegers were 'tourists of war' who came from Madrid for a few hours of entertainment. Willie Forrest came in a chauffeur-driven Rolls-Royce, once the property of a royalist nobleman. 'I took William Dobby, a visiting Labour MP, up a church tower from which you got a wonderful view of the Alcázar's courtyard. There was a machine-gun in the tower and Dobby couldn't resist the temptation to fire it at the fascists.'

Enrique Líster's offer to 'capture the Alcázar within 24 hours' if given full command of the operation was rejected for fear, he says, of offending the CNT who regarded it as their property, 'so all I got was one battalion.' As for the anarchists, 'they were having a holiday, red-and-black scarves everywhere, laughing and chatting with their girl-friends. Occasionally a few shots, that was all.' The only Republican success was non-military: arrangements were made for the safekeeping of the many El Greco paintings in Toledo.

Nationalist planes dropped supplies and messages of encouragement to the defenders; and on 21 September, by which time water was severely rationed and all but one of the 177 horses in the Alcázar had been eaten, Franco ordered the relief of Toledo. As miners summoned from Asturias managed to blow up one of the Alcázar's towers and assault guards from Madrid prepared for a final attack, Nationalist columns led by General Varela reached the city on 27 September. The Republican militia fled, with the spectacular exception of forty drunken anarchists who committed mass suicide by setting fire to a seminary in which they were quartered. The Nationalists took no prisoners and it was reported that the steep main street of Toledo was cascading blood and that wounded Republicans were killed by Moors in their hospital beds. On 28 September, in a final histrionic gesture for the photographers, the haggard, heavily-bearded Colonel Moscardó saluted General Varela, using the rebel password of 18 July – *sin novedad* ('nothing to report'). Next day General Franco, who had directed the campaign from Burgos, was appointed Head of State and Commander-in-Chief of the Nationalist armies.

While the Nationalist 'state' was moving towards unity of command there was little sign of coherence in Madrid, and despite the Toledan detour Mola confidently predicted that the capital would fall by 7 November, a date chosen as the anniversary of the start of the Bolshevik revolution.

On 4 September Largo Caballero had become Prime Minister of a 'government of victory' composed of Left Republicans, moderate and left-wing socialists, and Communists (the first to be included in a western administration). The social revolution seemed to have triumphed, but new tensions emerged. Largo admired the role of the Fifth Regiment; its discipline and its introduction of political commissars to indoctrinate militiamen and to keep a watchful eye on suspect regular army officers had made it outstandingly effective in the Guadarrama skirmishes. But he was beginning to resent the rapid growth of Communist influence. The decision to 'militarize' the various militias in the hope of creating a Popular Army roused the kind of resistance to central authority which it was designed to end in the name of greater efficiency. Plans to construct part of a defence complex of trenches languished because the necessary shovels and barbed wire did not

29 September 1936. General Franco with Colonel José Moscardó, commander of the besieged Nationalist troops (left), and General Varela (bare-headed) after the relief of the Alcázar.

arrive from Barcelona and building workers refused to leave paid civilian jobs.

Massing 25,000 troops for the attack, the Nationalists had by mid-October advanced to within fifteen miles of Madrid, causing further refugee problems to the harassed authorities. To capture a city with a population of more than a million was a far greater undertaking than the campaigns in Andalusia, Extremadura or the Basque provinces; but with successes behind them, and knowing that Soviet arms and advisers were arriving to boost the defence, the Nationalists pressed on with redoubled urgency. The first Republican opposition was brushed aside. Raw troops, unused to co-ordinated manoeuvres and tending to bunch together in open country, were cut down by machine-gun fire.

Despite the début of Soviet tanks, backed by units of the Fifth Regiment, Mola's columns had by 4 November captured Getafe airport on the outskirts of the city. Franco announced that the capital's liberation was imminent. A Radio Lisbon bulletin prematurely reported that the Caudillo had entered Madrid on a white horse. In what seemed a last despairing bid for unity Largo Caballero invited the CNT to join the threatened coalition. A national conference of the CNT authorized four candidates to enter the government: García Oliver became Minister of Justice, Juan Peiró Minister of Industry, Juan López Sánchez Minister of Commerce, and Federica Montseny Minister of Health. Federica Montseny explains that the decision was made 'to prevent the Communists seizing military and political control and to counteract those – some Republicans and Socialists – who were ready to end the war at almost any price.' But the move caused dismay – and fury – among many *cenetistas*. Federica Montseny's father told her that 'this means the liquidation of anarchism. Once in power you will not rid yourselves of power;' and when on 6 November the government fled from Madrid to Valencia with the excuse that it could not function efficiently in a war zone, the implication of so-called anarchists in such defeatism added to the contempt with which their 'collaboration' had been greeted.

Die-hard anarchists of the 'Iron Column' forced several ministers en route to Valencia out of their cars at gun-point. UGT (socialist) officials got similar treatment and all were held prisoner until CNT leaders in Madrid sent an order for their release. As trenches were dug and barricades thrown up in feverish haste, an atmosphere of near-panic revived the ever-lurking urge to strike at the enemy within while there was still time to do so. On 6 and 7 November, interpreting in their own fashion the fugitive government's orders that political prisoners should be transferred to Valencia, guards massacred about a thousand of them at the villages of Paracuellos de Jarama and Torrejón, shooting them into previously prepared trenches.

This was one way of acting on the ever-present banner slogan – 'Madrid Will Be the Graveyard of Fascism'. 'The people went into the streets to fight as best they could against the fascists,' says Lorenzo Iñigo, the CNT metalworker who was for a time secretary of the National Committee for Prisoners. 'They looked for them all over the city to kill them wherever they could be found. Not just the CNT but the entire Left, the whole anti-fascist spectrum, Communists, Socialists, Republicans. Contrary to what is often said, anarchists have always been sentimental. When they have used violence it has been in a passionate search for justice. Take the case of Melchor Rodríguez, the anarchist Director of Prisons. When, a few weeks later, Franco's planes were bombing Madrid and its periphery – and that was cold-blooded murder if you like – and people assaulted the prison at Alcalá de Henares wanting to kill the fascists there, he faced the mob and stopped them.' Fernández Cuesta, who was one of the prisoners at risk, confirms this. 'Rodríguez, a convinced anarchist but nevertheless a humane person, stood in front of the mob and said: "If you want to kill fascists go to the front. You're not coming in here."'

José Vergara, a statistician at the Ministry of Agriculture, remembers that after the government's departure on 6 November 'no one seemed to be in charge. The streets were practically deserted. There were some cars abandoned in the Paseo del Prado, but I didn't meet a single soul. A senior colleague asked me to find him a place to hide. At that point we felt that the war must have come to an end.'

General José Miaja, loyally Republican but with a mediocre military record, had been appointed supreme commander of Madrid's defence junta. Under the circumstances there was little he could do but call for determined resistance. When asked by some officers where to retreat in emergency he sardonically replied: 'To the cemetery.'

EDICIONES
BRIGADAS
INTERNACIONALES
VOLUNTARIOS INTERNACIONALES DE LA LIBERTAD
1936
1937
LOS INTERNACIONALES
UNIDOS a los ESPAÑOLES, LUCHAMOS CONTRA el INVASOR

CHAPTER THREE

THE INTERNATIONAL CIVIL WAR

For many people mention of the Spanish Civil War calls up the image of a large, sombre painting, by a man who had not lived in Spain since 1903, of a Basque town almost unknown outside Spain until it was saturation-bombed by German aeroplanes on 26 April 1937. Pablo Picasso, Guernica, the Condor Legion: a fitting trio to symbolize the relentless internationalization of the civil war.

On 17 October 1936, as the first recruits to the International Brigades arrived in Spain and the trials of Old Bolsheviks gathered sensational momentum in Moscow, the Communist paper *Mundo Obrero* published an open letter from Stalin which declared that 'the liberation of Spain from the yoke of the fascist reactionaries is not the private concern of Spaniards alone but the common cause of progressive humanity.'

The first appearance of Soviet tanks and planes in the defence of Madrid late in October and early in November made a tremendous impression, one which, says Teresa Pamies of the Catalan Communist party (PSUC), has never been quite forgotten. 'The USSR helped us, it sold guns to the government of the legitimate Republic. The guns were brought to Spain in their ships. Some of those Soviet ships were sunk in the Mediterranean by the fascists, and this feeling of mystical togetherness became a very solid feeling . . . which can't be stressed strongly enough and still continues.'

At first, says Alvaro Delgado, Nationalist planes had bombed Madrid with very little opposition. 'Then one day we saw some new machines in the sky, small ones we called *chatos* [snub-noses] flying at great speed, and another type we called *moscas* [flies], and they shot down some Nationalist aircraft. People started shouting "Long Live Russia!" and hugged each other. It was the first sign that maybe the war could tilt our way. It rekindled hope.'

Some Spaniards, while welcoming a supply of arms, resented the intrusion of foreign personnel. News of the impending arrival of the Comintern-recruited International Brigades did not delight the anarchists in Barcelona. CNT frontier patrols were at first instructed to prevent their entry, since it was believed that whatever the idealism of the multi-national volunteers they were the thin end of a Soviet wedge that would split and shatter the 'real' revolution. As the first Russian advisers tried to take the unruly Catalans in

OPPOSITE *During the civil war about 40,000 foreign volunteers from more than fifty countries were to fight for the Republic, 35,000 of them in the Communist-recruited International Brigades.*

October 1936. The first International Brigaders – from Europe – march through Barcelona.

hand, Durruti defiantly told Mikhail Koltsov, *Pravda*'s correspondent (himself recalled to Russia and liquidated about a year later): 'We shall not knuckle under either in Madrid or in Barcelona. We'll teach you Bolsheviks how to make a revolution.'

Koltsov and the *Izvestia* correspondent, Ilya Ehrenburg, who survived to write his marvellous memoirs, were half-amazed, half-amused by the buzzing turmoil of Barcelona in a revolutionary honeymoon so reminiscent of Russia in 1917–18. Looking back on that time Ehrenburg wrote that it reminded him of Eugène Delacroix's heroic canvases: 'Beyond the Pyrenees the romanticism of the past century smouldered briefly and flared up . . . there are many things that I can recall without emotion, but about Spain I feel a terrible tenderness and melancholy.' Not, like Madrid, under fire, Barcelona was a magnet for volunteers or fashionably leftist spectators from the West out to sample the revolutionary romanticism that in Russia had been suppressed or distorted by the Bolsheviks, in Europe by the fascists and the Nazis, but – for a few months – paraded there in antediluvian exuberance.

Not all the 'actors' in this theatre of ideological causes relished the role. Teresa Pamies criticizes the tendency to view the CNT and the POUM as 'immaculate angels at the temple of World Revolution', with the Communists, and especially the Soviet envoys, as spoil-sport villains. 'We had many Orwells in Barcelona, all looking for what André Malraux called "mon heure lyrique."' But the first great tourist invasion of Spain had curious side-effects.

In Madrid the Russians, with headquarters at Gaylord's Hotel, lived well and made no concessions to the proletarian-revolutionary style. José Vergara, always apprehensive because he had sent his wife and children to the Nationalist zone and was himself a neutral, benefited from the example of the saviours of the city. 'I still wore a suit, collar and tie, and was taken for a foreigner. I was never asked for my papers. Once, on the subway, some workers were grumbling about the government and one of them said to shut up because I could hear what they were saying. "What does it matter?" was the reply. "He's a Russian."' They assumed this 'Russian' didn't speak Spanish.

The vainglorious attitude of Mussolini and of some of his 'volunteers' in Spain – the first contingents arrived at Cadiz in December 1936 – infuriated their Nationalist 'allies', who were almost as delighted by the Italians' military disasters as were the Republicans. Majorca became an Italian naval and air base with Palma's main street, renamed the Vía Roma, sporting an idealized statue of handsome neo-Roman youths. Like German package tourists today, the Condor Legionaries lived in separate quarters – the best – and ate German food. It was easy for Spaniards to suspect that their war had been arranged by, and for the benefit of, foreigners.

There is little reason to suppose that Hitler or Mussolini anticipated, let

The first Soviet supply ship docks at Barcelona in October 1936. The Republic relied heavily on Soviet aid.

ABOVE *A Soviet fighter plane (nicknamed* CHATO *or 'snubnose'). The Republic bought many Soviet aircraft, and some 1,000 Russian pilots were to fly in Spain.*

CENTRE *April 1938. Air crews of the German Condor Legion are briefed at Granada airport for bombing raids in Spain.*

BELOW *Italian Savoia bombers in flight. Italy supplied some 600 aircraft to the Nationalists, also many tanks and about 75,000 'volunteer' troops.*

alone encouraged, the civil war – or that it was planned as part of a concerted fascist strategy: the conquest of Abyssinia, reoccupation of the Rhineland, subjugation of Spain. But both dictators, at first expecting a rapid outcome and never averse to fishing in troubled waters, were quickly embroiled. German and Italian transport planes airlifted the Army of Africa to the mainland. Portugal, whose dictator, Antonio Salazar, feared the proximity of a Red Republic, was pro-Nationalist from the start. At the end of July 1936 he offered to send troops to General Mola and even spoke of committing the entire Portuguese army. About 20,000 men of the Portuguese Legion eventually fought for Franco. Portuguese frontier police and military intelligence cooperated closely with the insurgents; Franco's brother Nicolás, established in Lisbon, was accorded ambassadorial status; the Republican navy's efforts to blockade Spanish ports were nullified by Salazar's permission for German supply ships, sailing from Hamburg under South American flags, to unload equipment in Lisbon, whence it was taken by rail to the Spanish frontier.

In the early stages of intervention Germany, Italy and the USSR were cautious, instructing 'volunteers' to keep a low profile; and they continued to leave options open by sending delegates to discuss the non-intervention policy favoured by Britain and France. Realizing that, like the League of Nations' resolutions condemning Italy's invasion of Abyssinia, this policy would remain almost entirely a verbal affair, they were able to pay lip-service to it for the next two-and-a-half years amid flurries of self-righteous accusations and counter-accusations.

Faced with Falange-like terrorist groups and powerful Catholic opposition, anxious to stay in office to push through at least a minimum programme of reform, the French socialist premier, Léon Blum, though sympathizing with the Spanish Republic, officially closed the Pyrenean frontier as a supply route on 8 August 1936. In this he was strongly encouraged by the British Foreign Secretary, Anthony Eden, who regarded what he called 'the War of the Spanish Obsession' as a tiresome menace to European peace coming just at the point when, it seemed, Mussolini's appetite for glory had been satisfied by the conquest of Abyssinia, Hitler's by the Rhineland.

Eden was fond of arguing that Britain already had experience of intervening in Spain during the Peninsular War of 1808–14 against the French occupation, and had received little gratitude from the Spaniards. Had not the Duke of Wellington, commanding the British expeditionary forces, complained that 'there is no country in Europe in which foreigners may interfere with so little profit as Spain'?

Jules Moch, a key figure in Blum's administration, remembers that Blum's instinctive reaction to news of the military rising was 'a feeling of moral and political obligation to aid the Spanish Republic'. But after a meeting in London on 23 July Blum told Moch of 'the extraordinary anti-European stance taken by Eden and his colleagues. Eden said that if war broke out in Europe over Spain, Britain would stay neutral, and therefore it would be wise

Paris, June 1936. France's socialist premier Léon Blum (centre) with Jules Moch (second from left), a member of Blum's administration. Blum's non-intervention policy limited aid to the Republic from and through France.

for France to do the same. According to Blum, the British attitude was that "we hate fascism, but we hate Bolshevism just as much. If there is a country where fascists and Bolshevists are killing each other, so much the better for humanity."'

On 8 August, then, the French border was closed, and on 5 September the insurgents captured Irún and permanently sealed off the Basque-French frontier at the western end of the Pyrenees. Juan Manuel Epalza, then a leader of the PNV (Basque nationalist) youth movement, states that 'the fall of Irún proved that the democracies were not going to help us. The knowledge that Léon Blum, the head of the Popular Front government, was the one who blocked the passage of the arms wagons we needed so desperately made our hearts sink into our boots. We were left completely cut off by land and had no contact with the outside world except by air – and we had no planes – or by sea. We Basques had always been sailors and there were plenty of ships available. But then they invented the Non-Intervention Committee, which put a stop to most of the arms shipments.'

Early in August an Anglo-French statement proposing a policy of non-intervention in Spain, initiated by Blum in the hope of at least limiting fascist aid to the insurgents, was accepted in principle by Italy, Germany and Portugal. On 9 September the Non-Intervention Committee held its first meeting in London.

Lord Home, who as Lord Dunglass began his political career in 1931 as a Conservative MP and from 1937 to 1939 was parliamentary private secretary to Prime Minister Neville Chamberlain, recalls the international crisis which influenced the British government's attitude towards the Spanish Civil War.

France was internally divided; the Italian invasion of Abyssinia had brought a European war perilously close; from autumn 1935 to summer 1936 part of the British fleet was at war stations in the Mediterranean; Japan was about to embark on a war of conquest in the Far East. 'In the 1930s,' says Lord Home, 'Mussolini was careering around in the Mediterranean and making all sorts of trouble, Japan was restive . . . a lot of people thought that Japan might be the first to declare war, and of course German rearmament was in full flood. So we were very apprehensive about getting entangled with any other situation.'

Geographically and ideologically nearer to the predicament of the Spanish Republic, the shaky French Popular Front coalition headed by the socialist Léon Blum saw non-intervention as a way of exerting diplomatic pressure while, whenever possible, turning a blind eye to arms shipments from or through France. 'Blum thought up the policy of non-intervention, which was not heroic at all, but nevertheless it was pragmatic.' Since the main immediate danger was a rearmed and aggressive Germany, Britain's policy of appeasement, or conciliation, was logical. 'I think that any democracy has to carry on a policy of conciliation, and you have to carry it pretty well to the limit. This was our policy, really I think that of all parties, towards Germany . . . to live with Germany and avoid war.'

Granted the danger of war with Germany and the possibility that, if the Spanish conflict developed into a major European war, Japan might seize the opportunity to overrun British positions in the Far East, non-involvement in Spain was, says Lord Home, 'geared to British interests. We needed all the arms we could get, in fact we didn't have enough when the war with Hitler started in 1939. Any arms sent to Spain would have been lost to our forces.' Such reasoning could seem cold-blooded and even immoral as pressure for commitment to the anti-fascist or to the anti-communist cause was applied by the rival regimes in Spain and by their vociferous supporters in Britain. Urging the moral obligation to defend democracy against the fascist threat, the Republican government 'naturally . . . tried to get as much as they could from both Britain and France . . . The House of Commons was very bad-tempered on this issue, emotions were very high . . . The Left supported the International Brigades and the Right was sympathetic in some ways to Franco.' R. A. (later Lord) Butler, then a parliamentary under-secretary at the Foreign Office, 'was the fellow who for two years or more had to bear the brunt of parliamentary attacks from the Left, and I remember that he earned the name of Stonewall Butler for that performance. But he stuck to what we considered to be the British interest, which was to keep out of this war.'

On German, Italian and Russian motives for intervening in Spain, Lord Home speculates that 'it suited Hitler to keep the situation boiling and to get France and Britain entangled if we were so foolish as to fall for that. I think Italy would have liked a quick Franco victory . . . and of course Russia was always willing to stir the pot all the time . . . '

Deep in the New Deal, grappling with the Depression and mounting unemployment, aware of a widespread isolationist mood and of the importance of the Catholic vote, President Roosevelt, though uttering ritual condemnations of the evils of dictatorship, resolved to stay out of the Spanish conflict. But United States neutrality, like French and British non-intervention, favoured Franco, since American companies took advantage of the Neutrality Act's failure to classify oil as war material and began sending tankers to Lisbon on 18 July.

On 30 September, in desperation, the Spanish Republic appealed to the moribund League of Nations. After leisurely deliberation the verdict was that the evidence for German and Italian intervention was too flimsy, being largely based on press reports; and that Spanish affairs would be better dealt with by an international Non-Intervention Committee which since 9 September had existed in London. As with Abyssinia, the machinery assembled to defend the victim of aggression was manipulated to favour the aggressor. The Vatican was more outspoken, Pope Pius XI virtually blessing the generals' 'crusade' with his denunciation of the Republican government's 'truly satanic hatred of God'.

The Non-Intervention Committee had on 14 September spawned a sub-committee, dominated by the representatives of Britain, France, Germany, Italy and Russia, with the ostensible function of monitoring the application of a policy which the last three member-states were determined to ignore in greater or lesser degree. Stalin had by the end of August decided to extend aid to the Republic. Intervention, if rightly managed, would enable him, despite his continuing massacre of actual or imaginary opponents in the USSR, to appear as the champion of bourgeois democracy.

On 8 October the USSR accordingly declared that in view of blatant violations of the non-intervention pact by Germany and Italy it would consider itself justified in following suit. The first cargoes of tanks, armoured cars, artillery, aircraft and lorries from Odessa were on their way, and by the end of October some 500 Soviet field officers, pilots, tank specialists, instructors and translators had reached Spain. Their often peremptory manner, the enthusiasm with which they were greeted, and, as a by-product, the rapidly increasing popularity of the Spanish Communist party (PCE), were already causing Largo Caballero to regret the necessity for their presence.

But the knot had been firmly tied by the decision, taken in mid-September by Largo Caballero himself and Juan Negrín, the Finance Minister, without consulting other members of the cabinet, to give Russia custody of most of Spain's 700-ton gold reserve, one of the largest in the world; for while the Nationalists were given extended credit for their shipments, the Republic had to pay on the nail for its requirements. Shipped from Cartagena in four ships and nearly 8,000 boxes, the gold was to be used as security for the purchase of supplies, including oil, mainly from the USSR, which was thus given very significant influence on the Republican war effort and on Republican policy in general. When the news of this deal broke, Azaña was horrified, Prieto wanted to resign.

Organized by Comintern agents under orders to cover their tracks, the supply of war material to the Republic too often degenerated into a hole-and-corner business offering ample opportunities for fraud and corruption to shady profiteers operating from 'import-export' offices all over Europe. Out-of-date or defective material reached the Republic by sea in tramp steamers with phoney certificates stating that their goods were bound for Greece, Britain, Latin America, even China.

Josep Tarradellas failed to persuade Largo Caballero to authorize the transfer to Barcelona of the plant of a cartridge factory near Toledo; and a request for foreign currency to buy equipment abroad was also rejected. The central government, says Tarradellas, did not want an arms industry in Catalonia, a decision that reflected the continuing power struggle between Madrid and Barcelona. That Largo's mistrust was not without foundation became apparent to Frederic Escofet when, hurried out of Spain to escape assassination, he was commissioned to purchase arms in Brussels. 'You'd find that if there were some guns on the market, for instance, there would be competition between buyers from Madrid, Barcelona and the Basque country, all bidding against each other.' Escofet found this 'sickening'. Where, in such a welter of mutual hostility and suspicion, was there any sign of Republican solidarity? Each faction seemed to be more concerned with the war to defend its own interests that might follow if Franco was defeated, rather than with the actual defeat of Franco.

The Non-Intervention Committee which, according to Joachim von Ribbentrop, the German representative, 'might have been better called the Intervention Committee', continued its tragi-comic sessions. Procedural finesse was designed to keep the Spanish war at arm's length. Neither the Republican government nor the junta headed by Franco was represented, and

BELOW LEFT *'Non-Intervention Poker': Low's cartoon of January 1937 shows Anthony Eden (hands tied behind back) at play with Blum and the three dictators.*

BELOW *This cartoon of the arch-appeaser Neville Chamberlain, with Mussolini and Hitler, appeared soon after the Munich Pact of 30 September 1938.*

'allegations' had to be presented by a committee member. Delay was ensured by stipulating that charges must be submitted in writing to the government accused and that no further discussion should take place until a written reply had been received.

Asked by Eden to 'see what's going on', Roger Makins (now Lord Sherfield), who had worked closely with the Foreign Secretary in Geneva as an adviser on League of Nations affairs, found that 'the strongest character on the fascist side was the Italian representative, Count Dino Grandi, a brilliant diplomat and a remarkably able and witty man.' He was supported by von Ribbentrop, the German ambassador in London, who was rather clumsy and unsubtle by comparison, but sessions were dominated by Grandi and Ivan Maisky, the Soviet ambassador, also a very able negotiator. Representatives of the minor powers – Belgium, Sweden, Czechoslovakia – generally said very little, and occasionally the Committee went into recess 'because the German, Italian or Russian representative had walked out.' But Lord Sherfield, convinced as he was of 'the rightness of the policies that Eden was trying to put into effect', points out that 'it suited all the powers to adhere to the non-intervention agreement. Neither the Germans, the Italians nor the Russians wanted the conflict to spread outside Spain; and the Germans were determined to limit the extent of their intervention.'

Lord Plymouth, the Committee's chairman, one of the parliamentary under-secretaries at the Foreign Office, was 'a very charming fellow but rather ineffective, and of course it was a very difficult committee to manage . . . It was clear to me, and to Eden, that with the Committee set up as it was, nothing could be done about it.' The best that could be expected was 'to keep intervention, which was virtually unstoppable, at the lowest possible level.' The Admiralty, says Lord Sherfield, 'was strongly opposed to the commitments which the enforcement of non-intervention policy would involve for the British Navy.' But he adds that 'it is certainly true that the British government was the only one which tried to observe the principles of non-intervention and also undertook a very substantial burden of enforcement by naval patrols and by stationing observers on the Portuguese-Spanish frontier.' Summing up, he maintains that non-intervention was not, as it was frequently made to appear, a hypocritical policy, and 'the fear that a Franco victory would mean that Spain entered the fascist camp was not borne out by events.'

By autumn 1937 Hitler and Stalin had reached the same conclusion – that German and Russian interests would be best served by prolonging the war in Spain. The strain on Italy, by far the most recklessly committed interventionist, would be increased, Hitler would be tied down.

Enrique Líster reckons that when the war ended the Non-Intervention pact, which Eden likened to a 'leaky dam, but better than no dam at all,' had leaked copiously – and overwhelmingly in Franco's direction. 'If the legionaries and the Moors had not been airlifted we would have had a complete victory within a few weeks – when we didn't have a single foreigner fighting on our side.' Most important to the Nationalists in terms of quality was the German contingent, about 10,000 at maximum strength, including instructors, technical specialists, and the 5,000-strong Condor Legion, an experimental tank, anti-tank and aircraft unit. Around 600 German planes were used in Spain – Messerschmitts, Heinkels and Junkers – and the 88-millimetre anti-aircraft guns did much to minimize Republican air superiority in the earlier stages. 'The other side,' continues Líster, 'had the Condor Legion, the Italian divisions, the Portuguese Legion, perhaps 90,000 Moroccan mercenaries – something like 300,000 men in all. On our side, we never had more than the 35,000 men of the International Brigades. As for arms supplies, the Russian arms we received were often better than the enemy's equipment, as was our aviation for a while. But in terms of quantity the enemy received much more, partly because much of what the Soviet Union sent was at the bottom of the sea, sunk by enemy submarines or captured from cargo ships.'

The real value of the International Brigades, says Líster, 'was in boosting morale. They were ambassadors representing millions of people in the world who were on the side of the Republic, on the side of Spanish democracy. Additionally, they played an important part in this or that battle.'

André Malraux, a kind of Gallic Byron, was the first to recruit an international group to fight for the Republic. Writer, adventurer and art connoisseur, he believed that only communism was capable of opposing fascism with force. After visiting Spain on 20 July, he was convinced that air power would be decisive and formed an 'Escuadrilla España' with about a dozen pilots – French, Italian, American, German. The aircraft he collected were of World War I vintage, some with a maximum speed of 70 m.p.h. After fighting with some success in Extremadura, at Toledo, in the defence of Madrid and in the retreat from Málaga, the squadron was disbanded, its ancient machines disintegrating after seven months in action.

Though not a member of the Communist party, the effervescent Malraux, president of the grandly-titled World Committee Against Fascism and War,

André Malraux, French writer, orator and man of action, inspired many volunteers to fight fascism in Spain.

inspired many young men to join the party and to volunteer for Spain. His freelance, bohemian initiative may have influenced the decision, taken in Moscow in September 1936 at the urging of Maurice Thorez, Secretary-General of the French Communist Party, and Willi Muenzenberg, head of Comintern propaganda in western Europe, to form 'international columns' of volunteers. The first recruiting drive was among Italian anti-fascists, but the idea spread among the many exiles or sufferers from fascist regimes. They saw the Spanish conflict as primarily a war against 'international fascism', a belated chance to strike a blow against triumphant reaction. Neither Azaña nor Largo Caballero was enthusiastic, for like the CNT they feared a Soviet takeover; but they went along with the idea in the hope that useful international publicity might accrue.

The sponsorship of an idealistic anti-fascist movement had obvious attractions for Stalin, not least to counterbalance increasing criticism of the Purge Trials. In Paris Muenzenberg and his lieutenant Otto Katz briefed Willie Forrest and another enterprising young communist journalist, Arthur Koestler, to 'establish a press agency in Spain to put across propaganda' linking the anti-fascist 'crusade' to Soviet support for Popular Fronts and collective security; for, as Forrest points out, 'the Spanish war was the last one in which the press had the field pretty much to itself as a moulder of public opinion. In World War II radio was a more powerful medium, now it's television.' After tossing a coin to decide destinations, Forrest went to Madrid, Koestler to Málaga. Comintern agents, headed by the Italians Palmiro Togliatti, Ettore Quaglierini and Vittorio Vidali ('Carlos'), redoubled their activity. Quaglierini supervised Spanish Communist party propaganda; Vidali, much concerned with the formation of the Fifth Regiment, became its chief political commissar.

The recruiting and transportation of the International Brigades now became the Comintern's main priority. Veterans of street-fighting against brownshirts or blackshirts in Germany and Italy volunteered in droves. From Paris Josip Broz, the future Marshal Tito of Yugoslavia, arranged passports, funds and travel routes for East European recruits. More than half the men were communists (those who were not were checked by members of the NKVD – the Soviet secret police) and the vast majority were working-class. Several hundred were long-term political exiles in Russia who had fought in World War I and in the 'international brigades' formed during the Russian Civil War of 1918–21. The first group of volunteers left the Gare d'Austerlitz in Paris in October 1936, travelling to their base at Albacete via Perpignan and Barcelona.

At Albacete they were sorted out according to experience and addressed by the three supremos of the Brigades: André Marty, celebrated for his part in a French naval mutiny in the Black Sea in 1919; the Italian Luigi Longo; and another Italian, Giuseppe di Vittorio. The length and thoroughness of training depended upon the time, weapons, ammunition and instructors available. Such slogans as 'Workers of the World, Unite!' appeared on the

walls of barracks once occupied by the civil guard. The ideological unity and the discipline of which Marty spoke were firmly and in due course harshly enforced – with Marty developing spymania and the German Walter Ulbricht supervising GPU heresy-hunters to ferret out 'Trotskyists'. But at the outset the spirit was one of hope and fierce comradely resolve.

Willy Burger, a Westphalian, had joined the German Communist party in 1927. After eighteen months in a concentration camp, he had escaped to France in 1935 to work for the Comintern under Otto Katz, and was sent on special missions. In October 1936 he volunteered for Spain and joined the Thaelmann Battalion, led by the novelist Ludwig Renn and composed mainly of Germans, but with a few English volunteers, including 18-year-old Esmond Romilly, a nephew of Winston Churchill. Everyone was given a Spanish nom de guerre and the volunteers travelled in a special train from Paris. From Perpignan coaches took them without trouble across the border at night. The first opposition they met was in Spain, from Catalan anarchists who tried to stop them going any further. At Albacete they were issued with old French uniforms. There was no time for training, and they were given aged Mexican rifles and rushed off to the defence of Madrid.

Kurt Goldstein, a German Jew, had joined the Young Communist League before leaving Germany in 1933, first for France, then Palestine. In Palestine many of his friends were jailed by the British authorities and he himself was beaten up by Zionists when distributing leaflets. His life had been an accumulation of such experiences. When he heard the news of Franco's rising

ABOVE LEFT *A snapshot of Ernest Hemingway (centre) in Spain. He wrote press articles, a play* (THE FIFTH COLUMN) *and a novel,* FOR WHOM THE BELL TOLLS, *about the Spanish War.*

ABOVE *The singer and actor Paul Robeson (centre) with black American International Brigaders in Madrid, 1938.*

and of German and Italian intervention he resolved to fight fascism in Spain. Two months later he sailed to Marseilles and took a boat to Barcelona.

Giovanni Pesce, whose family had lived in France since he was six, had worked in the mines from the age of thirteen, becoming a communist because of the exploitation he saw. He had begun to consider himself French until he read a manifesto urging Italians to fight fascism in Spain. So at eighteen he joined the Garibaldi Battalion of the International Brigades. The issues, he remembers, seemed so very simple. The party and the anti-fascist cause were beyond reproach. But though, looking back, he realizes that things were not so clear-cut, he believes that the Brigades played a vital part by inspiring Spaniards to fight fascism with greater determination.

Bill Bailey, a militant Communist who had been in battles with the police in the USA, did not tell his mother that he was going to Spain. But later he composed a letter of explanation to be delivered to her in the event of his death. 'You see Mom, there are things that one must do in this life that are a little more than just living . . . In Spain there are thousands of mothers like yourself who never had a fair shake in life . . . They got together and elected a government that really gave meaning to their life. But a bunch of bullies decided to crush this wonderful thing . . . That's why I went to Spain, Mom, to help these poor people win this battle, then one day it would be easier for you and the mothers of the future. Don't let anyone mislead you by telling you that all this had something to do with Communism. The Hitlers and Mussolinis of this world are killing Spanish people who don't know the difference between Communism and rheumatism. And it's not to set up some Communist government either. The only thing the Communists did here was show the people how to fight and try to win what is rightfully theirs.'

Like the fifty other volunteers with him Bailey was given $100, to satisfy French immigration authorities that he had some means of support, but was told: 'That's not spending money. Once you make contact in Paris, you'll turn this money over. And no screwing around or boozing on the ship. Don't mention Spain, you're passengers to Europe. We know there are government, even Franco, agents aboard. They may sidle up to you and try to get a conversation going. Stay clear of such people or you'll never make it to Spain.' Travelling third-class in the liner *Aquitania*, the crypto-volunteers docked at Le Havre in June 1937. In hotels at Carcassonne and Perpignan reservations had been made for 'a group of geological students'. Then, wearing rope-soled sandals, the men were shepherded by an ancient guide across the Pyrenees. At last 'we could see a long valley and an old Spanish farmhouse. The area looked like any scene of the back road country of Nevada. No horses, no cattle, just deer paths and brush and dried-up creeks. Many of us had travelled 8,000 miles to be able to stomp our feet on Spanish soil. As we walked towards the farmhouse we were shouting out within ourselves: "Hey, you bloody fascist bastards, Franco, Mussolini and Hitler. We've waited a long time for this opportunity . . . We may not be the most skilled soldiers in this world, but from here on in you're going to know we're here."' From Albacete Bill Bailey was transferred to the American volunteers' training camp at Tarazona. A few weeks later, after instruction in the use of rifle and machine-gun (only five live rounds were fired because of an ammunition shortage), 'we were ordered to move out and headed for the Aragon fronts.'

26-year-old Frank Deegan, an out-of-work Liverpool docker, had been a Communist since 1931, had taken part in the 1936 National Hunger March to London, and had been involved in other demonstrations, including at least one bloody fracas with Sir Oswald Mosley's blackshirts. He volunteered for Spain 'because I detested the inhuman capitalist system and believed that the international rich ruling class had ganged up to help Franco to defeat a legally elected people's government.' In May 1937 he travelled to London with another volunteer. In a café 'a comrade checked our credentials. This was necessary because there were government agents and stool pigeons hanging around. We had a medical examination and were handed a £5 note each with instructions to book tickets on the boat train to Paris . . . We had barely left the building when one of those despicable copper's narks tagged on and tailed us for hours. After a while we gave him the works, leaving him in a heap up a dark street. The government had introduced a law by which a British subject volunteering for the International Brigades would be liable to a fine of £100 – equal to a manual worker's wages for forty weeks – or two years' imprisonment.'

In Paris there was a rendezvous with 'Rita' – Mrs Charlotte Haldane, wife of the scientist Professor J. B. S. Haldane; then the train to Perpignan in a small group 'led by Josh Francis, who was a member of the aristocracy and spoke French, a chap named Reid who was a ventriloquist, two Welsh lads and two Scotsmen.' After a sixteen-hour night climb over the mountains (the French frontier police were now operating in earnest), Francisco Degano, as he became known, met other volunteers. 'Many were middle- and upper-class – students, academics, intellectuals, painters, sculptors, stage and film actors,

Paris, January 1937: collecting donations in a Spanish Republican flag. 10,000 French volunteers fought in Spain.

Of about 2,000 British International Brigaders, some 500 were killed and 1,200 wounded.

some from Hollywood. I felt rather self-conscious, just a common casual dock labourer. Inside the castle at Figueras were hundreds of men from almost every country in the world. It was a great feeling to be among them. After all the frustrations back home we were going to have the chance of getting to grips with the real fascist enemy.'

At Albacete he met several friends and acquaintances from Liverpool; and at the British volunteers' camp in Madrigueras the political commissar was 'a young Welsh miner from the Rhondda Valley called Harry Dobson. In charge of our training was Sergeant George Fletcher from Manchester. A Spanish family shared their food with me – eggs, fruit and vegetables were a welcome change from the barracks menu of beans and more beans.' At a daily wage of ten pesetas (about two shillings), the same as for soldiers of the Popular Army, the Brigaders, says Deegan, could hardly be described as 'Red mercenaries'.

The writer Stephen Spender recalls the Spanish civil war as 'a time when the individual felt that his personal contribution could make a real difference – that by joining the International Brigades he might actually affect the issue. For instance, Julian Bell [a nephew of Virginia Woolf] told me he thought that the war was being bungled and that if he went to Spain his military advice might help. Rather absurd perhaps, but that feeling that individual support and participation could make a difference was extraordinarily strong.' Julian Bell was killed a month after arriving in Spain when driving an ambulance for the British Medical Aid Unit. Other volunteers had time to become disillusioned. On the Madrid front Spender 'met a young English public schoolboy who said he had joined the International Brigades because he thought they were liberal republican organizations. Then he discovered that they were entirely Communist-run. He told me: "I'm going to spend the rest of my life walking up to that ridge a few hundred yards away and that will be the end of me." A few weeks later he was killed. I think there were many like him.'

As the first units of the International Brigades were rushed to Madrid, the mood in the capital was one of almost hysterical elation, symbolized by posters proclaiming 'Long Live Madrid Without A Government'. The tired, over-extended Army of Africa had failed to take the city by storm, but the breathing-space afforded by the Toledo diversion had not been used very effectively. Amid the confusion of vengeance killings, peasant refugees, and increasing tension between anarchists and communists, the comparative efficiency of the Fifth Regiment was almost uncomfortably obvious. General Miaja, head of the defence junta, and General Pozas, commanding what was called the Army of the Centre, found that their sealed orders had been put in the wrong envelopes. Reflecting the relative strength of parties or unions, the junta was inevitably dominated by the JSU (socialist-communist youth) and the PCE (Communist party). Russian advisers became suddenly influential and the Communist newspaper *Mundo Obrero* exhorted *madrileños* to 'emulate Petrograd'.

Recruiting was haphazard, individual initiative sometimes merely picturesque. Régulo Martínez met a man trundling a small cannon, which he claimed to have bought, to the Casa de Campo. 'We are on this side of the lake,' said the man, 'and the others are on the opposite side. I'll fire wherever they tell me it's needed.' Alvaro Delgado, serving in a shop when he was not roaming the streets with other boys collecting bits of shrapnel, saw some of the

The revolutionary atmosphere in Madrid is captured in this drawing by Luis Quintanilla of a soldier of the Communist Fifth Regiment.

employees join up on the spot when challenged by JSU militants. 'They just left the shop, were given some hand grenades and a rifle, boarded a truck or a tram, and went off to fight.' Lorenzo Iñigo remembers an example of clever improvisation. 'General Gardenal, an excellent artillery commander, with the few pieces of artillery he could muster, worked out a strategy for the whole of the bank of the Manzanares. He tied three or four 70mm guns to several trucks and stockpiled shells at various points along the river. The trucks would set off, with the guns tied to them, and fire off several rounds. Then they'd carry on half a kilometre to the next stockpile, and so on. This gave the enemy the impression that all that side of Madrid was completely covered by artillery, which helped to contain them a bit.'

Thousands of 'fascist' refugees, hiding in embassy premises or private homes, trembled for their lives. When asked which of his four columns would take Madrid, General Mola had referred to a 'Fifth Column' of Nationalists within the city – a thoughtless boast which helped to spur and to justify the anti-fascist pogrom. The nun Cristina de Arteaga, her shaven head covered by a wig, wearing civilian clothes and equipped with an Argentinian passport, eventually escaped by ship from Alicante; but not before enduring some moments of dramatic suspense during house searches. 'God gave us hope and we were calm, ready to die. We lived as in the catacombs and it was almost a joy.' Some of the fugitive nuns reached a pitch of reckless spiritual exaltation. 'One from our convent, in her twenties, told me when we said goodbye: "Sister Cristina, if I should be martyred it would be like a dream come true for me." A few months later militiamen searched the house where she was posing as a maid and guessed that she was a nun. She did not deny it and went away as if going to a party. We recognized her and another nun who was taken with her in photographs of the executed and collected their remains. It was like a celebration.'

Pilar Primo de Rivera, one of whose brothers, José Antonio, in jail at Alicante, was soon to be executed, while another, Fernando, had been shot in the Modelo, also escaped – to the Nationalist zone – after a series of narrow shaves. 'While I was underground I stayed in four different houses. In the last there was a radio. Because of the danger of detection I had to listen with the radio and my head draped in a towel. We heard a broadcast of the funeral of Onésimo Redondo, who had been killed in an ambush. We could hardly believe the sound of people shouting *Arriba España!*, and singing the Falangist anthem.'

Many right-wing fugitives spent the rest of the war in hiding. Enrique Miret Magdalena, the pious student who thought of himself as 'a moderate, Catholic Republican', was one of these, stuck for two years in a house which had been leased by the Paraguayan Embassy. The long internment was the more galling because in November 1936 it seemed almost certain that 'Franco's troops were about to enter Madrid'. There followed interminable days of boredom, bickering, talk of Red atrocities and fantasies about sadistic massacres of the Marxist fiends, starvation diet and incessant preoccupation

Republican posters, issued in Barcelona and written in Catalan, promote the war effort: LEFT 'Peasant! The revolution needs your effort.' BELOW LEFT 'You – what have you done for victory?' BELOW 'Industry for peace? No, industry for war!'

Republican posters inveigh against foreign intervention ('Rise up against the Italian invasion in Spain'), the clergy ('How the Church has sown its religion in Spain'), and fascism.

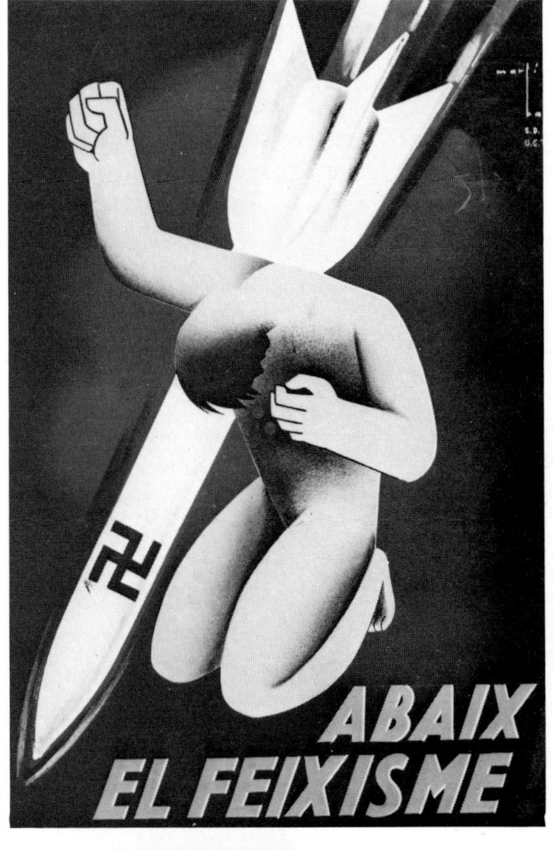

ABOVE *Propaganda posters stressed the need to concentrate on defending Madrid and presented the war as an anti-fascist crusade.*

LEFT *Refugees in a Madrid subway station. Junkers 52s began bombing the capital, virtually an open city, in late August 1936.*

with food and sex. Conversations were carried on in whispers in a room with blinds permanently drawn and crammed with sixty people – all in fear of informers or of blackmailing by minor embassy officials. For Miret Magdalena one of the few redeeming features was 'a Carmelite monk who disguised himself as an itinerant vendor, usually carrying a sack of potatoes, going from house to house to say Mass.'

By 6 November Nationalist troops had penetrated as far as the Casa de Campo, a park on the outskirts of Madrid. Next day UGT and CNT militiamen stemmed their advance in hand-to-hand combat, while floor-to-floor gun battles raged in the suburbs. Led by Enrique Líster detachments of the Fifth Regiment went into action, and on the body of an officer killed when an Italian tank was blown up a copy of the enemy's plan of attack for 8 November was found. Picked troops were accordingly concentrated around the Casa de Campo and the University, where the major attack was expected. They were joined by the pioneer International Brigaders, who after a triumphal progress from Albacete across the plains of La Mancha marched along the Gran Vía in corduroy uniforms and steel helmets. Other units arrived a little later, including the Thaelmann Battalion with Willy Burger and Esmond Romilly. In the next ten days the Brigaders performed a great service by showing Republican fighters how to take cover, dig protective foxholes, and conserve ammunition. But their casualties were terrible. Of about 3,000 most were killed or wounded. Willy Burger remembers that in one day, during fighting around the railway track, the Thaelmann Battalion lost over 600 of its 700 men in casualties.

Comintern publicists so effectively trumpeted the heroism of the Brigades that they were widely assumed to have saved Madrid, though the Nationalist momentum had in fact been halted before they arrived. Feared for their mobility and sharpshooting in the open, the Moors had been outmatched by the fury and expertise of Spanish militiamen in close-quarter street combat. But as Líster reiterates, the appearance of 'these well-turned-out men singing the Internationale and other songs in various languages was a terrific boost to morale, proof that the democratic world was on our side.'

On 18 November 1936 Italy and Germany recognized Franco's junta as the government of Spain; and Italian and Condor Legion aircraft intensified their bombing of an open city with no air-raid shelters and precious little in the way of anti-aircraft guns. Like other *madrileños* Alvaro Delgado was used to artillery bombardment but found the air raids unnerving. 'More than thirty planes at a time – the screams, the flashes in the sky, the lights going out, the way the ground shook. Nothing compared to the war in Europe later – the bombs were then tiny things – but to us they seemed like super bombs.'

At this point shrapnel and incendiary shells were pumped into the city centre and the working-class suburbs at the rate of 2,000 an hour. At night waves of German bombers repeated the dose. On 17 November about 500 people were killed, but far from cowing the populace this barrage stiffened resistance, and panic was followed by intense curiosity. Aerial combat was

A Nationalist stronghold in a Madrid suburb is dynamited after six months' tunnelling underground.

treated as a free entertainment and police were posted to urge spectators to seek shelter.

Incessant shelling and bombing seemed likely to wreck Madrid's war industry, scattered around the city in small workshops, until 25-year-old Lorenzo Iñigo, general secretary of the CNT metalworkers' union and a member of the defence junta, had the idea of concentrating the engineering works in one bomb-proof place: a newly completed but as yet unused subway tunnel. When Miaja referred this proposal to Valencia and got a discouraging response, Iñigo went ahead regardless. Plant and personnel from the workshops were moved to the tunnel, smoke extractors were fitted in lift-shafts, a canteen was installed. The entire intricate operation was completed in six weeks, including an inventory of plant and arrangements for compensation to the owners. 'So we set up our big factory untroubled by air raids. Instead of the five or six hours the men had been working above ground, we worked a ten-hour day.'

Madrid without a government, or with its own more representative junta, was showing plenty of initiative. But Iñigo was frustrated when War Minister Prieto, who had already tried to veto the arms tunnel, refused funds to buy some much-needed Swiss machinery. 'Prieto was sure Madrid would be captured and the machinery with it. So we still couldn't make cartridge cases and had to improvise with spent cases collected at the fronts. We filled them with the lead bullets which were the best we could produce.'

Above ground too improvisation was hectic and ingenious. Advancing German tanks were knocked out by militiamen who crawled to within a few yards and hurled grenades at the tracks. A crash training course was arranged for Spanish crews of the Soviet tanks that replaced ancient Renaults. Most of the volunteer drivers were taximen, since at least they had experience of driving. Precision instruments, including radios, were ripped out, flags were used for signalling, and gunners simply looked through the sights and fired. Outraged Soviet experts were told: 'We can't go by the book. There's a war on.'

Among the many deaths in ferocious house-to-house fighting two epitomized the rivalries and murky undercurrents of a very political war. On 14 November Durruti led a column of 4,000 anarchists into Madrid, perhaps in a bid to eclipse the glory attributed to the Fifth Regiment and the International Brigades. When, armed with 50-year-old Swiss rifles bought by Russia on the 'free' market, his column broke under machine-gun fire during a frontal assault in the Casa de Campo, the presence of a Soviet 'adviser' led to speculations that the débâcle had been deliberately arranged to discredit the CNT. Having talked of the need for discipline and unity, Durruti was regarded by the hard-line anarchists as too 'collaborationist'. When he was mortally wounded on 19 November it was strongly rumoured that an FAI purist, or alternatively a Communist assassin, had been responsible. But Eduardo de Guzmán, who was with Durruti in his last hours, insists that he was hit by enemy machine-gun fire.

Durruti, whose close comrade Francisco Ascaso had died during the assault on the Atarazanas barracks in Barcelona four months earlier, had indeed been trying to reconcile anarchist spontaneity with the demands of political power and military realities; and he seemed to be emerging as a 'sensible' or 'pragmatic' anarcho-communist. His death was mourned not only by huge crowds in Barcelona but by politicians of all shades who feared that the CNT had lost its most responsible and charismatic leader. Juan Molina, now deputy secretary of defence in Catalonia, mourned him as a friend, remembering how, exiled in Brussels in the late 1920s, Durruti and Ascaso had given the proceeds of their bank robberies to the cause and had worked at their trades – one as a mechanic, the other as a waiter or dish-washer, reading widely in their spare time to educate themselves. 'Lola and I mingled with the crowds, dazed and desolate. I did not have the heart to attend the official funeral ceremony. Ah! Durruti was a man, as good as he was tall – nothing exceptional as a speaker, but he could sweep the people along.'

Hans Beimler, political commissar of the 12th International Brigade, was killed in similar circumstances. A former Communist deputy in the Reichstag, he had escaped from Dachau by strangling an SS guard and using his uniform. There was a theory that he had been disposed of by a Communist killer as a 'deviationist', and that nine Brigaders at Albacete had been murdered to suppress the real cause of his death. But according to Willy Burger, present in the Casa de Campo when Beimler was shot, the bullet came from a sniper hidden among some olive trees. As an anti-fascist hero Beimler was given a funeral almost as impressive as Durruti's. Willy Burger, who escorted his body to Barcelona via Alicante, Valencia and Tarragona, was amazed by the crowds that gathered everywhere.

The Nationalists' process of homogenization did away with such eccentricities as the *requetés*' battle finery – tasselled forage cap, jack-boots, knee-hugging breeches and bull's pizzle switch – in favour of drab battle-dress: green serge blouses, green serge trousers pulled in at the ankle. And on the Republican side, as the Fifth Regiment and the International Brigades set an example of more conventional discipline, it was decided to form a Popular Army on the same lines. The remains of the old regular army were mingled with the militias in 'mixed brigades', officers were called from retirement, uniforms of a sort contrived, discipline enforced. The days of taking a vote by show of hands before an attack were numbered, the independence of union or party militias was threatened. The clear implication was that the workers' control honeymoon was over.

The social and political mixing involved did not appeal to the more class-conscious members of the CNT and POUM. Anarchists bridled at the whole conception of imitating the fascists with a hierarchy of rank, saluting, kow-towing to the government, and accepting 'unity' with communists and bourgeois officers. People's War Schools were bad enough, but the establishment of the CNT's own Bakunin Training Centre and García Oliver's appointment as director of officer training schools seemed positively blasphemous. Anarchist newspapers talked of making revolution not war, criticized pay differentials, proposed that soldiers' councils should run the army, and jeered at 'neo-militarism'. *POUMistas* shared the suspicion that the anti-militia decree was a Stalinist trick when Líster was appointed to lead the first mixed brigade. Earlier illusions of solidarity with the civil guards (renamed the National Republican Guard) and the *asaltos* evaporated as they reverted to their role of internal security; and it was noticed that the frontier guards were now mostly communists or socialists.

Timoteo Ruiz, a corporal in the Fifth Regiment, welcomed militarization. 'We needed discipline. At the start of the war I used to see anarchists leave the front at the end of the day to sleep more comfortably in a village.' Líster denies that militarization and social revolution were incompatible. 'We were making a revolution at the same time as fighting a war – giving land to the peasants, arms to workers, factories to committees. The anarchists refused to accept this, or some of them did. Eventually I had plenty of anarchists under my command who fought as well as communists.'

The high command, which remained in the hands of career officers, did, he thinks, lack confidence in the people, and so, like Azaña and Prieto, were essentially defeatist. 'I always had to watch my back. Prieto wanted the communists to fail.' Such people 'could not imagine the transformation of the *milicianos* into an army of 1,200,000 or conceive that thousands could show real military ability even if they hadn't attended a military academy.' But Líster agrees with Ruiz that 'we tried to organize an army that was much too similar to the one we were fighting.' The element of surprise, of initiative, was lost. 'Perhaps we should have fought a different type of war, using guerrillas much more.'

Until March 1937 Madrid remained the most active front as Franco and Mola renewed their attempt to encircle a city which seemed to have become thoroughly sovietized. There was a sudden spate of films glorifying the Russian revolution and Soviet achievements. Alvaro Delgado, who like many *madrileños* went to the cinema partly to keep warm in a winter when fuel was in very short supply, preferred American musicals 'like the one with Fred Astaire and Ginger Rogers dancing the conga'. But there was no escaping the Soviet presence. 'There were triangular towers in the streets with huge portraits of Marx, Lenin, Stalin and La Pasionaria, wall posters of them too. Almost everyone in the Politburo was represented, with suitable slogans, often La Pasionaria's "Better to die on your feet than to live on your knees".'

Yet privilege in rations, living quarters, and medical treatment for the Soviet élite began to cause an undertow of resentment. Largo Caballero, envious of the growing reputation of La Pasionaria and of other communists who had stayed on in Madrid, began to have visions of a Soviet coup d'état. The popularity of General Miaja was at least partly due to his known antipathy to Russian experts. Attending the PCE's celebration of the anniversary of the Bolshevik revolution, Régulo Martínez was angered by La Pasionaria's harping on the heroic role of the party in the defence of Madrid, and reminded her that the *people* were fighting for their city as they had fought in times past. 'The communists were put out by what I said, but the *madrileños* stood and cheered.'

The ammunition shortage was such that by January 1937 infantry were sometimes issued with blank cartridges to create an impression of activity; if they were lucky they got 20 rounds each instead of the customary 300. Deploying 40,000 Nationalist troops, General Orgaz launched a major attack in the valley of Jarama south-east of Madrid on 6 February. Soviet planes established air superiority, Soviet tanks slowed the enemy's advance, and the 15th International Brigade, with volunteers from 23 nations, including 600 Englishmen, about the same number of Americans, and some IRA veterans (who faced General Eoin O'Duffy's fascist Blue Shirts), fought gallantly in what Líster rates as 'one of the bloodiest battles ever fought on open ground'. There were around 10,000 casualties on each side. Both claimed a victory, but the result was a stalemate. The really significant fact was that in its first real baptism of fire the hastily assembled Popular Army had proved itself a match for the Moors and the legionaries.

Only eleven days of feverish preparation separated the end of the battle of Jarama on 24 February and the start of a new Nationalist thrust, this time to the north-east at Guadalajara. Much depended on the performance of 35,000

Guadalajara, March 1937. Light artillery is brought up to resist the last major Nationalist offensive on the Madrid front.

Italian troops, fresh from an easy victory at Málaga, with a full complement of tanks, mobile artillery and fighter planes. Mussolini anticipated a crushing Italian victory. But initial blitzkrieg successes were halted by heavy rain followed by snow, ice and fog. General Orgaz's simultaneous offensive from Jarama failed to develop. Bombed and machine-gunned from the air, menaced by heavy Russian tanks, the Italians wilted when counter-attacked by the 11th Division, led by Líster and including the German 11th International Brigade, and the 14th Division led by the anarchist Cipriano Mera and including the 12th International Brigade – spearheaded by Italian volunteers of the Garibaldi Battalion whom General Roatta had described as 'brothers of the Marxist rabble we smashed in Italy'. The subsequent rout of Roatta's corps – 3,000 dead, nearly 1,000 captured, 4,000 wounded – was a terrific boost to Republican morale and caused cruel glee among Nationalists.

Giovanni Pesce, who took part in the Garibaldi Battalion's final attack, remembers that the scenes which followed the Republican victory were amusing and, often, rather moving. Several times he saw 'fascist' and Garibaldi Italians embrace each other with cries of excited recognition – 'Hey, you come from Milan, don't you?'

The battle of Guadalajara ended the Nationalist bid to take 'fortress' Madrid, and did something to offset the capture of Málaga which virtually completed the Nationalist conquest of Andalusia. Directed by Queipo de Llano, this predominantly Italian victory was something of a pushover thanks to the Republican government's inability to spare reinforcements or ammunition to another front. Demoralized by CNT-UGT rivalry, amounting at times to open war, the *malagueños* showed little inclination for determined resistance when communications with the city were cut. On 3 February 1937, a mere seventeen days after the opening of the offensive, the attack on Málaga began. Victory on 7 February was followed by what was probably the bloodiest repression since Badajoz. There had been about 2,500 killings in the previous seven months and Queipo whipped on the reprisals. Refugees on the coast road to Almería were strafed by planes and pursued by tanks. Many were shot, others died of exhaustion or starvation. 4,000 are said to have perished in the first week of the new regime. The Italian ambassador complained to Franco that the massacre was 'a moral question affecting the reputation of both Spain and Italy'.

The British government intervened to save the life of the Hungarian Arthur Koestler, correspondent of the London *News Chronicle*, who had been imprisoned in Seville under sentence of death for spying – not without reason since he was a Comintern agent. But Eden's efforts to prod the Non-Intervention Committee into action were unsuccessful. During discussions of the undeniable presence of tens of thousands of Italians at Málaga and Guadalajara Maisky accused Italy of 'ever-increasing intervention', to which Grandi replied that he hoped not a single Italian 'volunteer' would leave Spain until the war was won.

Yet with Spain as the outstanding international problem in Europe, the Committee had to contrive at least a semblance of control – especially naval control, since between November 1936 and May 1937 the Nationalists and their fascist allies had sunk, damaged or impounded nearly forty cargo ships, mostly British, Russian or Scandinavian, en route to Republican ports. The very mention of a naval patrol caused Sir Samuel Hoare, First Lord of the Admiralty, to grumble to Eden that 'we are getting to a point when, as a nation, we are trying to stop General Franco from winning.'

But by 19 April 1937 the Committee had worked out a plan for surveillance of all Spanish land and sea frontiers, and had even agreed the design for a non-intervention pennant. Italy and Germany eagerly accepted an arrangement whereby they patrolled the Mediterranean stretch of the Republican coast while England supervised the Basque-Santander coast and, with France, the Franco zone coasts, including Morocco. There was no naval inspection of the Portuguese coast.

Britain's involvement was complicated by the Nationalist junta's claim to be the only legal government and therefore entitled to belligerent rights at sea, which included the stopping and searching of ships of any nationality and the blockading of enemy coasts. The Admiralty sought to avoid unpleasant clashes by instructing naval commanders not to accompany merchant vessels into Spanish territorial waters. On 6 April 1937 the Nationalists announced a blockade of the Bilbao-Santander coast – to which British freighters, backed by widespread public sympathy for the Basques and encouraged to take risks by the huge profits from such 'smuggling', carried food and other supplies.

There was heated argument in the press and in the House of Commons about the humiliation of permitting a rebel clique to search British ships, and

Fifi Roberts in Bilbao, April 1937, after the SEVEN SEAS SPRAY *had broken the Nationalist blockade.*

the ineffectiveness of the blockade was demonstrated when, on 20 April, the *Seven Seas Spray* steamed into Bilbao harbour unscathed: a feat which forced the British government to cancel its veto on merchantmen trying to run the blockade. Fifi Roberts, the daughter of the captain of the *Seven Seas Spray*, still wears the gold brooch presented to her at 'a slap-up celebration banquet' in Bilbao. Nineteen at the time, she vividly remembers the adventure. 'We left Swansea in March 1937 to unload coal at Savona in Italy. Then we were told that the ship had been chartered to the Basque government and that we were to sail to a port near Alicante where we were to load salt. At Gibraltar we took on coal and set course for Bilbao. When we were nearly there we received a radio message that we were to obey naval instructions and proceed to St Jean de Luz.'

A week later, on 19 April, 'we heard that the non-intervention patrol was to become effective that evening. After a talk with a Basque representative my father agreed to take the risk of running the blockade and informed the senior naval officer of his intention. We left St Jean de Luz that night on a darkened ship, arriving at Bilbao early next morning, and were welcomed by the hooting sirens of the fishing fleet. The people of Bilbao treated us like VIPs. As we sailed down the long, narrow river there were people in every window on both banks, cheering and waving sheets, shouting "God bless you!" and making the sign of the cross. I never felt so humble. They had only four days' stocks of food left. Children used to gather at the foot of the gangway begging for scraps.'

The main Nationalist military effort had been switched to the northern front, concentrating on Vizcaya, the last surviving province of Euzkadi (the Basque Republic). The ruling Basque Nationalist party, the PNV (Partido Nacionalista Vasco), Catholic and conservative, was interested only in independence, not in social revolution or in defending or promoting democracy. Its relations with anarchists, socialists and communists were minimal or hostile. Since Basque troops refused to fight outside their own territory there was little attempt to coordinate operations with the neighbouring regions of Santander and Asturias, anyhow regarded as dangerously 'Red'. As earlier in Irún and San Sebastian, the PNV was firmly opposed to the scorched earth, industry-wrecking methods favoured by some left-wing militants; and also to reprisal massacres of 'fascist' prisoners. The Basque army, predominantly composed of PNV soldiers known as *gudaris*, numbered around 30,000 and, uniquely in the Republican zones, was attended by a corps of chaplains who not only celebrated Mass but kept watch on the morals of the troops and did their best to 'form the minds of the conscripts in the Christian tradition'.

This staunch Catholicism made the non-Navarrese Basques' refusal to join the Nationalist crusade doubly infuriating. On 27 March 1937 General Mola's pre-campaign proclamation reflected this: 'I have decided to end the war rapidly in the north . . . If surrender is not immediate I shall raze Vizcaya to the ground. I have the means to do so.' While his opponents, cut off from the central Republican zone, received little more aid than had Málaga in its hour of need, Mola could dispose of 50,000 well-equipped Navarrese (Carlist), Moroccan and Italian troops, and Italian and German planes had command of the air. The first hint that Mola's proclamation was more than rhetorical came on 31 March, when Junkers-52s of the Condor Legion bombed Durango, a defenceless country town behind the front. 127 civilians, including two priests and thirteen nuns, were killed and 120 died later in hospitals.

The next stroke of apparently premeditated aerial terror occurred on 26 April when, after a disappointingly slow advance over hilly, forested terrain sprinkled with tank-traps and barbed-wire barriers, the Condor Legion saturation-bombed Guernica, the ancient (and still the spiritual) capital of Euzkadi. Apart from its almost sacred significance to the Basques – the Tree of Guernica was venerated as the site where, in olden times, Spanish kings had sworn to respect regional rights – Guernica was a market town, well behind the lines, where the only target of conceivable military interest was a river bridge whose destruction would hamper the retreat towards Bilbao, around which a defensive 'ring of iron' had been constructed.

Neither the bridge nor the historic tree with its adjoining parliament house was in fact destroyed, but just about everything else was. Townspeople who survived the attack described it as happening in three waves: the dropping of explosive and shrapnel bombs by Junkers, machine-gunning of people in the crowded market-day streets by Messerschmitt and Heinkel fighters, and a

The Basque market town of Guernica, deserted after saturation bombing by German and Italian planes on 26 April 1937.

final devastating shower of incendiary bombs. The town was almost literally razed; at least 200 people died and many more were wounded in the $2\frac{1}{2}$-hour raid. Fifi Roberts, who with her father was taken to see the shambles on 27 April, found it 'soul-destroying to see the refugees coming away, some pushing wheelbarrows or handcarts, perhaps with a donkey or a pony. It looked as if there were only three buildings still standing. The whole place seemed to have been evacuated. There wasn't a soul about.'

It is still not certain who was directly responsible for the attack. Both Mola and Franco are said to have been angered by such experimental Teutonic overkill. But though such 'total' tactics were never repeated, the Durango-Guernica 'example' was undoubtedly effective in demoralizing the defenders of Bilbao. Lord Plymouth's suggestion that the Non-Intervention Committee should call upon both Spanish 'parties' not to bomb open towns came to nothing; Ribbentrop and Grandi countered with a protest that the subject should not be considered in isolation from 'general humanitarian aspects'. But in the propaganda battle which followed, the Basques and the Republic were victorious.

Eyewitness accounts of the raid were attested by the British consul in Bilbao as well as by foreign correspondents who hurried to Guernica. Ignacia Ozamiz and her children were in a shelter during the raid. 'The hospital,' she says, 'was bombed, killing 25 children and two nuns . . . When the *gudaris* told us we could leave the shelter, we saw that our house and everything in sight was burning . . . How could they say that the Reds had done it, when they hardly had a single plane, poor souls?'

But in Salamanca Luis Bolín, chief of foreign press relations, probably under German pressure and certainly influenced by the anger of Mola's Navarrese troops, maintained that Guernica had been blown up by the Basques with the object of discrediting the blameless Nationalists. A later version had Republican planes dropping bombs to detonate charges of dynamite placed in the sewers; and this was coupled with a denial that any 'Nationalist' aircraft had been in action on 26 April, which did not exclude the possibility that German and Italian planes had been involved.

Twenty years later it was still a crime in Franco's Spain to say that Guernica had been destroyed by the Nationalists, or at least in the course of the Nationalist 'crusade'. Bolín's attempt to shift the blame had admittedly been preceded by equally unscrupulous atrocity-mongering on both sides. The Comintern virtuoso Otto Katz had startled correspondents by claiming that the churches of Catalonia had been wrecked by 'fascist' bombers. Claud Cockburn, an apt pupil, had, at Katz's bidding, invented a wholly imaginary battle full of 'democratic' heroism and 'fascist' villainy which, he later wrote, 'emerged as one of the most factual, inspiring, and at the same time sober pieces of war reporting I ever saw.' Bolín's lie was designed to exonerate the Condor Legion, Cockburn's to speed the flow of arms from France to the Spanish Republic. The Nationalists had one considerable advantage – a powerful new German radio transmitter which ensured that their propaganda could be heard throughout Spain.

The Nationalist advance continued, though at the cost of heavy casualties. Mola's death in a plane crash on 3 June did not disrupt the slow but inexorable process, and on 19 June, with only three airworthy planes to defend the city while police guarded factories against sabotage and prisons against mob violence, Bilbao fell. Euzkadi was no more and its government fled to Barcelona. Warned by the reaction to the Málaga massacres and the Guernica incident, Franco restrained the victors' reprisals. But it became a crime to speak or teach the Basque language and there was a severe purge of 'disloyal' schoolteachers. The iron ore mines, blast furnaces, rolling mills and chemical factories of Bilbao and other industrial centres were now under Nationalist control.

As many as 200,00 people had fled from Bilbao, most of them soon to return. But after Guernica the evacuation of children – their health threatened by the famine caused by blockade and the influx of 100,000 refugees from Guipuzcoa – had begun. By mid-June more than 13,000 had been taken away, 4,000 to England, the rest to France, Belgium, Switzerland and the USSR. Returning to the north coast at Aviles, near Gijón, after a voyage to Valencia, the *Seven Seas Spray* spent five weeks being fitted out for a different cargo. 'Water tanks were put on deck and ladders let down into the holds,' says Fifi Roberts. 'We spent the day on the beach while the Basques did the work. Eventually we took on board 2,500 refugees, including a government official

October 1937. Basque refugees arrive in France after the fall of Gijón completed Franco's conquest of northern Spain.

with his family, so we all had to give up our cabins. I slept on luggage piled over a stack of picture frames. We sailed to Bordeaux and after disembarkation the ship was fumigated.'

Among the refugees were the Ozamiz children. 'We had lost them, we had lost everything,' says their mother. 'For eight months I had no news and didn't even know where they were. Perhaps in Russia – that would have been the worst thing. Then Nationalist newspapers reported that a ship with many children on board had been sunk.' In fact, after reaching France the children spent some time in a transit camp where, says Koni the eldest girl, 'we all slept on the floor. Gradually we were sent off to other places. Those in charge would say: "Form a line and tell us where you would like to go." When we said we'd like to go to England because we had aunts there, it was too late, the quota had been filled. So the four of us – holding tight to each other so as not to be separated – tried for Belgium, but that quota was filled too. It looked as if it would have to be Russia. But luckily, with about thirty others, we stayed in France, in a big castle said to have belonged to Napoleon. They looked after us fantastically. We were given a haircut, new clothes, excellent medical care. We had dancing lessons and were taken to the theatre. In the summer we went to a camp where there were all sorts of games and we played with French children. I think the socialist metalworkers' union had adopted us and I still remember the socialist songs we learnt.'

CHAPTER FOUR

FRANCO'S SPAIN

When Málaga fell in February 1937 the only looted item which interested Franco was a religious relic. Said to be a hand of St Teresa of Avila, it was stolen from a convent near Ronda and discovered in the baggage of a captured Republican officer. Sent to Franco's headquarters in Salamanca, it was kept at his bedside as a talisman.

The characteristic Nationalist mixture of religiosity and military pomp was to be monumentally summarized after the war in the Valle de los Caidos (the Valley of the Fallen), a colossal memorial to the victims of the civil war. On a hillside near the Escorial, a gloomy half-palace half-monastery built by King Philip II in the sixteenth century, Franco decreed the planting of a huge granite cross, perhaps the largest Christian symbol ever erected. Beneath it a granite crypt bigger than the nave of St Peter's in Rome, which took workmen (often prisoners of his regime) ten years to tunnel, was made to rumble and blare with a ceaseless organ-assault of military marches and triumphal hymns. Here, complete with the remains of José Antonio Primo de Rivera and of Franco himself buried in front of the high altar, is the essence of what passed for the sublime in Franco's Spain.

Though his Asturian wife Carmen was noted for her piety, Franco was not – until the generals' rebellion had been promoted, first to a 'movement' and then, with the blessing of the Church, to a crusade against 'anti-España.' Cristina de Arteaga remembers her younger brother, later killed on the northern front, asking her in all seriousness: 'If we die to defend God and Spain, shall we go to heaven as martyrs?'; and she believes that, with the heavy burden of his responsibilities as Commander-in-Chief and Head of State, Franco himself reached spiritual maturity.

Short and in 1936, aged 44, distinctly plump, Franco was renowned for personal courage and feared as a martinet with a high-pitched, almost priestly, voice and a singular lack of imagination and humanity. Socrates Gómez thinks that Franco can best be characterized as 'the Head of State who signed the most death sentences in the history of Europe'. José Antonio Primo de Rivera told Serrano Suñer that during their infrequent meetings he was baffled by Franco's total absorption in military affairs. Serrano Suñer himself was struck by Franco's lack of, even contempt for, political strategy – 'he was

OPPOSITE *'One Fatherland, One State, One Leader': children of 'the New Spain' before a poster of Franco in the Nationalist zone.*

purely a tactician.' Pilar Primo de Rivera comments on his typically Galician stolidity. In the 1940s Sir Samuel Hoare, then British ambassador in Madrid, was exasperated by the Caudillo's 'imperturbable complacency . . . like a doctor with a big family practice and a good bedside manner.' For the monarchist Pedro Sáinz Rodríguez, Franco was not so much reticent as intellectually null: 'A lot of the time he didn't have anything to say. He was a sphinx without a secret. The only thing he loved was his career.'

Yet this dour, un-Duce-like figure had an icy presence and a core of steely obstinacy. After vainly trying to extract concessions from Franco in 1940, Hitler remarked that he would prefer to have several teeth drawn rather than endure such a frustrating experience again; and he said that when he mentioned the Nationalist debt to Germany for aid supplied during the civil war, Franco had made him feel 'almost like a Jew trading in the holiest possessions of mankind'. Fond of lush ceremonial but shunning personal publicity, this naval paymaster's son was not, as General Primo de Rivera had been, the kind of man who could pass as the fallible, extrovert father of the national family. Primo's swashbuckling grandee style was anathema to this essentially prim, bourgeois Victorian paterfamilias.

Franco had no coherent, clear-cut political philosophy. As the first director of the military academy at Saragossa and as Chief of the General Staff he had worked with total dedication, training cadets on the German model and then reorganizing the army: a task which included the dismissal of many officers appointed by the Azaña administration of 1931–33 and the reinstatement of those who had been retired on political grounds. This in itself was an indication of his leanings which, as the Saragossa cadets well knew, were unmistakably authoritarian, and obsessively anti-Bolshevist. Though he kept clear of anti-Republican plots for five years he would wholeheartedly have endorsed Primo de Rivera's *pronunciamiento* of 1923 with its contempt for 'professional politicians who are responsible for the period of misfortune and corruption which began in 1898 and threatens to bring Spain to a tragic and dishonourable end.' Franco's own proclamations, and his behaviour when in power, carried exactly the same message.

In 1924 he had, with other officers who had served in North Africa, been prepared for a coup which involved arresting Primo when the latter showed signs of abandoning the Moroccan protectorate: a decision which, if it had been enforced, would probably have guaranteed Republican victory in the civil war. He had been irritated by the pro-Republican antics of Queipo de Llano, who in a typically coarse but quotable phrase remarked that the letters UP (short for Primo de Rivera's Union Patriotica) could equally well stand for Public Urinal. But until the aftermath of the February 1936 elections Franco's attitude to the Republic was watchful rather than hostile. He was not ready to overthrow it, but determined to protect Spain against the Marxist menace and regional separatism. Justifying the savagery of Yagüe's repression after the Asturias rising of October 1934 he told a press conference that 'this is a frontier war and the fronts are socialism, communism and any other political systems which attack civilization to replace it with barbarism.'

For Franco, 'bolshevism,' the revolt of the unwashed, undisciplined masses, was the ultimate horror. But he seldom allowed his personal prejudices public expression, even after he had permitted himself to be dragged into the limelight on 18 July 1936. Beside Queipo's wilder rantings or Mola's apoplectic abuse of Azaña – 'a monster who seems more like the vile experiment of a new Frankenstein than the fruit of a woman's love' – Franco's speeches were models of restraint.

His military and administrative ability were unquestionable, his sense of timing impressive, and his lack of political commitment an asset when dealing with the various Nationalist factions. Mola, the Carlists' candidate for supremo, was known to be hostile to the Falange. Queipo was a newly-reformed 'Red' rake. By the end of August 1936 Sanjurjo, the monarchist choice, and General Goded, captured in Barcelona, were dead. Don Juan, the son of Alfonso XIII, was virtually arrested on his way to the front near Pamplona and ordered to return to France: 'Mola didn't want any more political problems,' says Vegas Latapié, who with other monarchists

General Franco and (beside him, in glasses) General Mola in Burgos, capital of Nationalist Spain.

had travelled to Cannes to pluck the prince from exile. Mola depended on Franco and his negotiators for Axis aid in order to campaign effectively. José Antonio Primo de Rivera was in jail. The rapid advance of the Army of Africa, directed by Franco, and the relief of Toledo, decreed by Franco, had by the end of September 1936 greatly enhanced the prestige of 'the young general'.

Committed solely to the concepts of national unity and law and order, he was, rather like Oliver Cromwell, able to apply them to troublesome allies as well as to outright enemies, not hesitating to discard yesterday's props when they had served their turn. Abstemious, a non-smoking and non-philandering workaholic, there seemed to be no chink in Franco's armour of righteousness. There was an unenthusiastic inevitability about his choice as Generalissimo and Head of State in Salamanca on 28 September. At a meeting of military leaders including Mola and Queipo, Yagüe made it clear that the Legion wanted Franco; and though there was criticism of his assumption of political as well as military authority, this was soon overcome by the busy persuasion of General Alfredo Kindélan, commanding the air force, and Franco's own brother Nicolás. Talking to Vegas Latapié in later years Queipo summed up the situation: 'There were only three candidates – Franco, Mola and myself. If we had appointed Mola we would have lost the war. I was politically undesirable, so that only left Franco.'

On 1 October, taking over the powers hitherto exercised by a junta headed by General Cabanellas, Franco was installed with due pomp and ceremony in Burgos. Crowds acclaimed him as the new Caesar; posters proclaimed 'One Fatherland, One State, One Leader'; Radio Castilla announced that 'tonight you are going to hear the authentic voice of Spain, the voice of the Caudillo, the chief, the guide . . . General Franco is going to speak. Viva Franco! Viva España!' Apart from some passages of bellicose patriotism the speech was characteristically cautious. Industrial workers were offered a vague guarantee that their rights would be respected; peasants were assured of sympathetic treatment; the party system was to be replaced by some less divisive method of ascertaining the will of the people; the Church would be upheld and taxation reduced. The question of whether Franco was acting as Head of State in perpetuity, or as head of a provisional government, was left unanswered.

Five days later, at a banquet in honour of an envoy who had brought congratulations from Hitler, Franco expressed admiration for 'the new Germany' and indicated that a restoration of the monarchy was not at present on the agenda. With heavy financial contributions from Juan March and other rich capitalists and from the exiled King, whose example was followed by most people of wealth in the Nationalist zone (and by the British and German business communities), Franco's position was strengthening. A further important boost came when on 18 November Germany and Italy committed themselves by officially recognizing his regime: a move which was reflected in the gradual substitution of the term 'Nationalist' for 'insurgent' in the world press. This recognition posed its own problems of how to prevent a

General Millán Astray, the much-wounded founder of the Foreign Legion with its slogan 'Long live death!', arrives to inspect female Falangists in Saragossa, September 1936.

sell-out to Axis interests that would make palpable nonsense of Franco's patriotic propaganda, already being ridiculed by Republican cartoonists. By January 1937, after the failure to take Madrid, he had been forced to accept a team of German and Italian advisers; and as a condition for even more substantial aid he was soon under heavy pressure to accept direction of military operations by a full-blown Axis general staff with himself as a Nationalist figurehead.

More slowly, therefore, than he might have wished, Franco moved to grapple with what he saw to be the most urgent task, that of 'creating a common ideology among the co-fighters for liberation'. Threats of social ostracism or worse spurred donations to the cause. 'Capitalists!' said one press appeal, 'the National Movement, salvation of Spain, permits you to continue enjoying your dividends and rents. If you hesitate to lend your moral and material assistance generously, not only will you prove yourselves unpatriotic but ungrateful and unworthy of living in the strong Spain which is being reborn.'

In August 1936, at a ceremony in Seville, the red-and-yellow monarchist flag was adopted as the Nationalist standard. Queipo likened it to 'the blood of our soldiers unstintingly shed and the golden harvests of Andalusia'. General Millán Astray, the much-wounded founder of the Foreign Legion, bellowed the slogan 'Viva la muerte!' ('Long live death!'), adding 'Death to all the Reds!' Ignoring the presence of thousands of Moorish mercenaries,

Franco and church dignitaries give the Falangist salute after a service commemorating the death of José Antonio Primo de Rivera.

José Maria Pemán, a monarchist writer who was the regime's leading literary apologist, spoke of Spain's 'providential mission to save the civilized world, expelling Moors, battling with Turks, baptizing Indians.' Now the enemies were 'red and cruel Asiatics, again threatening Europe. This is a holy war, a crusade. We fight for love and honour, for the paintings of Velasquez, the plays of Lope de Vega, for Don Quixote and the Escorial!'

But the windy rhetoric of violence and nostalgia concealed a worrying lack of unity. Some generals, notably Queipo in Andalusia, continued to rule their regions like viceroys with little reference to the Caudillo. Old Guard Falangists were alarmed by the mass influx of time-serving 'new shirts' who knew little and cared less about the original aims of the movement, and they were angered by the failure to consult them about Franco's elevation. In the absence of José Antonio Primo de Rivera and Fernández Cuesta, the old shirts were led by a junta with Manuel Hedilla, a former mechanic from Santander, as chairman, and they tried to keep alive the revolutionary content of falangism as expressed, for instance, by Onésimo Redondo in July 1936: 'Spain must be proletarianized, must become a nation of workers . . . The capitalists, the rich, will be traitors to the fatherland if they persist in their incorrigible egoism, their refusal to see the trail of hunger, poverty and misery they leave in their wake. Bread for all, justice for all, these are our slogans.' Nationalist censors were kept busy suppressing Falangist attacks on the generals' reactionary attitudes, often in the form of quotations from José Antonio's more radical speeches. At this stage Pilar Primo de Rivera was numbered among the Falangist opposition, which was encouraged by the German ambassador, General von Faupel.

The anti-clericalism of the Falange embarrassed Franco in his attempts to gain full support from the hierarchy and the Vatican. Having established his headquarters in the archbishop's palace in Salamanca, Franco began to hear Mass regularly and to make pointed references to Spain's glorious Catholic tradition. Far more effective than such manoeuvres was the news of the 'Red' massacres of priests, monks and nuns. Without prompting, the clergy of 'White Spain' were soon accusing contrite congregations of the sin of having tolerated Jews, freemasons, atheists and trade unionists and demanding that the persecutors of the Church should be exterminated.

Monarchist sentiment was rooted in the medieval past. But the more fanatical Carlists imagined that they were fighting another Carlist war to restore an absolute monarchy, and their proposal to establish a Royal Military Academy to train officers in traditionalist ideals as well as in military matters was treated by Franco as an act of treason. The academy was forbidden and the Carlist leader Fal Conde exiled. Vegas Latapié, editor of *Acción Española*, which tried to give monarchism a semblance of intellectual respectability, knew that he and his associates were a tiny minority when they dreamed of 'a king who would govern as well as reign,' with laws 'approved by a parliament chosen not on the one-man-one-vote system but by the authentic forces in the country.' Their corporative state would, they hoped, genuinely represent municipalities, unions, agricultural and commercial interests, unlike the fascist 'caricature' where delegates were nominated and controlled by the government. Vegas Latapié, who had narrowly escaped exile for his part in smuggling Prince Juan into Spain, further irritated Franco by suggesting that education by press and radio would be more effective than firing squads. He was given the job of purging schoolteachers as a member of the Culture and Education Commission of the provisional government.

Proven teaching ability was the last consideration. Malicious denunciations, often made by parish priests, alleging atheism, infrequent Mass attendance, or regional patriotism, were enough to cost a teacher his or her job or to involve transference to another province. Vegas Latapié did what he could to protect teachers against such absurd charges as 'having knelt on one knee only when the Host was elevated'. But the reports of the provincial commissions roused the contempt of the 72-year-old political philosopher Miguel de Unamuno, rector of Salamanca University, who added some sarcastic comments of his own before passing the documents to the city's civil governor. A Basque celebrated for a paradox-mongering brilliance which had made him a household word for intellectual vitality and independence, Unamuno had been exiled for criticizing Primo de Rivera's dictatorship, and as a Republican deputy in 1931 he had been equally outspoken about the shortcomings of Azaña's administration.

Taken together with the repudiation of the Republic by other prominent intellectual leaders, who had fled abroad to denounce Red atrocities and excessive communist influence, Unamuno's welcome for the generals' intervention as 'necessary to save western civilization, the Christian civilization which is threatened' had been a prime propaganda asset. But his support was qualified by the assumption that the war was being fought to create 'an honourable republic'; and he had been shocked by the murders of García Lorca, of a fellow university professor, and of Juan Crespo's uncle Dr Casto Prieto, the Republican mayor of Salamanca and a close friend.

The Madrid government had responded to Unamuno's attacks by dismissing him from his post as lifelong rector. But he was just as critical of Nationalist jeers at Basque and Catalan separatism. At a meeting held in the great hall of the university, very close to Franco's headquarters, on 12 October 1936 to celebrate the Day of the Race (the anniversary of Columbus's discovery of America) and chaired, in the Caudillo's absence, by Unamuno, the old word-warrior was provoked into his final, rather magnificent, public fling of defiant nonconformity.

Among those on the dais with Unamuno were Millán Astray – with his black eye-patch, empty sleeve and thirteen gold-braid wound-stripes the very epitome of reckless, mindless militarism; Vegas Latapié, representing the Commission for Culture which had arranged the event, with his friend Pemán wearing a Falangist blue shirt; and, at the last moment, Franco's wife Doña Carmen escorted by a guard of honour which included Juan Crespo. Fidgeting beneath a huge portrait of Franco, Unamuno was forced to listen to a succession of sycophantic tirades from professors, culminating in a flowery oration by Pemán. Several speakers had referred to Basque and Catalan nationalism as 'a cancer which should be cut out from the body politic'.

Vegas Latapié noticed that after these remarks 'Unamuno began scribbling some notes and ceased to listen to the speeches. According to the programme he was not supposed to speak, but when the evening finished he took the floor. Of course nobody could stop him because he was presiding in lieu of the Head of State.' Crespo watched Unamuno, whose lectures he had attended as a student, closely. 'He had taken an envelope from his pocket. He was wearing

A rare photograph showing Franco's wife, Unamuno and Millán Astray (with eye-patch), during the ceremony at Salamanca University at which Unamuno made a scathing impromptu speech on 12 October 1936.

Miguel de Unamuno, scholar, controversialist and Rector of the University of Salamanca.

what he always wore, a dark blue suit with a high-necked black jersey. He stood up and began to speak, and at once I realized that this was something out of the ordinary. "You talk about the Basques and the Catalans," he said, "but here is your bishop who is Catalan and tries to teach you the Christian doctrine you don't want to know; while I, a Basque, have spent my life teaching you to read and think in the Spanish language, of which you are ignorant."' Then, remembers Vegas Latapié, the rector denounced atrocities on both sides. In Nationalist Spain women, sometimes wearing religious emblems, went to gloat over executions; in Republican Spain women were sometimes the executioners. Hatred without compassion could not win minds, to conquer was not to convince.

At this point, says Crespo, Millán Astray got to his feet 'and flapping his empty sleeve like a penguin, cried "Death to the intellectuals!" and other things which I couldn't hear, there was such uproar. Don Miguel tried to answer this madman, but whatever he said was inaudible.' Some officers drew their pistols and Millán Astray's bodyguard 'thrust his sub-machine-gun into Don Miguel's chest. Doña Carmen pushed the gun aside and, signalling to her guard of honour, led Don Miguel down the steps while our officer supported him on the other side. He could hardly walk, he let himself be carried along as we cleared a path with our rifle butts and put him into a car.' Driven from his club with cries of 'Red!' and 'Traitor!', Unamuno was finally dismissed from the rectorship, this time by the Nationalists. In letters written before his death two months later he spoke of 'a stupid regime of terror' whose real enemy was 'liberalism, not bolshevism'.

To prevent some inflamed patriot from assassinating him, Unamuno was provided with an armed bodyguard on the few occasions when he left his house after that impromptu speech. There was no mention of it in the Nationalist press, but several versions were current; as when Unamuno is said to have deplored the 'senseless paradox' of Millán Astray's legionary slogan and to have lamented that such a person 'should dictate the pattern of mass psychology. A cripple who lacks the spiritual grandeur of a Cervantes is wont to seek ominous relief in causing mutilation around him.'

Hearing a garbled account of his death and believing that the Nationalists had executed him, Unamuno's sons, who were in Madrid, both volunteered for the Republican armed forces. One was wounded, losing an eye soon after going into action. There was a last, cruelly ironical twist to the sequence. Anxious, it seems, to make some public gesture of respect, Falangists asked the family's permission to act as pall-bearers at the funeral, saluting the coffin as it slid into its niche and performing the fascist-inspired ritual of crying 'Comrade Don Miguel de Unamuno!', with the reply 'Presente!', quite as though the deceased rector was a Falangist martyr.

The legend 'José Antonio, Presente!', still to be seen in fading letters on the walls of Spanish churches, commemorates the chief martyr in the Falangist roll-call of honour. Several attempts to rescue him by offering large bribes to anarchist leaders in Alicante had failed. A proposal to exchange him for a prisoner of the Nationalists was rejected by Azaña; and his own offer to fly to Salamanca to try for a negotiated peace did not meet with favour in either zone. Tried and sentenced to death on 17 November 1936, José Antonio Primo de Rivera was executed on 20 November as the anarchist leader Buenaventura Durruti lay dying in Madrid.

The execution took place before the government in Valencia had confirmed the sentence. On 19 November the government was still debating the question, says Socrates Gómez, with Prieto arguing that José Antonio should be freed and allowed to go to Salamanca, where his presence might well embarrass Franco and cause serious political divisions. 'Then came a telegram from the civil governor in Alicante saying that local militants were threatening to kill all the prisoners unless José Antonio was executed. By 9 o'clock that night the jail was surrounded and danger imminent. I told Azaña himself of the situation. Communications continued during the night, but at dawn José Antonio was shot – not by an army firing squad, as was the rule, but by members of the group which had issued the ultimatum. The government had the choice of risking the deaths of all the prisoners or summoning troops from the front to attack these bandits. In the end it was powerless to resist their blackmail.'

In a last testament the Falangist leader had expressed his hopes for a 'government of unity' with a majority of moderate socialists and Left Republicans. 'You see,' says Serrano Suñer, 'José Antonio didn't want the coup for its own sake, but to *avoid* civil war. When it failed to achieve that he offered to parley with the generals, leaving as hostages his aunt, who was like a mother to him, and one of his brothers, but the Republican government stupidly rejected this idea. Facing death, José Antonio spoke these moving words: "May it be that my blood is the last Spanish blood to be spilt in civil war. May it be that the Spanish people, so full of fine qualities, can at last find peace, a homeland, bread and justice."'

José Antonio's sister Pilar was kept in suspense by the mystery surrounding his fate. 'There were rumours that he had been seen, that some journalists had visited him. The uncertainty about whether or not he was alive was a constant concern. Franco must have known, but probably didn't want to undermine morale. After some months we were told the truth and had to accept it and keep fighting despite this terrible absence.'

In fact the myth of *el ausente* (the absent one) was useful to Franco since it postponed a final decision about the leadership of the Falange and gave time for rivalries to intensify. His relief at the news of José Antonio's death showed in an uncharacteristic display of malicious glee. Serrano Suñer recalls 'a very violent scene. One day we were having lunch and Franco said to me: "You're always talking about this man, his splendid virtues and his courage and so forth, but I've heard that he was unable to walk to his execution, he was so frightened." At that I went wild and shouted: "It's a lie! Cowards!"' There is a story that Franco so deeply resented the mass appeal of *el ausente* that he maintained that José Antonio had been handed over to the Russians, who had castrated him.

Vegas Latapié was disgusted by the 'absolutely fascist' atmosphere created by the cult of the Caudillo. At the end of a banquet which he attended with his friend the Count of Rodezno, an eccentric Carlist, 'everybody stood up to sing the national anthem with arms outstretched in the fascist salute. I said to the count: "This is ludicrous." He had merely raised his hand, saying: "It's far more comfortable this way." In the cinema everyone had to salute when Franco appeared on the screen.'

A touch of quasi-imperial exoticism was added by Franco's Moorish bodyguard, and journalists wrote of the need to exorcize 'the liberal, decadent, masonic, materialist and Frenchified' spirit and to 'impregnate ourselves with the spirit of the 16th century, imperial, heroic, proud, Castilian, spiritual and chivalrous.' In accordance with this costume drama mentality, there was a purge of 'objectionable' street names, hotel titles, even menu listings; all had to be hispanicized. The assault on liberalism had sartorial implications. Nudity in infants more than two years old was considered indecent, bathing trunks were banned, plunge necklines, short skirts and bare (female) arms banned. Formal salutations were required: whereas in the Republican zone it might well be dangerous to use the word 'God' except as an expletive, in White Spain the prescribed 'Red' greeting – *Salud* (health) – was one to avoid. An order for the early closing of bars and cafés was unevenly observed. But booksellers had a bad time of it since the index of forbidden publications was comprehensive. Public and school libraries were purged, bookish citizens found themselves at the mercy of anonymous informers, the prejudices of the illiterate or the philistine were flattered by a literary *limpieza* (cleansing) which frequently culminated in a bonfire of books.

Perhaps no Nationalist satrap better personified the ideal of *limpieza* than Major Bruno Ibañez of the civil guard, who began his reign of all-out terror in

Castellón, June 1938. A nun in charge of war orphans gives the Falangist salute after the Nationalist occupation.

Córdoba in September 1936. Ostentatiously pious and fond of proclaiming that 'Spain, in its essence, is nothing more than twenty centuries of struggle for Christianity,' he not only fed the firing squads at a rate which eventually alarmed even Queipo de Llano but launched a major purge of the cinema and of literature. Córdoba province, he announced, was to be cleansed of 'every book pernicious to a healthy society', and with the threat of a court-martial hanging over them people hastened to surrender to the flames any volume which could conceivably be construed as subversive. Within two weeks nearly 5,500 books were destroyed.

Francisco Poyatos, the public prosecutor, was an equally good example of a rarer species, a Spanish liberal repelled by totalitarianism in whatever guise. He takes pride in 'having been fired by the Reds for being a fascist and by the fascists for being a Red'. To achieve that distinction he had to endure some hair-raising experiences, not least that of finding himself in Córdoba at the height of Don Bruno's manic purification. Walking through Madrid in the early hours to plead for the life of a colleague who had been taken to a *checa* (party interrogation centre), he had heard screams and constant volleys of gunfire in the Retiro park. Towards the end of August 1936 he received an anonymous phone call: 'Wherever you hide we'll find you and kill you.' The protection of assault guards and the kindness of a police inspector enabled him and his wife to get away to Paris, an example of Republican justice and humanity which he never forgot. But becoming restless, he wrote to Franco offering his services as a lawyer and was told that he would be welcome. Despite a warning from his wife, who had stayed in Almería, he still believed

Seville, September 1936. General Queipo de Llano, well-known for his bloodthirsty radio threats, at a military parade.

that if there was so much evil in the Republican zone the Nationalists had to be better. 'I actually imagined that I would be on the side of the angels.'

His first jolt came in Algeciras, where he was arrested on the outlandish charge that he had been a communist candidate in Almería before the war. Transferred to a prison in Seville, he was released after four days when Queipo de Llano intervened. His arrival in Córdoba, where he had been sent to resume his duties as a public prosecutor, was no less traumatic. Having been notified of his dismissal by the Republican authorities in Madrid, he was told three days later that he was to be suspended on suspicion of being a Red. The local military commander offered sympathy, but the knowledge that he was under Queipo's protection did more to spare him from the attentions of Don Bruno.

As a lawyer concerned with justice, Poyatos took a gloomy view of the wanton waste of life in both Spains. But in much of the expanding Nationalist zone the war was a distant affair which could be left to the generals, and life for the 'clean' bourgeoisie was much the same as in Primo de Rivera's time. Bullfights and festivals were resumed, social life ticked over at the traditional tempo. There was no lack of food or fuel, and plenty of opportunities for patriotic service. The workers had been shot or put in their place. Taxation was not excessive, inflation controlled, export business in wines and farm produce booming, wheat prices guaranteed. It was not difficult to obey the clergy's exhortations to thank God for Franco and for economic and political stability.

But what of the workers and peasants? Did they have much reason to be grateful? From Tetuán Franco had proclaimed: 'Fear nothing, Spanish working people. Our movement is dangerous only for those who live like princes, for those who use trade union funds without rendering accounts, for those who do nothing but attack the Republic.' From Seville Queipo appealed to the workers of Andalusia and Extremadura: 'Does disorder, anarchy and gangsterism suit you better than a government which imposes freedom from above? The real freedom, which ends where that of your neighbour begins.' Were such statements propaganda or did they presage some tangible benefits after the destructive turmoil of 1931–36?

The inadequacy of the agrarian reform of 1932 had angered peasants throughout Spain. CNT or UGT agitators, with their emphasis on collectivization, were often viewed with suspicion or hostility, as was proved when, within a day of the rising and with the support of most small- or medium-holding Catholic peasants, Old Castile, León, Galicia and part of Aragon were firmly held by the insurgents. Peasants from those regions provided – apart from the Army of Africa – the best troops to the Nationalist forces. Peasant farmers, themselves sometimes employers of labour, did not need to be told of the importance of law and order. Since Franco's name was associated with this blessing, they too thanked God for Franco.

Born and bred in the village of Castrogeriz near Burgos, Florentino Villandiego and Agapito Anton Pérez, whose families both owned small plots of land, admit that 'before the Republic the *caciques* were too powerful', but otherwise have little but criticism for the UGT's domination of the village in 1931–34. There was, they say, chaos and victimization in reverse. 'The union secretary was the new *cacique*: he would only give work or confiscated land to his members. If you were right-wing and didn't belong to the union you would get nothing. So we had to join. He was even controlling the bosses, who had to put up with workers they didn't want.' For Florentino and Agapito 'religion, work and the family are the most important things', and though they dared not express their feelings both were angered and distressed by the burning of religious effigies. They maintain that 'when the war started it became clear that most of the villagers were right-wing. Some of the Left were imprisoned, others were killed. Many escaped. One of us went off to fight with the Falange, the other stayed in the village because he was married. We didn't know about the rest of Spain, but we think it must have been like this everywhere, otherwise the war would not have happened.'

Tales of forced collectivization in the Republican zones helped to stiffen the resolve of the Florentinos and the Agapitos. They left to fight for their often impoverished independence or stayed at home, working unstintingly. For them the war brought peace and stability. They could get on with farming again and forget what Franco called 'petty politics'. There was even a hint of wartime democracy, with *señoritos*, the sons of the gentry, lending a hand on the land. Husbands, sons and sweethearts were killed at distant fronts, but that was the fault of the Reds. It was not a lovely war, but it often brought a sense of unity and common purpose that had for long been missing.

The peasants who jointed the armed forces were, in a sense, primarily defending the interests of the rich. But for men and youths who may never have have travelled farther than the provincial capital, the war offered a glittering prospect of seeing the big cities where politicians and profiteers lived in inconceivable luxury and sin, trembling as the day of reckoning drew near. Whatever happened there would be free travel, free clothing, free food. So, in a very real sense, this was a war of liberation for peasants whose lives had always been tightly circumscribed.

For factory workers who became soldiers there was much the same sense of release. For those who stayed behind there would be no strikes but regular work. They were denied the heady delights of experiments in workers' control, but were spared the headaches and political friction that went with them. Nationalist Spain, too, could boast some bold experiments. 'Social equality is nonsense,' said Queipo de Llano in March 1937. 'Look at nature, at the work of God, and you will see that no two things are equal.' But he said it when inaugurating a workers' housing scheme in Seville: and with virtually dictatorial powers Queipo was able to promote his idiosyncratic brand of republicanism. He not only banished strikes and unions on pain of death but he did more for social welfare, agriculture, and the expansion of industry than Seville and its environs had known since the days of the enlightened despot-kings of the 18th century.

He cajoled financial backing for a textile plant, raised money to reclaim 240,000 acres of marshland for rice fields, abolished employers' associations as well as workers' unions, forbade the dismissal of employees without reference to a regional labour office, protected tenant farmers by decreeing a moratorium on mortgage payments, and carried out an agrarian reform of sorts by distributing to 'loyal' peasants land donated by big proprietors or confiscated from 'Reds'. Once the worst of the bloodletting was over, Queipo, by no means the drunken, incompetent clown of Republican propaganda, proved himself an imaginative administrator. When he had ceased to utter extravagant nightly threats he used the radio to ridicule Republican politicians, particularly Azaña; and even to tell his huge audience that if, unthinkably, General Franco should be guilty of betraying the true interests of the Spanish people, he, Queipo, would as a sincere patriot feel constrained to fight the Caudillo.

With his theatrical swagger and leery joie de vivre, Queipo was probably the most effective publicist on either side, certainly the one with the widest popular appeal. But by mid-1937 the uninhibited rule of this Cavalier Nationalist was being scrutinized by the Roundheads in Salamanca. In February 1937 old shirt Falangists and hard-line Carlists, sharing a grudge against Franco's political presumption, met in Lisbon to discuss merging the movements. Nothing came of this; but Franco, thinking along the same lines, was determined to create a unified Nationalist party, led by himself, with a programme that would placate the various squabbling monarchist and Falangist factions.

The task was entrusted to a newcomer in the Caudillo's entourage, 36-year-old Ramón Serrano Suñer. Though an outsider without any official position, he became – very soon after his arrival in Salamanca in February 1937 – so powerful under Franco's protection that he was sarcastically known as 'El Cuñadisimo' (supreme brother-in-law). Elegant, ambitious, sharp-witted, and for long Franco's only close political associate, he rapidly replaced the easy-going Nicolás Franco as right-hand man. A strenuous critic of 'degenerate' democracy since 1934, his contempt for the Republic had been sharpened into hatred by the deaths of his friends Fernándo Primo de Rivera and Ruiz de Alda in the Modelo Prison, by the shooting of his two brothers, and by the execution of José Antonio. Ironically, the man who was to lend a lasting stability to Franco's regime by a mixture of ruthlessness and political sleight-of-hand had escaped from a private clinic in Madrid in a female disguise which was just good enough to deceive the guards: 'I put on a wig which my sister had brought in her bag. It wasn't very good, it didn't even cover my head properly, but on the other side we stuck a beret.'

Serrano Suñer's problem was how to give the military dictatorship a consultative façade, composed mainly of delegates from the less radical sections of the Falange, the Carlists and the monarchists. With the advantage of being able to offer posts of influence in the proposed establishment he held talks with leaders of all three factions and with generals and Church dignitaries. His adroit manipulations widened the existing divergence

Family group, Burgos 1937. Franco and his brother-in-law Ramón Serrano Suñer with their families.

between 'separatists' and 'collaborators' in the Falange, which was trying to set up its own national council.

At midnight on 19 April Franco broadcast a decree which summarily united the Falange and the Carlists, incorporating them and other Nationalist groups in a new hold-all party with what Vegas Latapié describes as 'possibly the longest name in the world, the Falange Española Tradicionalista y de las Juntas de Ofensiva Nacional-Sindicalista' (usually abbreviated to FET-JONS). Already Head of State and Commander-in-Chief, Franco now became the leader of the FET, whose uniform was to consist of the Falangist blue shirt and the Carlist red beret. The resentment caused by this compromise is well brought out in the story of how the Carlist Rodezno, asked by some bare-headed Falangists why he was wearing ordinary clothes, replied: 'Because I can't put my blue shirt in my pocket.'

Mola and Queipo reluctantly agreed to the unification. Hedilla, encouraged by the mischief-making German ambassador, refused the offer of a place on the new 'political secretariat,' but on 25 April was arrested, and, some weeks later, sentenced to death on a charge of treason. Serrano Suñer, who had master-minded this coup, now claims the sentence was commuted at his insistence. 'I told Franco that it would be a grave political misjudgement and after a long conversation he said: "All right, all right. But you'll see how our weakness will cost us dear one of these days."' But Hedilla spent the next four years in solitary confinement and the Falangist rebels came to heel. Appointed Secretary-General of the FET, Serrano Suñer owed his power partly to being an outsider, with many enemies and no personal following, whose loyalty to Franco would be guaranteed; but he denies that the decree of unification aimed to smash the 'real' revolutionary Falange: 'The spirit of the Falange was the main factor in the unification. The proof of this is that Dionisio Ridruejo [a young Falangist leader from Valladolid] and other radicals were with me. They stayed for as long as they believed that Falangist doctrine would be the basic ideology. Later Franco developed a personal power and we were no longer needed. He had collaborators who never questioned him. Then a political organization, a huge bureaucracy, was built around him and this was Franquism.'

The chief objective, he says, was 'to avoid internal conflicts. If the rearguard was disturbed by political rivalries the war effort would be disrupted, as happened in the Republican zone.' Enrique Líster admits that whatever the means by which Franco seized dictatorial power he made pretty good use of it. 'Foreign aid was important, but a unified command was important too. This is what we lacked in our camp.'

Some Falangists discussed the possibility of kidnapping Franco, but found little support for such a drastic step. Nothing could be done in the midst of war, says Narciso Perales, who with other revolutionary Falangists had hoped for a rapid coup to restore order throughout Spain as a prelude to 'making the falangist revolution'. Enforced militarization in December 1936, when he estimates that there were about 100,000 armed Falangists at the fronts, had dealt a severe blow to the political power of the Falange. Now Franco was seizing the chance to create the kind of old-fashioned military dictatorship despised by true Falangists. For radical Carlists like Jaime del Burgo, the young student leader from Pamplona, unification meant betrayal by their leaders and victory for the flashy, foreign ideology of the Falange. He felt humiliated that Carlism should have been tamed by a decree rather than 'perishing in a great battle'. *Acción Española* monarchists, says Vegas Latapié, had to accept a *fait accompli*, though 'in principle' opposed to it: 'We didn't want any parties, preferring an organic system of corporations.' But with Hedilla and many other uncooperative Falangist chieftains in jail and no sign of any coherent opposition, Franco and Serrano Suñer had scooped the pool, conjuring up a mass political movement from the bewildered or indifferent members of already demoralized factions.

The only possible protest was a negative one, and the young monarchist Juan Crespo, still on guard duty at Nationalist headquarters, made it, though not without trepidation. 'The square was crammed with people chanting "Franco, Franco, Franco". He made a speech from the balcony just above me. When I went off duty I composed a statement addressed to the commander of our militia saying that I was returning my palace guard's uniform and resigning from the militia as a protest against His Excellency's speech. I couldn't see why, because a man banged his fist on the table, we should all have to believe the same thing. I thought there might be some kind of reprisal, so instead of going home I presented myself to the Victoria Regiment as a volunteer and was assigned to the 13th Battalion.'

February 1939. Women of Auxilio Social, the Nationalist welfare organization, dispense food to children after the capture of Barcelona.

Though in due course three women – Pilar Primo de Rivera, Mercedes Sanz Bachiller (the widow of Onésimo Redondo), and Maria Rosa Urrica Pastor (the Florence Nightingale of Nationalist nurses) – were appointed to the 'advisory' national council, women's role was seen as strictly 'complementary'. Launched in October 1936 in Valladolid by Mercedes Sanz Bachiller, the Auxilio Social, eventually headed by Pilar, established centres throughout Nationalist Spain. Founded to care for the orphans of the repression and for elderly displaced persons, it developed into a welfare network for the needy in general, providing accommodation, maternity homes, food and medical treatment. The 'Margaritas of Tafalla', a Carlist women's organization, ran a hospital and a soldiers' welfare service, and 'foster mothers' of the Auxilio Social sent photographs, letters and small gifts to their 'foster sons' at the fronts.

In October 1937 a decree required all able-bodied women between the ages of 17 and 35 to enrol in some form of social service. A sizeable army of female auxiliaries rallied to the flag. But there was no place for women in positions of political authority, no La Pasionaria or Federica Montseny, no *milicianas* at the fronts. In keeping with the Caudillo's new-found piety, the tone was solemn and prudish. The Margaritas had to 'promise on the Sacred Heart of Jesus . . . to observe modesty in dress: long sleeves, high necks, skirts to the ankle, blouses full at the chest . . . To read no novels, newspapers or magazines, to go to no cinema or theatre without ecclesiastical licence . . . Neither publicly nor privately to dance the dances of this century, but to learn the old dances . . . Not to wear make-up as long as the war lasts.'

February 1938. Franco with his cabinet: at far left, Serrano Suñer, Minister of the Interior; third and fourth from right, Fernandez Cuesta, Minister of Agriculture, and Sáinz Rodríguez, Minister of Education.

Addressing the national council of the Falange's Women's Section in February 1938 Pilar Primo de Rivera vowed that 'we shall never put women in competition with men because they will never succeed in equalling men. If they try, women will lose the elegance and grace that complement a man's qualities.' She now contrasts women's role as defined in such statements with attitudes in Republican Spain. 'Divorce, abortion, they had no sense of the family. There was chaos, a flood of weird things. In the Nationalist zone we were guided by the Church, by Catholic morality, and everything was much more constructive and orderly.'

'First the fathers are shot, then the children get charity,' ran a cynical comment on the work of the Auxilio Social. In December 1936 Hedilla had appealed to Falangist investigators 'to do everything possible to prevent anyone from satisfying personal vengeance. Ensure that the man who from hunger and desperation voted for the Left is not punished or humiliated. We all know that in many places there are people of the Right who are worse than the Reds.' But such an appeal had little effect on new-shirt Falangists thinking of their own careers and the known ruthlessness of the Caudillo. And when military justice replaced random killings, the terror was hardly less indiscriminate.

A horrified Francisco Poyatos watched 'trials' during which up to twenty 'criminals' were dealt with in so many minutes. 'There wasn't even time for them to make statements . . . it was even worse than the executions without trial, because it was making a mockery of justice, giving an appearance of legality to something which was not legal at all. And also, as I learnt later,

BELOW LEFT *Captured Republican troops are forced to give the Falangist salute.*

BELOW RIGHT *Pilar Primo de Rivera with members of the Women's Section of the Falange beneath the Falangist yoke-and-arrows emblem.*

Franco insisted that only one in five people could be acquitted, that was the highest proportion.' Summing up his experience of repression in both zones, Poyatos comments: 'There was nothing which happened in one zone which did not happen in the other, no crime which the other side didn't also perpetrate. But the moral difference is striking, because in the Republican zone it was popular fervour which spilled over and killed people; in the Nationalist zone it was those in authority who cold-bloodedly condemned people to death . . . talking about a Holy Crusade in God's name, which is blasphemy.'

Serrano Suñer states that Franco refused a suggestion that he should delegate the task of supervising the purges to a committee. 'He felt that this would detract from his authority as commander-in-chief. There was absolutely nothing that I personally could do.' Long before the war ended Juan Crespo had ceased to believe in God-and-the-Fatherland slogans. 'Hundreds of thousands of people were massacred and for every family it was a complete world. I went on fighting because my disenchantment didn't mean that I identified with the slogans of our enemies, who killed in the name of universal socialism and the brotherhood of man or whatever.' Imprisoned in Bilbao, Ernesto Castaño had reason to be grateful for the way the Basque authorities protected Nationalist prisoners against lynchings by infuriated mobs during the bombing of the city. 'We were actually given guns and ammunition to defend ourselves if need be.' On 18 June 1937, when Bilbao was about to fall, he and other prisoners were released and escorted by prison officials to the Nationalist lines.

Castaño had been 'simple enough to think that Franco was fighting a clean war without violence for violence's sake.' He was soon disillusioned by a monarchist officer who confirmed what Castaño had refused to believe – that in Salamanca alone about 5,000 people had been executed. 'He said that Franco's behaviour had made him wish that the rising had never taken place.' Castaño was further shocked by the Church's failure to use its influence to end the repression. Far from doing so, it had either encouraged bloodlust in a spirit of 'crusade' or had kept quiet, making an unholy alliance with Franco in return for extensive privileges. For Castaño, who had 'found God in prison when I was sentenced to death,' this was the foulest betrayal.

The nun Cristina de Arteaga, on the other hand, still maintains that whatever their excesses the Nationalists *were* fighting a crusade. 'The Pope said so, didn't he? The Church could forgive the people who murdered priests and nuns, burned churches and convents, and attacked religious education; but it would surely have been impossible for the Church to bless them? It was natural to support an army fighting for religion and faith.' Father Alejandro Martínez Gil, whose brother, also a priest, had been shot, argues that the Church was 'reactionary' because 'the Left has always kicked and beaten the Church to the right.' Held in a prison hulk in Gijón harbour for some months, he was disturbed by the Nationalist repression but not surprised that most of the bishops came out for Franco. 'You can't really blame them for thinking

ABOVE LEFT *Variously described as 'the smiling general' and the saviour of Christian civilization, the portly, middle-aged Franco has his portrait painted.*

ABOVE RIGHT *Generalissimo Franco with his Moorish bodyguard as seen by a hostile cartoonist.*

that the Republicans, who also sometimes talked of their crusade, were children of the Devil.'

Cardinal Gomá had described the war as a punishment for the godlessness of the Republican leaders. Only two prelates, the Archbishop of Tarragona – who had been saved from assassination by President Companys – and the Bishop of Vitoria, criticized Nationalist atrocities, particularly the shooting of Basque priests. The rest, before finally committing themselves, waited for Franco to discipline the equally 'godless' Falange and for the Pope to give his blessing to the crusade. The first requirement was met by the unification decree; the second by the Vatican's full approval of the Nationalist cause after the collapse of Basque Catholic resistance.

On 1 July 1937 the bishops issued a collective letter unequivocally supporting Franco: 'The war is an armed plebiscite . . . On one side spiritual values are defended by the insurgents who rose to defend law and order, social peace, traditional civilization, and religion. On the other side, the worship of materialism – call it Marxist, communist or anarchist – which wants to replace Spain's ancient civilization with the new "civilization" of the Russian Soviets.' Three months later the Vatican confirmed its recognition by sending a nuncio to Salamanca. The Church reaped its reward in a rigidly enforced restoration of religious teaching in the schools, where classrooms were adorned with portraits of the Caudillo and images of the Virgin Mary. Church attendance was obligatory for all military and civilian officials. The Jesuits, dissolved (not for the first time) in 1931, were welcomed back as 'a peculiarly Spanish Order', thus proving the accuracy of a popular proverb – 'Night and the Jesuits always return.' A parade-ground religiosity was the keynote of White Spain. And the Republican government made what gestures it dared to appease Catholic opinion, permitting freedom of private worship in August 1937, allowing refugee Basques to worship publicly in Barcelona, and authorizing chaplains to be attached to some Popular Army units.

The unification decree of April 1937, crowning Franco with a triple tiara of power, was followed in August by a decree requiring all officers to affiliate to the FET and announcing that the Leader would in due course appoint his own successor. *Franquistas*, as his more devoted followers now began to be known, trumpeted the virtues of 'the paladin of Western civilization'; posters of 'the smiling general' and eulogistic biographies were distributed. Carefully-screened and intellectually inferior teachers and professors filled the gaps in schools and universities left by the dismissal or liquidation of 'Red' incumbents who, according to Franquist propaganda, had been the beneficiaries of 'a Jewish-Marxist-Masonic conspiracy' to corrupt the Spanish mind. After heavy fighting, Republican offensives at Brunete near Madrid and at Belchite and Teruel in Aragon were frustrated. The stalemate at Madrid continued, but on 19 October, with the capture of Gijón in Asturias, the campaign in the north was completed. The Nationalist zone now covered two-thirds of Spain and victory seemed to be well within sight.

Summoned by Serrano Suñer (a fellow ex-CEDA deputy) in November 1937, Castaño was offered a government post in charge of the new 'vertical' trade union system. As a believer in the 'family' approach to management-labour relations with which he had founded the Agrarian Bloc back in 1932, he declined the offer. Two months later the Agrarian Bloc was dissolved and its archives seized. Fernández Cuesta, released from jail in Valencia in exchange for Justino de Azcárate, brother of the Republican ambassador in London, in the hope that he might stir a Falangist rebellion, was rapidly absorbed into the regime as secretary-general of the consultative national council; and in the cabinet formed in February of what was pompously called the Second Triumphal Year he was appointed Minister of Agriculture. 'I didn't know a beetroot from a potato,' he says, 'but anyhow agrarian reform was impossible in a divided Spain.'

Ministers were required to take an oath of allegiance in a ceremony staged in the ancient monastery of Las Huelgas near Burgos and described by Serrano Suñer as 'fervent, devout, like a vigil in arms'. Some of the politicians, notably the monarchists Sáinz Rodríguez (Minister of Education) and Vegas Latapié, found the occasion vulgarly ostentatious as they were made to swear 'in the name of God and His holy evangelists' to fulfil their duty 'with the most exact fidelity to the Head of State, Generalissimo of our glorious armies, and to the principles which distinguish the Nationalist regime.' Neither Sáinz Rodríguez, who had joined the government on the understanding that the day the war ended he would resign ('so I was a minister of the uprising not of the regime'), nor Vegas Latapié lasted for long. The former's sarcastic comments soon brought him into disfavour and he went, not unwillingly, into exile.

Vegas Latapié, who had a particular aversion to the *Cuñadisimo*, lobbied to vote him off the national council, an unforgivable sin. He resigned as secretary-general of press and propaganda and enlisted as a private in a Falangist unit, later joining the Foreign Legion.

Vegas Latapié describes Serrano Suñer as 'an absolute carbon copy of a Nazi. He imagined that he was going to play Hitler or Mussolini to Franco's Hindenburg or Victor Emmanuel.' Serrano Suñer himself does not deny that he and Franco anticipated a German victory in World War II, but asserts that the real Nazis were to be found among disgruntled old-shirt Falangists. 'I was never a Nazi, even before their barbaric deeds were known. I argued violently with the racist philosopher Alfred Rosenberg, telling him that there was a huge gap between us because, despite what Azaña said, the Spanish people are largely Catholic and we Spaniards believe in the moral unity of mankind. As a Latin and a Catholic I had a love for Italy, yes, and because of it those Falangists used to denounce me at the German embassy and in Berlin when they went there.' The 'upstart' brother-in-law, one of the few experienced politicians in the Nationalist junta, became the target for malcontents of every nuance. But even as a scapegoat he was valuable to Franco.

Dionisio Ridruejo pressed for a labour charter based on Falangist principles, which, so far as they had been formulated, seemed to favour a federation of autonomous industrial unions, set within a planned economy. But the Labour Charter promulgated in March 1938 was much nearer to the 'vertical' syndicalism of Italy. Many of its proposals sounded progressive enough – a minimum wage, social insurance, family allowances, holidays with pay, safeguards for tenant farmers. But the operative concept was 'the vertical trade union as an instrument in the service of the State . . . which recognizes private enterprise as the source of the Nation's economic life.'

Essentially this was not fascism – a closer parallel might be with the paternalist regime figure-headed by Marshal Pétain in Vichy France – but a restoration of pre-1931 capitalism with the support of the police and the army. The workers' standard of living would be 'raised as and when the Nation's superior interest permits'. Strikes and go-slows were classified as treason. An impressive pyramid of local and national corporations, culminating in a national corporative assembly, was more useful as a source of bureaucratic patronage than as an economic solution. Two other decrees established a rigid press censorship and, in tune with Franco's declared war on separatism and the regime's ideal of 'Unity, Totality and Hierarchy', formally rescinded the Catalan autonomy statute of 1932.

Franco's severest problem was with his fascist allies; and the apparent concessions to fascist doctrine in the Labour Charter may well have been at least partly designed to placate them. Mines in Morocco were requisitioned from French and British owners and 60 per cent of Rio Tinto iron ore production diverted to Germany, whose envoys pressed for a near-takeover – and were frustrated by Franco's insistence that as head of a provisional government he was not empowered to conclude any such deal. German

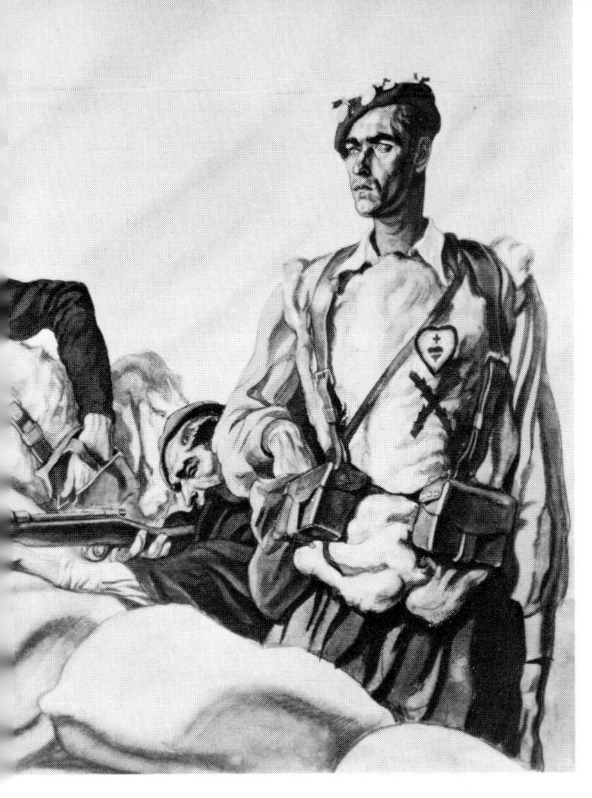

ABOVE LEFT *A Carlist* requeté *from Navarre with Sacred Heart medallion known as a 'bullet-stopper'. Painting by Carlos Saenz de Tejada.*

ABOVE RIGHT *A Moorish soldier enjoys a smoke after earning a 25-peseta reward for knocking out a Russian tank. Painting by Carlos Saenz de Tejada.*

pressure became so intense that, as one story has it, Franco vowed in private to forgo German aid and fight a guerrilla war, since he was determined not to sell any Spanish territory. But as a condition of continuing aid he was forced to raise the upper limit for foreign investment in Spanish companies from 25 to 40 per cent and ultimately to 75 per cent.

He also had to tolerate the transformation of Majorca into an Italian colony and to swallow the affront of the Condor Legion's apparently unauthorized bombing of Guernica and the Italians' independent glory raids on Barcelona. But when, in August 1937, Basque officers in Santoña negotiated a separate surrender with the Italians, hoping for more humane treatment, the Nationalist General Dávila acted promptly to prevent the arrangement. Basque refugees were forced to leave two ships on which, with Italian permission, they had embarked. One was the *Seven Seas Spray*. When the soldiers had been removed Captain Roberts and his crew were kept in captivity for more than a month.

Scuffles between Spanish and Italian troops were not infrequent. The Germans laughed at Italian inefficiency, the Italians complained of German arrogance. General Adriano Mantelli, then a young ace pilot who was credited with shooting down 22 Republican planes, remembers that in an interview with Mussolini he answered the Duce's query about the effectiveness of foreign intervention by saying that most Spaniards realized that the Italians were fighting for the same ideals, whereas the Germans were just testing war machines.

In his dealings with troublesome and greedy allies, both of whom despised his regime for its lack of a clear-cut (i.e. fascist) ideology, Franco had one great advantage over the Republican government. Unlike Stalin, the Axis dictators of Germany and Italy did not have a party or propaganda machine of their own in Spain, and the unification coup had made doubly certain that they would not. The separate Falangist, Carlist, CEDA and monarchist militias had been 'militarized' – absorbed into the Nationalist army – at much the same time and for the same reasons as applied in the other Spain. By early 1937 some 4,000 'provisional lieutenants', mostly middle-class university students or graduates, had been commissioned after a three-week crash course supervised by German instructors. Juan Crespo, the young student from Salamanca University, attended one of the courses. 'The instructors could hardly speak any Spanish and gave orders in German. We guessed what they meant.' These hastily-trained officers were to form the backbone of the Nationalist army, which by the end of 1937 was, like the Republican army, about 500,000 strong: larger, in fact, than any in Europe except the French.

20-year-old Crespo chose to lead a unit of Moorish *regulares*, 'because, with the Legion, they were the shock troops; and they had such a spectacular, theatrical kind of uniform, the blue *djellaba* and the red cap, not a thought of camouflage.' He denies that the Moors were particularly ferocious. 'I learned a lot from them. They knew everything: how to deploy, how to use hand grenades, the main assault weapon, to the best advantage; and they were excellent sentries, much more patient than Spaniards. As for raping and looting, they were kept in check by their officers. I came across only one case of rape and had the culprit shot. Since we did not stay in captured towns or villages, but moved on, the real villains may have been the ordinary troops on garrison duty.'

But though by April 1938 the Nationalists had fought their way to the borders of Catalonia and controlled a stretch of the coast above Valencia, there was growing dissatisfaction with Franco's performance. His decision to relieve the Alcázar at Toledo in September 1936 was thought by some critics to have wasted the chance to capture Madrid. Now the decision to advance to the Mediterranean seemed to have squandered the opportunity to complete the conquest of Catalonia and capture Barcelona. General Diez Alegría, in 1938 a liaison officer with the Nationalist High Command, reckons that Franco 'had the typical qualities of an officer used to colonial campaigns. He was a first-class tactician but not such a good strategist . . . To my mind the most serious strategic mistake was made in March 1938, after the battle of Aragon. After capturing Gandesa we advanced towards the river Ebro. There were hardly any troops on the other side. If we had crossed the river then, Catalonia could have been taken very easily, even more easily than it was later . . . But it was decided to retreat and divert towards Valencia. Why? I think there was a fear that if we advanced through Catalonia, the French might intervene . . . But in my view this decision prolonged the war by a year.'

There were other considerations. Speaking at a Falangist banquet held in Burgos on 19 April to mark the anniversary of the unification, General Yagüe, who was temporarily relieved of his command in consequence, praised the

Juan Yagüe, Army of Africa commander and critic of Franco's military and political strategy.

effectiveness of the Republican army, referred to the Germans and Italians as 'beasts of prey', and criticized the repressive mania which kept in jail thousands of men who could be useful to the Nationalist war effort.

But Franco was not in a hurry. In the winter of 1936–37, when Italian troops began to arrive in Spain, he had emphasized that his policy was not so much to defeat armies as to conquer territory, 'accompanied by the necessary purges'. Even in 1938 Franco preferred slow, grinding campaigns to blitzkrieg. Yagüe's speech had raised hopes for negotiations in the Republican government, but 'whoever desires mediation serves the Reds or the hidden enemies of Spain,' said Franco in a speech delivered on 6 June 1938, adding that to make peace now would be to risk another war later. The job, in fact, had to be finished, the cleansing thorough. A subservient press rammed home the Caudillo's message. 'In the name of Spain's historic destiny, of its martyrs and heroes, the fatherland demands the unconditional victory of Franco.'

CHAPTER FIVE

REPUBLICAN SPAIN: WHAT ABOUT THE REVOLUTION?

WHILE Franco and Serrano Suñer were taming their rebels and trying to keep their allies at bay, Largo Caballero faced the far more daunting task of contriving a semblance of Republican unity and resisting Soviet domination. The result was a tale of three mutually hostile cities, of a rumbling civil war within the civil war.

Peasants and industrial workers were busy making their revolution and revelling in what amounted to a dictatorship of the proletariat with its inevitable accompaniment of Red terror; but improvised union and party militias were having little or no success on the battlefield. The prestige of the USSR and of the rapidly growing Spanish Communist party rocketed after their spectacular contribution to the defence of Madrid. Soviet aid in the form of planes, tanks, guns and military advisers had coincided with the first appearance of the International Brigades and the emergence of the Fifth Regiment under such leaders as Enrique Líster. With its disciplined *esprit de corps* and concentration on the immediate priority of winning the war, this regiment was to form the backbone of the Popular Army.

'It became clear,' says Líster, 'that we were entering a long war and would need an army which could stand up to the enemy's professional troops. The real start of that was the Fifth Regiment. We called it the Fifth Regiment of Popular Militias at first, but what we quickly organized was a military unit which grew to 70,000 strong. There was a medical corps, a service corps, and we had formed companies, battalions and brigades before the 10 October 1936 decree creating the first six brigades of the Republican Popular Regular Army. Only one of these was not composed of contingents from the Fifth Regiment, which provided four of the six commanders. I was responsible for assembling and organizing the first mixed brigade, including soldiers of the old regular army. The birthplace of the Popular Army was Madrid. Elsewhere months passed before union and party militias were militarized, with consequent lack of efficiency and discipline.'

Madrid, governed by a defence committee after the flight of the government to Valencia, was, to the envy of Largo Caballero and the militants of Barcelona, basking in the glory of having made at least one heroic slogan – '*No pasarán!*' (they shall not pass) – come true. The impact of Soviet aid seemed

OPPOSITE *A militiaman and militiawoman on the Madrid front, July 1936.*

Largo Caballero, 67-year-old Republican prime minister, rides (on white horse) to visit an outpost in the Alto de León.

the more miraculous since, unaware of the transference of the gold reserve to Russia, many people imagined it to be a gesture of altruistic solidarity. Among those who hastened to join the Communist party were many career officers and JSU leaders, including Santiago Carrillo, the future leader of the PCE. In the government, Largo Caballero's close friend, foreign minister Alvarez del Vayo, became a fervent *comunizante* (fellow-traveller).

Largo Caballero himself, who had been billed as the Spanish Lenin, reacted angrily to being treated as a pawn in the power politics of the Comintern, whose agents manipulated the PCE despite some opposition from its secretary-general, José Diaz. Resisting pressure to merge the Socialist and Communist parties, Largo Caballero strove to restore the authority of the government while preserving essential liberties and revolutionary gains.

A half-condescending, half-threatening letter of advice from Stalin suggested that he should forget about social revolution during a war and be careful not to antagonize foreigners by confiscating their property, or peasant farmers by allowing anarchists to dragoon them into collectives, or the middle classes by treating them like enemies. Incessantly chivvied by the Soviet ambassador, Marcel Rosenberg (himself soon to be recalled and liquidated), Largo Caballero finally exploded: 'Out you go! You must learn, Señor, that we Spaniards may be poor and may need help from abroad, but we are sufficiently proud not to tolerate a foreign diplomat trying to impose his will

Manuel Azaña, prime minister 1931–33 and president of the Republic 1936–39.

on the head of the Spanish government. And as for you, Vayo, you ought to remember that you are a Spaniard instead of arranging with a foreigner to exert pressure on your own Prime Minister.'

Communism's attraction for an anti-fascist volunteer and its contempt for 'infantile leftist' revolutionaries is a central theme of Hemingway's novel *For Whom the Bell Tolls*. Robert Jordan, an American volunteer who, though not a Party member, has accepted communist discipline because it gets things done and therefore seems 'the soundest and sanest for the prosecution of the war', listens to the Russian journalist Karkov (Mikhail Koltsov) telling his tale of three cities: 'In Madrid you feel good and clean and with no possibility of anything but winning. Valencia is something else. The cowards who fled from Madrid still govern there. They have only contempt for those of Madrid. Their obsession is the weakening of the commissariat for war. And Barcelona. You should see Barcelona. It's still all comic opera. First it was the paradise of the crackpots and the romantic revolutionaries. Now it is the paradise of the fake soldiers who like to wear uniforms, who like to strut and swagger and wear red-and-black scarves. Valencia makes you sick and Barcelona makes you laugh.'

For Spaniards who resented Soviet domination and for whom the sacrifice of principle in the name of anti-fascist unity represented a moral defeat that made the war hardly worth fighting, Barcelona was the capital of dissent, the

Barcelona, September 1936. Three militiamen are married in a 'revolutionary wedding' conducted by a union official.

keeper of the revolutionary conscience. In Valencia the four anarchist ministers were the only ones who stood by Largo Caballero in the last analysis. In Madrid the CNT prison director Melchor Rodríguez struck a blow for human rights by exposing the existence of communist *checas* (interrogation centres) in which prisoners, sometimes men who had been released by the Republican authorities, were tortured. These revelations were used by Largo Caballero to dissolve the communist-controlled defence committee and to force the resignation of José Cazorla, the communist chief of public order.

But it was in Barcelona, far from the fighting fronts, that the luxury of political debate and revolutionary experiment was most riotously indulged. 'Now,' proclaimed a workers' committee which took over the running of the Metro, 'we set out on the great adventure!' The dam of authority had burst, caution and misgivings were overwhelmed in a wild and festive flood.

Sweeping into Aragon at the head of his column in August 1936, Durruti cocked a snook at Communist policy by encouraging villagers, sometimes rather less than gently, to form collectives; and in reply to a journalist who predicted that victory would only be achieved amid a rubble of ruins, Durruti retorted: 'We are not afraid of ruins. We have always lived in slums and holes in the wall. We, the workers, built the palaces and cities and we can build new ones to take their place – better ones. The bourgeoisie may blast their world before they leave the stage. But we carry a new world in our hearts.'

Even a keen young communist like John Cornford, a writer-poet fresh from Cambridge University who for a while found himself, curiously enough, in a militia unit of the anti-Stalinist POUM on the Aragon front in the autumn of 1936, was affected by the dissident atmosphere. He liked the German volunteers he met but was puzzled when four of them explained that they had left the Communist party because the Comintern had 'deserted the revolution'. Writing to his girl-friend Margot Heinemann he began to reveal doubts about communist policy in Spain. 'It isn't easy to get straight, but roughly in Catalonia things are like this. There is a Left Republican government. But in fact the real power is with the workers. There are 50,000 or more armed workers . . . but the Anarchists predominate. 75 per cent of industry in Barcelona is already socialized, and mostly worked by the Anarchists. Assisted by the militia there is a peasant war raging in the countryside . . . The Anarchists appear to be preparing to attack the government after the fall of Saragossa . . . I fear that the Party is a little too mechanical in its application of People's Front tactics. It is still concentrating too much on trying to neutralize the petty bourgeoisie, when by far the most urgent task is to win the anarchist workers . . . '

In Barcelona, Cornford reported, there was 'a real terror against the Fascists. But that doesn't alter the fact that the place is free – and conscious all the time of its freedom . . . The palace of a marquis in the Rambla is a CP headquarters . . . It's as if in London armed workers were dominating the

Lenin Barracks, Barcelona, early January 1937. POUM militia about to leave for the Aragon front. In the background can be seen the tall figure of George Orwell.

streets – it's obvious that they wouldn't tolerate Mosley or people selling *Action*. It is genuinely a dictatorship of the majority.' For Catalan manufacturers and businessmen the experience was alarming rather than exhilarating: 'like being on a plane which you know is going to crash,' as one of them put it. Through contacts in the British Independent Labour Party (ILP), George Orwell, arriving in Barcelona in December 1936, joined the POUM militia. 'It was a novelty to be in a town where the working class was in the saddle,' he wrote in *Homage to Catalonia*. 'Even the boot-blacks had been collectivized and their boxes painted red and black. Waiters and shop-walkers looked you in the face and treated you as an equal . . . No private motor cars, they had all been commandeered . . . revolutionary posters everywhere, flaring from the walls in clear reds and blues . . . Except for a small number of women and foreigners there were no "well-dressed" people at all . . . There was much in it that I did not understand, in some ways I did not even like it, but I recognized it immediately as a state of affairs worth fighting for.' In England Orwell had found that 'this business of class-breaking is a bugger.' In Barcelona it seemed that the barriers were down.

In the factories, workers often found themselves in control because many owners had fled, gone into hiding, or been shot. The taboos of an intensely conservative and religious country were comprehensively challenged – by 'revolutionary weddings'; by legalized abortion, decreed, for the first time in Western Europe, by the anarchist minister of health, Federica Montseny; by radical feminists proclaiming that 'as long as any woman is kept as an object and is prevented from developing her personality, prostitution continues to exist'; by female employees raising the question of equal pay and demanding an end to sexual harassment at work; by fanatical advocates of the single wage, for instance in the Tivoli theatre, where a celebrated tenor counter-attacked by announcing that 'since we're all equal now, I shall collect tickets and one of you can sing the lead.' When the Catalan surrealist painter Salvador Dali wrote to a friend suggesting that he should come to Barcelona to launch 'an historic project . . . a Department for the Irrational Organization of Daily Life,' he got the reply: 'We don't need you, it's perfectly organized already.'

Nowhere was enthusiasm keener than among the female zealots of the recently-founded JSUC (United Socialist Youth of Catalonia), a branch of the still tiny Communist PSUC (United Socialist Party) which was affiliated to the Comintern. They were convinced of their mission to canalize and clarify the muddy waters of revolutionary turbulence around them. 'I don't think there'd ever been so much singing in Barcelona,' says Teresa Pamies, then an 18-year-old dressmaker who had joined the JSUC on the outbreak of war. 'I'd held meetings in cafés where we talked about the revolution and sang revolutionary songs. Then suddenly the revolution broke out and I couldn't have asked for more.'

Sadly she had to accept that others, including members of her own family, did not share her dogmatic élan. Her father, a peasant in Balaguer, admired

ABOVE LEFT *18-year-old activist Teresa Pamies addresses a mass meeting in Barcelona.*

ABOVE RIGHT *Luis Companys, President of the Generalitat (Catalan parliament).*

Trotsky, and several close relatives belonged to the POUM. Yet when, following the Comintern's Popular Front line, the JSUC formed a female youth movement with the Left Republican Esquerra (ERC) and the Young Libertarians, invited to join, asked if the POUM had been invited, 'our automatic reply was: "Trotskyists? Never. They are enemy agents." So we lost the Young Libertarians. I knew in my heart that my relatives could never be enemy agents. Yet I wasn't obeying Moscow's instructions when I attacked the POUM, I just wanted to believe what Moscow was telling us.' The POUM's constant attacks on Stalinism and the Soviet show trials merely confirmed the impression that it was 'objectively fascist'.

There were arguments over the name of the group. 'At first we thought of Union of Catalan Girls, but some members were over 30. Someone suggested Young Catalan Flowers, but that was too corny. Finally we settled for Young Women's Alliance as that had a nice respectable ring.' Problems did not end there. During the first congress JSUC extremists objected to a large portrait of President Companys on stage and demanded that it be replaced by a photograph of Lina Odena, a Communist *miliciana* who had shot herself with her last bullet after killing several Moors in a gun-fight near Granada. 'The Esquerrans left the stage in a huff and the JSUC offenders, expelled from the meeting, walked out singing the Young Red Guard anthem.' Remembering the cries of 'Don't touch President Companys!' and 'What about Lina

Odena!' Teresa Pamies later realized how almost impossible it was to 'put forward a common programme that would include the basic needs our people were screaming for. The ERC might want to cooperate, but like most middle-class Catalan nationalists they felt, deep down, that the PSUC wanted to turn Catalonia into a Soviet Republic.'

The alliance between the rapidly-expanding PSUC and the ERC, led by Companys and his lieutenant Tarradellas, was indeed an uneasy one. On the need to curtail fancy revolutionary experiments, to end the people's terror, to impose law and order by taking police power from the CNT-dominated Militias Committee, and to restore the authority of the Generalitat (Catalan government) – all in the name of efficiency and winning the war – they were fully agreed: especially as the PSUC's main hope of gaining political power was through the Generalitat. But as the advocate of a strong central government the PSUC, which was in effect the Catalan Communist party, did not approve of the ERC's determination to keep Catalonia autonomous.

At the end of July 1936 Companys had, without consulting Madrid, upgraded himself from President of the Catalan government to President of Catalonia. This assumption of virtual sovereignty meant little at a time when the real power was with the Militias Committee – which forced the withdrawal of three PSUC leaders who had been invited to join the Generalitat. The POUM (Partido Obrero de Unificación Marxista), itself a fusion of two Left communist parties, had taken that title on the insistence of the Marxist theorist Andrés Nin, a former secretary of Trotsky.

Still for the moment all-powerful, the Militias Committee in Barcelona continued to tackle the formidable task of restoring public order with its street patrols, organizing industrial production and food supplies, and co-ordinating the campaign to liberate Saragossa – where, lacking the support of civil and assault guards, the CNT had not been a match for the army garrison. Eduardo Pons Prades, then a boy of 16 dashing about the city on his bicycle as an errand boy, remembers it as a time when libertarian ethics burst exuberantly from theory into practice. 'The first building to be destroyed by volunteers from several unions was the women's prison, then came the blitz on centres of moral corruption – cabarets, bars, brothels – especially in the notorious Barrio Chino [a red-light district]. There were arguments. Realists would say: "So you've closed the brothels. Where will men go now?" Hotheads would reply: "They can find girl friends and get married." "Maybe, but that can't be done overnight. Why not shut the brothels gradually, so that people can get used to the idea? The same with the bars. What about the people who work in them, the waiters and so on? What will they do for a living?" "We'll teach them another trade." "Yes, but what, where and how?"'

Libertarian veterans like Lola Iturbe did what they could for their exploited sisters by opening 'anti-brothels' where out-of-work prostitutes could learn to sew, cook and do other household chores. But the salvationist scheme was soon sabotaged by the demands of militiamen who, though they might be entertained by visits from Teresa Pamies and other members of the Young Women's Alliance who went to the front to organize literacy classes, poetry readings and agitprop meetings, expected sexual satisfaction when they got to Barcelona on leave. 'So,' says Pons Prades, 'things started up again, though not on the same scale as before.' Instead of making a clean sweep of sin libertarian moralists found themselves acquiescing in army brothels as part of a social welfare programme.

The libertarian ideal of free unions with no marriage ceremony, based purely on love and ideological compatibility, was also modified by wartime exigencies. 'In the past free unions had been made between responsible, educated adults,' Pons Prades remembers, 'but now the idea of free love spread among young people in the recklessness of the time . . . Many were getting together and then splitting up and the CNT decided that there must be some form of control. Mothers were complaining that their daughters had vanished to live with some boy whom they hadn't even met . . . So we invented revolutionary weddings, popularly known as "parapet weddings" because the husband might be killed and his widowed girl could at least produce documentary evidence of the union.'

This came about, says Pons Prades, 'after a debate at the woodworkers' union. One of the speakers was a Catholic who was respected by all despite his religious views. He maintained that these young couples should be shown the meaning of love and mutual responsibility. What he had said made a deep impression on most of us. "Don't forget that Jesus has been described as the first anarchist," said one comrade.' The ceremony, with a union official as registrar, was an anarchist version of the Church's for-better-or-for-worse formula. Three copies of the certificate were made, one for the union archives, the others for the wedded couple.

Theoretically the marriage could be dissolved if the couple presented themselves at union headquarters, justified their wish to separate, and handed over their certificates: whereupon all three pieces of paper would be burnt. In fact, says Pons Prades, realism again prevailed. 'The president of our union, a very amusing man from Seville, would take the fellow aside after the ceremony and tell him: "What we said about burning the certificates isn't quite as easy as you may think. Don't come here pestering me without giving the matter very careful consideration, because if you do I'll give you such a kick in the balls that you'll remember it for the rest of your days, right? So off you go, comrades, I hope you'll be happy, long live the revolution."'

Belated realism also influenced the CNT's decision to enter the Catalan government. On 27 September four anarchists took over the departments of health, supply, defence (García Oliver) and the interior. Andrés Nin became councillor for justice. Juan Comorera, a PSUC leader, was in charge of public services. Three ERC men, with Tarradellas as Prime Minister (or chief councillor), held the more important posts. It could be argued that the CNT had merely formalized the political power which it had exercised for more than two months. But this victory for the 'pragmatists' led by García Oliver was seen as a moral defeat by thoroughgoing anarchists who were not deceived by the ploy of rechristening the Generalitat 'Regional Defence Council' to avoid the shame of being in a *government*.

On 1 October 1936 the Militias Committee was dissolved and the various local workers' committees were replaced by Popular Front-style village or town councils. This was a further setback for the CNT, which had already, on principle and for the sake of anti-fascist unity, refused to take full power on 20 July 1936 when the Militias Committee had been formed. 'This Committee was actually the revolution's most authentic expression,' says Federica Montseny: and apart from the central committee in Barcelona, there were anti-fascist committees throughout Catalonia, the Levante and Aragon, and in parts of Extremadura and Andalusia. In her view their dissolution was 'a great mistake. We agreed to the destruction of a popular entity created by the revolution and joined something (the Generalitat) which was controlled by political forces that had been unable to confront fascism but were now resurfacing.' As in nearly all revolutions, she says, the professional politicians manoeuvred to regain the authority they had temporarily lost.

A few weeks later four anarchists, including Federica Montseny, committed what, to some of their followers, was the unpardonable sin of entering the central government. As Minister of Justice in Caballero's administration García Oliver began by ordering the destruction of all convict files, a loss which was attributed to fire caused by an enemy air raid. 'Justice,' he said in a speech on 31 January 1937, 'cannot be restricted within the bounds of a profession. Not that we totally despise books and lawyers, but there have been too many laws and too many lawyers. When relations between men become what they should be there will be no need to steal and kill. For the first time let us admit, here in Spain, that the common criminal is not an enemy of society. He is more likely to be a victim. Who dares say that he would not steal if driven by hunger and the need to feed his family? Man, after all, does not proceed from God but from the cave, from the beast. Justice, I firmly believe, is so subtle a thing that to interpret it one has only need of a heart.'

He defined *paseos* as 'justice administered directly by the people in the complete absence of the traditional legal machinery,' and issued a stream of bold decrees – annulling penalties for all crimes committed before 15 July 1936; making black-marketeering a criminal offence; creating labour camps for Nationalist prisoners; abolishing court fees; giving women a legal identity for the first time; and legalizing 'parapet weddings'.

The achievements of Durruti, García Oliver, Lorenzo Iñigo, Melchor Rodríguez, and Popular Army commanders like the former builder Cipriano Mera – to name but a few – not only proved that the anarchist movement could match socialists and communists in leadership potential, but revealed how much proletarian talent had been stifled. And the surge of workers' control in Barcelona gave scope for sensible initiative as well as for crackpot utopianism. Describing the socialization of the Catalan wood industry – one of the most successful enterprises, employing about 40,000 people – Pons Prades remarks that 'if I were a Catholic I'd call it a miracle.'

In one form or another collectivization was put into practice throughout Republican Spain. In Asturias fishermen collectivized the docks, their equipment, and canning factories; mining communities collectivized retail outlets, paid wages in kind, and issued vouchers to exchange for meals at public canteens. In Alicante and other Mediterranean ports docks and public utilities were managed by CNT-UGT committees. In Madrid around 30 per cent of industry was affected, in Valencia around 50 per cent. But this great social revolution, the war aim which meant most to millions of workers, went furthest in Catalonia. There, by the end of October 1936, when a collectivization decree tried to regularize the process, something like 70 per cent of all enterprises including at least 2,000 industrial and commercial firms, were involved.

But the war imposed strict limitations. Stocks ran out and could not be replaced; foreign factory owners were unsympathetic; the home market contracted with every Nationalist advance; raw materials were hard to come by; skilled workers left for the fronts; inflation and a huge influx of refugees

Barcelona: a collectivized garment-making workshop. At first even barbers and bootblacks were collectivized.

A Barcelona café collectivized by the UGT, the socialist General Workers' Union.

played havoc with the economy. Ambitious schemes for social insurance, six months' annual holiday, higher wages, and the establishment of health clinics and schools for employees' children had to be postponed or modified. The collectivization of small shops was recognized to be a mistake, and one which drove many small businessmen into the PSUC as the defender of private property rights. The October decree exempted all firms with less than a hundred employees. The dream of totally decapitating hydra-headed capitalism had to be abandoned and a mixed economy tolerated: though not, as Josep Tarradellas explains, without some violent protests.

During a debate on the decree 'things got so heated that at one point a CNT delegate pulled out a gun and shouted: "You are an agent provocateur, a Franquista, you don't want the factories to succeed under workers' control!" Fortunately he was surrounded and disarmed.' Though praising the workers 'who saved our collectivized industries after many owners had fled to France, Switzerland or Burgos,' Tarradellas admits that the Generalitat's grip on the banks gave it a powerful pull. 'The CNT was reluctant to share control, but as economic councillor I ordered the banks not to release any money to collectivized businesses without permission. So the workers had to come to terms.'

Baffled by the complexities of a big city economy, so many collectives were driven to rely on government funds and technical advice that what began as a competitive welter of workers' control was to a large extent transformed into a nationalized network complete with form-filling and a sizeable bureaucracy. Some of the side-effects ruffled egalitarian sensibilities. Union leaders, now virtually executives in a major socialized industry, started wearing white shirts and ties, and the change was resented. Pons Prades heard one worker muttering: 'They start by wearing different clothes and who knows how they will end?' Yet the mutterers were often the kind of *cenetistas* who had fought shy of taking authority with the excuse that it was against their principles to give orders. As a result ex-owners were enticed to cooperate by being offered double a worker's wage and, more important, protection from assassination.

The murder of one ex-owner, who had stayed on because he had treated his workers well and thought he had nothing to fear, seemed particularly grotesque. The murderer, a young worker from the province of Córdoba, was caught by a CNT patrol, says Pons Prades. When asked why he had done this, he replied that though he had only once seen his victim, he hated the man 'because he looked just like the *cacique* who owned our village, the bastard who ruined my father's health and forced us to emigrate.' Pons Prades could not help pitying the peasant killer. So much hatred had accumulated in him and in so many others like him that it was hard to blame them for taking revenge. And he reflected that most of the 'uncontrollables' responsible for the worst of the terror in Barcelona were embittered immigrant workers.

The nationalized wood industry was perhaps the best example of integration, involving the entire process from felling, sawing and transporting the timber to manufacturing and marketing it. Sent ahead on his bicycle to collect the keys of the offices of the Owners' Association, Pons Prades witnessed the earliest stages of the reorganization. The owners of small workshops were persuaded to merge so that production could be streamlined; new, properly ventilated factories were built; and a central office block completed in just 55 days, such was the enthusiasm.

All the wood in the eastern Pyrenees had been collectivized, and Pons Prades went on several buying trips. At first villagers were often suspicious of the anarchists from the big city, who had to convince them that they were not thieves – and occasionally had to back persuasion by a threat of force. Timber was exchanged for money, furniture, or whatever the peasants needed and happened to be in stock. A barter system was used when dealing with other collectives: for instance, an agrarian collective in Aragon would receive manufactured goods in return for its produce. The value of goods was calculated in man-hours and a skilled factory worker's hour was worth the same as a peasant's. The food collected in such deals was either sent to the front or sold through cooperatives in Barcelona.

The large, well-articulated wood industry offered its workers, 80 per cent of whom belonged to the CNT, benefits such as an Olympic-size swimming pool, a gymnasium and a solarium. Yet though there were no strikes or organized protests there was a feeling that the workers were losing control. 'It turned out that when the administrative committees were formed, 16 out of 22 were managed by ex-owners or their sons, people who because they had been better educated knew how to do their sums. You had to know this for such a huge enterprise to function smoothly,' says Pons Prades. 'Knowing your craft or showing good will was not enough. Sums were the important thing.' The problems of 'alienation' in big nationalized industries, of how far the state should intervene to create a wholly directed economy, were earnestly debated. In a half-directed economy individual collectives blundered on with a cut-throat competitiveness sometimes keener than in the bad old days. There was little attempt to channel profits from successful enterprises to help worthy but struggling groups. The inability of the improvised armaments industry to achieve more than half its potential production was largely due to the Generalitat's inability to raise enough funds to buy new equipment and the central government's refusal to do so for fear of encouraging Catalan separatism. This increased the dependence on Soviet aid and strengthened the position of the PSUC. The POUM scathingly attacked the selfishness of 'syndical capitalism'; and Horacio Prieto, a CNT leader, complained that 'this is not anarchist collectivism. It is a new capitalism more disjointed than the old system . . . rich collectives refuse to recognize any responsibilities . . . No one seems to understand the complexities of the economy, the dependence of one industry on another.'

Political tensions bedevilled the question of rural as much as urban collectivization: a tension heightened by the fact that though a majority of landless labourers might favour workers' control, an obstinate minority of peasant farmers thought they had it already. They quite often formed cooperatives, but were generally hostile to collectivization, especially if imposed by militant ideologues from the towns or cities. In this they were encouraged by the Communist party, many of whose members were hard-bitten conservative peasant proprietors or tenant farmers.

There were, it is estimated, some 2,500 rural collectives – in Andalusia, Valencia, Murcia, Castile and, most notably and under CNT direction, in Aragon. The abolition of rents and the burning of property records was almost universal but otherwise the pattern varied. Sometimes the village land as a whole was collectivized, together with the shops, the barber, the blacksmith, the carpenter and the local doctor and pharmacist. Sometimes confiscated land was distributed among the peasants. In other places a mixed private-cum-collective economy was the rule. In isolated villages in Aragon and Andalusia the regime was particularly austere. Money was abolished and all transactions made by barter or ration-tickets. Confiscated money might be pooled and issued to villagers by committees if an application was approved – perhaps to travel some distance to visit a relative or to seek specialized medical treatment.

It was a crude and sometimes oppressive system, yet for many peasants it was a genuine revolution. Short-lived everywhere, it lasted longest – into 1938 – in parts of Aragon, where the CNT claimed that by May 1937 there were 450 collectives with about 180,000 members. Durruti regarded it as an experiment which, apart from testing libertarian theories about the just society, was

The anarchist militia chief Buenaventura Durruti (right) on the Aragon front. He was mortally wounded in Madrid on 19 November 1936.

justifiable in terms of the war effort since production would increase and peasant farmers would not be able to hold back supplies to release on the black market. But since collectivization was put into practice under pressure from anarchist columns, how far could the result be described as libertarian?

Durruti, anxious to restrain those who favoured drastic measures to overcome peasant resistance, regretted the necessity for taking his men to the defence of Madrid. A Council of Aragon, headed by Joaquín Ascaso, a cousin of Durruti's close comrade, was established; and though describing itself as an advisory body concerned to 'foster collectivization as a contribution to the war effort,' it looked suspiciously like a CNT dictatorship. Largo Caballero reluctantly recognized the Council as the *de facto* government of Aragon – which, Ascaso provocatively announced, was 'the Spanish Ukraine', whose libertarian achievement would not be destroyed by Marxist reactionaries, as had happened to the Ukrainian anarchist leader Nestor Makhno in 1921. As the Aragon front stagnated, CNT troops seemed to be providing protection for 'their' collectives rather than threatening the Nationalist hold on Saragossa.

Aragon did not resemble the Ukraine in fertility of soil; nor, as a region mostly occupied by peasant farmers noted for their toughness and independence, was it a promising field for collectivization. On a large scale this only made economic sense with substantial mechanization, plenty of time and capital, competent technical advice, and patient leadership, none of which was possible during the war. There was a feeling that Aragon was being treated as an agricultural colony of Catalonia; and though the antagonism of the central government, and especially of its Communist members, to the Council probably helped to check the zeal of anarchist militants, 'private peasants' who chose, when they were allowed, to opt out of a collective were sometimes penalized by the withholding of seed and similar sanctions; and their land was not registered 'in order to counterbalance the spirit of egoistic proprietorship'. These 'individualists' might also be forbidden to employ outside labour, even if it was voluntary help from a relative or neighbour, and were often segregated in separate cafés.

Ironically, while the CNT went on a collectivist rampage in Aragon, Catalonia remained overwhelmingly a countryside of peasant smallholders. Only about eighty collectives were formed. Josep Solé Barberá, a Communist lawyer who had taken over the administration of justice in the town of Reus, where UGT influence was strong, states that 'sometimes the CNT tried to impose collectivization by force, though in south Catalonia there was a long tradition of cooperativism. When patrols from Barcelona attacked the village of Fatarella and shot several people I counter-attacked with assault guards and militiamen from Tarragona. The peasants, who had fled, later came back and re-established their cooperative.'

In Aragon, as in most regions, distrust of agricultural machinery, seen as the creator of more unemployment, was overcome with difficulty. In northern Aragon, near Huesca, Orwell watched peasants using antiquated, much-mended ploughshares 'which barely scratched the soil', and noted that 'spades, among a people who seldom possessed boots, were unknown; they did their digging with a clumsy hoe like that used in India.' After inspecting a harrow which, consisting of hundreds of flint-chips jammed into a plank-board, 'took one straight back to the later Stone Age', Orwell was horrified by the 'poverty that was obliged to use flint in place of steel'; and confessed that he had 'felt more kindly towards industrialism ever since'. Cars, tractors, and motorbikes requisitioned from former landlords helped to make life a little easier, and in some of the more prosperous and progressive collectives a special effort was made to equip schools – where, in a daring innovation, boys and girls came to learn together – with rationalist textbooks and even with ciné-projectors to show educational films.

OPPOSITE
A poster urging Catalan farmers to sell their produce through agricultural collectives and not on the 'free' market.

But in poorer villages where illiterate day labourers predominated, delegates' committees sometimes had to turn to small landowners to manage the accounts and run the administration. Peasant farmers, forced to bring

MERCAT
LLIURE
ESPECULACIÓ
NO ENVIEU ELS VOSTRES PRO-
DUCTES AL MERCAT LLIURE
VENEU-LOS A TRAVES DELS
SINDICATS AGRICOLES

their produce to the common stock, resented being issued with rations like so many paupers. Much confusion was caused when, having decided that the abolition of money was a mistake, collectives coined their own currencies, perhaps tin discs punched from a metal sheet by the blacksmith. In a time of improvisation and bumpy transition, production did not, overall, increase and the supply of food to the fronts was irregular.

The fact that collectives paid no taxes and, even where socialists controlled the committee, tended to disregard official directives, did not endear them to the central government in Valencia. The known hostility of Negrín and of Vicente Uribe, the Communist Minister of Agriculture, affected morale. Intent on braking a runaway, ramshackle people's revolution that itself, after the first few heady months, had lost impetus and confidence, Communist propaganda increasingly attacked the Aragon experiment as an 'inhuman tyranny' sustained by terror; and with some justification criticized the arrogance and high living of swashbuckling anarchist '*caciques*' and especially of Joaquín Ascaso and the 'gangsters' of the Council of Aragon.

In January 1937 Vicente Uribe, who favoured collectivizing only land belonging to Nationalist supporters, grudgingly legalized the collectives 'during the current agricultural year'. The obvious message was that, in this phase, in some ways redolent of the Spanish struggle between centralism and the *patria chica*, the Spanish Ukraine in particular was doomed as soon as the harvest had been gathered.

Both sides regarded the war as a battle for the mind, a campaign of social hygiene. Mola saw Azaña as an intellectual Frankenstein monster befouling traditional Spanish decencies. 'Priests,' said an Andalusian peasant, 'are sub-human. They begin by not marrying, which is not decent.' In Nationalist Spain progressive teachers were purged and classrooms resanctified; in Republican Spain education was cleansed of clericalism and rescued for rationalism.

La Barraca, García Lorca's touring theatre company, was no more, but the spirit of the cultural missionaries of 1931–33 lived on. In Madrid the Casa de Cultura Popular was housed in an aristocrat's requisitioned mansion and staffed by eager university students. Within a month three hundred libraries had been assembled, and two art exhibitions, transported in lorries, had visited the nearest fronts.

For teachers who took over schools formerly run by priests or nuns it was easier to change textbooks than to dissolve prejudices. Pupils resisted desegregation of the sexes and resented the removal of religion from the curriculum. A striking example of the will to enlighten and the hunger for knowledge was the formation of a body of cultural shock troops who attacked ignorance and illiteracy in the barracks and the trenches. The classroom might be a rough shelter contrived by the soldiers, the blackboard as often as not a large sheet of paper. In summer 1937 young Pons Prades was given the job of motivating a bunch of sullen peasant conscripts from La Mancha. 'When I saw them climb down from the lorries I thought they were all

A 'cultural militiaman' teaches how to read and write – and how to dig effective trenches.

middle-aged – short, stooping, their faces burnt black and furrowed by sun and wind . . . They were thinking that now, after being exploited all their lives, they were being driven to the slaughter.' They showed no aptitude for the simplest military training and no conception of why they were undergoing it. Pons Prades gathered a few of the more articulate men and asked them to explain how it had been in their villages. Then he told them: '"In this war we're risking our lives so that when you go back to your villages conditions like those you've lived in will be over. If we win the war the land will belong to the community. If there are hardships they will be shared by everybody, the same if there is abundance. That's what we're fighting for and what some of us will die for." Those peasants changed completely. Next day in training they set themselves to it and even made suggestions.'

Military defeats seemed only to spur the urgent quest for knowledge. Late in 1938 on the Madrid front the French aviator and writer Antoine de Saint-Exupéry visited 'a school 500 metres from the trenches . . . A corporal was teaching botany, carefully peeling away the petals of a poppy. Around him were bearded soldiers, their brows knitted in the effort of concentration . . . They had been told: you are brutes, you have only just left your holes, we must save you for humanity. And with heavy feet they were hurrying towards enlightenment.'

For Teresa Pamies the war meant an enormous sense of liberation, especially for women, taking over men's jobs and proving the absurdity of traditional estimates of what they could not, or should not, do. She remembers, too, that even in the worst of the air bombardments and food shortages, concerts, lectures and political rallies were always crowded. 'At theatres where only the rich used to go – no more furs, long dresses or pearls, but eager audiences of workers and soldiers.' There were musical comedies as well as Catalan and Spanish classics, even an anti-prostitution anarchist drama entitled *Woman, Don't Sell Yourself.*

Pablo Casals was a star attraction, and many well-known foreign actors came to Barcelona to perform, some of them International Brigaders. Nicolás Guillén's poetry readings were massively attended, and one of his poems was broadcast to the enemy over loudspeakers: 'I don't know why you should think/That I hate you, soldier/We are, after all, the same thing you and I/You are poor, so am I . . . ' New cultural magazines were born every week. The American poet Waldo Frank read his poems in the street. Paul Robeson sang. In June 1938 the Generalitat organized a Book Day and there were record sales. The young women of the Alliance sometimes arranged more frivolous events like grand dances with the Betty Boop Orchestra. Advertising went revolutionary as in the workers' committee version of the Caldolla Soup jingle: 'Woman is no longer a slave/Not even a slave to her pots and pans/Because now all she needs for her soup/Is a magic Caldolla cube/Oh Caldolla, Caldolla . . . '

One of Teresa Pamies' most treasured possessions was a blue-and-white Komsomol (Soviet Youth Organization) skirt given to her by the Soviet consul in Barcelona, Vladimir Antonov-Ovsëenko. A small man with long white hair and lively blue eyes behind thick lenses, he sometimes invited members of the JSUC executive committee, including Teresa Pamies, to lunch at the consulate: a treat to which they looked forward, because there would be delicacies unobtainable anywhere else in Barcelona. But, like the lively *Pravda* correspondent Mikhail Koltsov, Antonov-Ovsëenko, an Old Bolshevik intellectual who had led the assault on the Winter Palace in Petrograd on 7 November 1917, was soon to be recalled to Moscow and liquidated in Stalin's purges.

What was his crime? Perhaps to have been too friendly with anarchist and POUM leaders – particularly Andrés Nin, whom he had known in Moscow – whose uncompromising idealism reminded him of his own youth. Perhaps to have criticized the policy of starving Barcelona and the Aragon front of arms to weaken the main threat to Communist domination. Pere Ardiaca, then editor of the PSUC paper *Treball* and a member of the party's executive committee, denies that this was a deliberate policy. 'You should have seen the huge demonstration in Barcelona when the first Soviet supply ship arrived. People of all parties turned out to greet it. I know that the anarchists complain that Soviet military aid went only to Communist units. This is not true. Those weapons had to go to the busiest fronts. How could we send them to the

Aragon front when the enemy was about to conquer Madrid? It would have been suicide.'

Enrique Líster, too, denies that CNT troops were starved of weapons. 'In the early days they had more weapons in Catalonia than we had in Madrid, because they had captured so many arms from the barracks and arsenals when the rising in Barcelona was quelled. But often the anarchists hid the weapons – we uncovered them many times, keeping them for the second round, so that they could impose their will after the defeat of Franco. They were sharing out the lion's skin before they killed the lion. The lion was in front of us, and whilst we Communists dedicated ourselves on the battlefield and in the rear to doing all we could to win the war, they dedicated themselves to preparing for the postwar battle. They didn't understand that, in that second round which they foresaw, the ones who would gain the upper hand were those who had striven hardest to win the war. Some anarchists, like Durruti, of whom I formed a high opinion, did try to establish military discipline; and when they were incorporated into Popular Army units – I had several hundred of them under my command – the anarchists fought as well as anyone else. But those behind the lines continued their manipulation, their tricks, just like Prieto and Azaña. That was the real problem.'

Juan Manuel Molina tells a different story. 'Our men were going to the front with 10, 15, 20 rounds of ammunition, all that could be supplied from hastily-improvised munitions factories in Barcelona. No heavy artillery, no air cover. Ships would arrive in Barcelona harbour, but they weren't allowed to unload, they had to go to Valencia. Once a ship arrived carrying 3,000 machine-guns which we desperately needed. With them we could have taken Huesca, Teruel and Saragossa and that might have changed the course of the war. I was Undersecretary for Defence and I telephoned the central government and begged permission to unload those guns. It was refused and the ship was torpedoed and sunk. We could have won the war in the first few months if we had received any decent weapons. But the Russians didn't want the CNT to have any military success.'

The POUM leader Enric Adroer agrees with Molina and adds some bitter comments of his own. 'The rising succeeded mainly in Spain's poorest regions, the sparsely populated rural areas. We had all the industry and manpower. The communists' policy prevented an early victory. They wanted the war to drag on so that fascism would be kept busy here. They also wanted to prevent the CNT and the POUM from winning any victories. That's why they didn't unload a single firearm in Barcelona. Only one Soviet ship was unloaded there and it was a food cargo. Soon after 20 July 1936 the CNT and POUM columns reached Saragossa, Huesca and Teruel. We could have created eight, maybe ten new divisions from a very militant proletariat and overwhelmed the enemy in Aragon. A major offensive could have been launched from there with a better chance of success. All we needed was weapons.'

In *Homage to Catalonia*, an account of his experiences in Barcelona and with

POUM leaders Julián Gorkin (second from left) and Andrés Nin (second from right) in Barcelona.

the POUM militia on the Aragon front, George Orwell reports: 'The thing for which the Communists were working was not to postpone the Spanish revolution till a more suitable time but to make sure that it never happened . . . There is very little doubt that arms were deliberately withheld from the Aragon front lest too many of them should get into the hands of the Anarchists, who would afterwards use them for a revolutionary purpose; consequently the big Aragon offensive which would have made Franco draw back from Bilbao, and possibly from Madrid, never happened . . . The whole tendency of Communist policy was to reduce the war to an ordinary non-revolutionary war in which the Government was heavily handicapped. For a war of that kind had to be won by mechanical means, i.e. ultimately by a limitless supply of weapons; and the Government's chief donor of weapons, the USSR, was at a great disadvantage, geographically, compared with Italy and Germany. Perhaps the POUM and Anarchist slogan, "The war and the revolution are inseparable," was less visionary than it sounds.'

With the dissolution of the Militias Committee and the growing power of the PSUC, prompted by its Comintern adviser, the Hungarian Ernö Gerö (who in 1956 as deputy premier supported the Soviet suppression of the revolt in Hungary), the Generalitat was plainly determined to end or dilute what remained of workers' control. Its two obvious targets, the CNT and the POUM, were far from united. When, in December 1936, at Communist insistence, Andrés Nin, the only POUMista in the Generalitat, resigned, there had been little protest from the CNT, which chose to dismiss the incident as just another tedious Marxist squabble.

The anarchist-communist feud smouldered on. The libertarian youth

LEFT A Republican warning to 'avoid venereal disease – as dangerous as enemy bullets', and BELOW a poster informing militiamen that 'Illiteracy blinds the spirit. Learn or study, soldier.'

'Until victory or death': a Republican poster issued by the POUM.

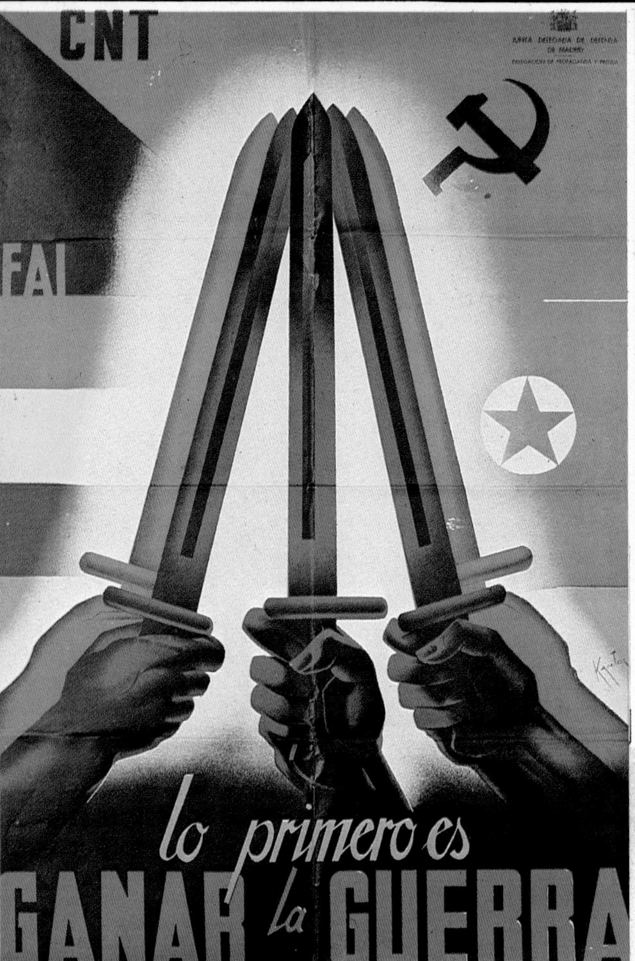

Republican posters urge unity.
ABOVE 'The first thing is to win the war' – revolution will presumably come later.
RIGHT 'All the militias merged into the popular army'.

leader Lorenzo Iñigo recalls that in Madrid the murder of two anarchists, found with CNT cards stuck in their mouths, was avenged by the shooting of four communists, found with party cards stuck in *their* mouths. In Barcelona a slanging match followed the appointment in January 1937 of Juan Comorera, a PSUC leader, as food minister. He accused his anarchist predecessor of incompetence and the CNT returned the charge when a bread famine, due to a poor harvest, caused riots which were dispersed by assault guards (enemies of the people now to their former comrades-in-arms). There was deep resentment at the erosion of workers' control through the government's monopoly of credit and the dominant role of 'state delegates' in the larger collectivized concerns. As stocks ran out production faltered and short-working became common. Wages could not keep pace with inflation. Recriminations intensified.

In February the FAI threatened to break the fragile unity of Caballero's Popular Front government in Valencia by withdrawing the anarchist ministers unless arms were supplied to the Aragon front. Soon afterwards the FAI captured a shipload of weapons in Barcelona harbour. García Oliver refused to surrender them unless the government met the FAI's demands. Another, separate struggle, between two parties of the revolution, was being fought in the headlines of their respective newspapers. At a PCE (communist party) conference in Valencia early in March José Diaz made a violent attack on the 'Trotskyists' of the POUM as 'agents of fascism hiding behind revolutionary slogans'.

Throughout the spring of 1937 tensions were stretched to breaking point. Anarchist patrols in Barcelona stepped up their private terror. *La Batalla* and *Solidaridad Obrera* condemned plans to militarize the remaining workers' militias as part of the plot to wreck the revolution. On 26 March the CNT members resigned from the Generalitat when Tarradellas decreed that 'political' patrols should disband and that all unions or political parties must surrender their arms. Not until 16 April was a new government formed. Caballero dissolved the communist-dominated Madrid defence junta and ordered a purge of communist political commissars in the Popular Army. Almost at the same time, late in April, the finance minister, Dr Juan Negrín, further inflamed anarchist feelings by sending carefully selected *carabineros* to take over the Pyrenean frontier posts which since 18 July had been controlled by anarchists, several of whom were killed in a skirmish in Puigcerdá. A prominent UGT leader, Roldán Cortada, was murdered in Barcelona, and his funeral turned into a massive PSUC-inspired anti-CNT demonstration. The anarchists claimed that Cortada had been murdered by the communists, partly because he had criticized Comintern methods, partly to justify police repression. With both sides preparing for a trial of strength, the Generalitat cancelled the May Day processions for fear of armed clashes. But on Monday 3 May the shots which sparked off a five-day turmoil of almost inextricable confusion were fired.

Following the assertion of governmental authority at the frontier posts, the

Generalitat decided to end CNT control of the telephone exchanges in Barcelona, Tarragona and other centres. It seemed intolerable that the CNT should be able to monitor conversations between government ministers, let alone that a militant telephonist should interrupt a call from President Azaña to President Companys with the comment that the service should be used for more important purposes.

'I was at the switchboard with two others on 3 May,' says Enriqueta García Cervera. 'A few anarchist guards were nodding off in the corridor. At about 2 p.m. I saw several trucks stop outside the Telefónica. The next thing I knew was that after disarming the sleepy sentries, assault guards lined us against the wall, telling us not to touch the switchboard and nothing would happen. Firing began from anarchists on the floor above. We were kept under arrest until 10 p.m. when the next shift arrived, though I was allowed to go to the canteen for a quick brandy. When I walked out, there were big crowds around the building and a few scattered shots could still be heard. Four days later we were allowed to return to work. There were no anarchists there any more. Only assault guards.'

Pere Ardiaca had been present at a PSUC central committee meeting when Rodríguez Salas, the police chief (a PSUC man), announced that he had received orders to occupy the Telefónica. 'We told him he must obey those orders. We realized that they could cause a serious confrontation, but things couldn't go on as they were. The government had to act.' Pons Prades, who on 2 May had seen members of the defence committee of Pueblo Seco, the working-class district where he lived, taking out pistols and hand grenades they had hidden beneath a church, was stopped by JSUC patrols when, after visiting his sick mother, he was bicycling back to work on 4 May. 'They asked for identification. When I showed my CNT card one of them said: "This isn't worth a piece of shit." I asked if it was now illegal to belong to the CNT and was told: "Not yet. But watch your step. As Comrade Comorera has said, you are just a tribe of defeatists."'

Barcelona, 3 May 1937. A casualty of civil war within the civil war, as anarchists and POUMistas fought to defend their revolution against what they saw as a communist conspiracy to stifle it.

Reaching a CNT barricade, Pons Prades was told that the communists were out to sabotage the revolution, taking over the collectives and forcing the workers to come to heel just as they had in Russia. This time, militants vowed, they would make the revolution properly and pack the treacherous politicians off to labour camps where they could join the fascist counter-revolutionaries. Fury greeted a broadcast by García Oliver and Federica Montseny, backed by an editorial in *Solidaridad Obrera*, 'appealing for us to lay down our arms. García Oliver even went so far as to say that we should embrace the assault guards because we were sons of the same fatherland fighting the same fascist enemy. There were some vicious comments about these ex-comrades who had forgotten that a revolution is made in the streets, not in government ministries. Some threatened that "when we lay hands on those Judases we'll put a couple of bullets in them." One of our union leaders said that only the social revolution made the war worth fighting. If that was to be abandoned the war might as well be brought to an end.'

'I have often been reproached,' says Federica Montseny, 'but my conscience is clear. I spoke on the radio and sat in President Companys' office answering calls from CNT, POUM and PSUC leaders. I calmed people down, made them understand that the fratricidal conflict had to end or the fronts would collapse and the war finish shamefully. And so bit by bit I won a cease-fire. I am happy to have done what I did.'

'The communists didn't dare attack us directly because we were too powerful,' says Juan Molina. 'We didn't give any orders to our members, they reacted spontaneously. The PSUC offices and the barracks of the Karl Marx battalion – the only military unit we didn't control – were surrounded.' While the CNT demanded the resignation of Rodríguez Salas and other PSUC councillors, Molina contacted anarchist commanders at the front who were proposing to march on Barcelona. 'I told them to stay where they were and restrained coastguard ships and shore batteries which wanted to fire on the Generalitat building. I felt that we were in full command of the situation, as on 20 July 1936. I was just waiting for an order from our leaders to finish the job. But the order never came.'

The POUM very reluctantly entered the fray, and their offer to form a united front against the PSUC-Generalitat 'counter-revolution' was rejected by the CNT, itself split between the moderates of the middle-aged official leadership and youthful revolutionaries. Meantime the POUM leadership was challenged by a no-compromise faction known as the Bolshevist-Leninists. As an example of the almost farcical chaos Enric Adroer cites the case of a group of English volunteers, including Orwell (then on leave after four months in the tedium and squalor of the stagnant Aragon front), who came to POUM headquarters asking what could they do to help. 'We had to think of something. So we gave them some machine-guns and told them to take up position on a rooftop opposite with the task of guarding the party offices against a possible attack. Then we forgot about them. When the fighting ended on 8 May these comrades appeared and said: "Well, we've

Republican assault guards from Valencia sent to Barcelona to crush the May rebellion.

done our duty, but can you please tell us what's happened in Barcelona?"'

Orwell found the rooftop vigil 'strangely peaceful' and read a succession of paperbacks despite the 'hellish noise' of street-fighting, particularly loud where the headquarters of the CNT and the UGT faced each other. He 'dimly foresaw' that when the conflict was over, 'the entire blame would be laid upon the POUM, the weakest party and therefore the most suitable scapegoat.' And it was 'infuriating to come back to Barcelona ravenous for a bit of rest and comfort' and have to spend his time 'sitting on a roof opposite civil guards as bored as myself who periodically waved and assured me that they were "workers" (meaning that they hoped I would not shoot them), but who would certainly open fire if they got the order to do so. If this was history it did not feel like it.'

Symbolic of the dangerous maelstrom in which it was hard to tell friend from foe was the brief ordeal of Richard Bennett, who like John Cornford had left Trinity College, Cambridge, to volunteer for service in Spain and, after a spell on the Aragon front, had joined Radio Barcelona as 'the Voice of Spain'. Confronted by two heavily-armed militants who burst into his room demanding 'Whose side are you on?' he cannily replied: 'Yours.' But when the shooting ended on 8 May after renewed appeals for 'a return to normality' had been reinforced by the arrival of several thousand assault guards from Valencia and the presence of ships of the Republican navy in the harbour, it was estimated that 500 people had been killed and 1,000 wounded. And when the *asaltos* occupied Pueblo Seco, says Pons Prades, 'the first thing they did was to burn the libraries of our union and of the Young Libertarians, just like the Nationalists, who when they captured a place massacred the books before they started on the people.'

Many conspiracy theories have been put forward to explain the May Events. 'The POUM didn't provoke the Telefónica incident. It was a communist manoeuvre,' says Enric Adroer. 'It's clear that the whole thing was a Stalinist plot aimed at the POUM,' says Juan Molina. Pere Ardiaca is convinced that the POUM and the CNT did provoke a show-down. Teresa Pamies has serious doubts. Tarradellas admits that he and Companys were playing a dangerous game with the PSUC, but in view of the need to establish good relations with the Russians does not see that there was much alternative. The sudden recall of Antonov-Ovsëenko, 'who understood the anarchists and was sensitive to other points of view,' may, he thinks, have been disastrous to any hope of compromise. 'The Generalitat lost its grip and I must share the blame. The central government seized control of public order, our autonomy was eroded, and I saw that the war was lost.'

Azaña considered that 'all the materials for a conflagration were there without the novelettish explanation of a foreign power being involved.' Orwell reached the same conclusion – 'the fighting was only preconcerted in the sense

Federica Montseny, anarchist, feminist, and Spain's first woman minister, appeals for an end to fratricidal strife.

The anarchist leader Juan García Oliver, who as Minister of Justice also appealed for a ceasefire in Barcelona.

that everyone expected it. There were no signs of any definite plan on either side.' Probably the Comintern plan was to replace Caballero and then deal with 'deviationists' in Catalonia; just as the PSUC's objective, set by Gerö, was to gain power in the Generalitat and then invite the central government to move in. But since the Barcelona riots had happened, dividing and demoralizing the CNT – which soon withdrew from the central government and from the Generalitat – and further isolating the POUM, they were ruthlessly exploited.

With the war in the north going badly as Mola's army closed in on Bilbao after the Guernica outrage, it was not difficult to whip up feeling against the 'saboteurs' in Barcelona, nor to represent the POUM as the heart of a conspiracy against the Soviet saviours of the Republic. In the International Brigades, says Frank Deegan, political commissars put it about that anarchist and POUM troops had been 'fraternizing with the fascists, even playing football and swopping cigarette cards with them.' Only a tiny minority of the POUM was Trotskyist, but as an anti-Stalinist gesture its leaders had invited the exiled Trotsky to come to Catalonia – though he had fiercely criticized their policies.

On 9 May in Valencia José Diaz harangued a large political rally: 'Who if not the Trotskyists inspired the criminal putsch in Catalonia? Everyone knows it. Why is the government not treating them like fascists and exterminating them without hesitation?' Largo Caballero was under pressure to suppress the POUM. He refused, but when the communist ministers threatened to resign, and were followed by moderate socialists, including Prieto and Negrín, he too found himself isolated, and resigned on 17 May.

His successor opened the way to settle accounts with the POUM. Dr Juan Negrín, born into a wealthy upper middle-class family in Las Palmas, was a physiologist of international reputation and the kind of socialist who had no time for delinquent revolutionaries. Married to a Russian and multilingual, he was a sophisticated cosmopolitan realist willing to sacrifice the POUM for the sake of the Soviet connection. Clever, energetic, and no mere puppet, he had no personal following or wide popularity. In this he resembled Serrano Suñer. His academic standing and anti-revolutionary views seemed likely to commend him to the British and French governments; but for many Spaniards he was a symbol of Soviet domination.

The dismantling of worker-power in Catalonia was vigorously pursued. Anarchist patrols were dissolved. General Pozas, a *comunizante*, was appointed Captain-General of Catalonia and took command of the Catalan armed forces. Catalan policemen were transferred to other parts of the Republican zone. More collectivized industries were firmly 'nationalized'. The remaining CNT and POUM militias were disarmed and military discipline enforced along the Aragon front. On 28 May the POUM paper *La Batalla* was banned. Two weeks later Orlov, the GPU chief in Spain and virtually director of the communist-dominated Servicio de Investigación Militar (SIM), told Colonel Antonio Ortega, Director-General of Security, that the time had come to arrest the POUM leaders and that he could produce evidence that they were part of a fascist espionage network.

On 16 June the POUM was outlawed and forty of its leaders arrested. 'We had just held a meeting of our executive committee,' says Julián Gorkin, editor of *La Batalla*. 'When we returned to our headquarters the guard there said he'd heard that agents had come from Madrid to arrest us. Andrés Nin refused to believe this. We went upstairs to Nin's office – he was political secretary of the POUM – to discuss the news. Then a committeeman came in to tell me that the police had arrived and were taking Nin away. I went out onto the balcony and watched him going off very calmly surrounded by the police. I didn't imagine that I would never see him again and that a terrible tragedy was unfolding that would end in his death five days later.'

Nin was dealt with separately because, as Enric Adroer puts it, 'he had been more an ideological enemy of the Soviet Union than the rest of us as a result of his connections with Trotsky and with all the left-wing opposition to Stalin in Russia in the 1920s.' In 1927 Stalin had vetoed Nin's nomination as secretary-general of the Spanish Communist party. He was, in fact, a classic case of the man who knew too much, and the main quarry in the POUM witch-hunt. If he could be made to sign a confession similar to that which had been concocted for the Moscow purge trials, implicating all his associates, the POUM would be linked with the alleged international fascist conspiracy and the Moscow trials would seem to receive sensational justification. But, says Gorkin, who had been in Moscow at the same time as Nin, he did not break under torture and intensive interrogation at a GPU *checa* near Madrid. 'Since they couldn't force him to agree to lies about the POUM belonging to the Gestapo or to confess that we had unleashed the May struggles to help Franco, they simulated a kidnapping in which two guards were left with their hands tied and German banknotes and other compromising documents were scattered in his cell to give the impression that he had been sprung by the Gestapo. He was then shot.'

While the communist press in Spain and elsewhere repeated the story that Nin had refused to endorse, the other POUM leaders were submitted to a lengthy ordeal which, says Gorkin, proved that the Comintern was now in effect run by the NKVD. With four other members of the executive committee he was taken to Valencia. Released from prison there, they were 'kidnapped and taken by NKVD agents to a *checa* in Madrid. Fortunately the CNT not only expressed solidarity with us in various protests but infiltrated the SIM. An anarchist guard smuggled out a letter from me to the Director-General of Security which may have saved our lives.' The framing of the POUM had not gone according to plan. Gorkin, Adroer and the other 'defendants' stayed in prison until finally brought to trial in Barcelona in October 1938. But thanks largely to a vigorous international campaign of protest which made the GPU think twice about creating any more martyrs like Nin, they all survived.

Fenner Brockway was a prominent British organizer of this campaign. In June 1937 he led a delegation to Valencia to investigate the death in prison of Bob Smillie, the son of a Scottish ILP leader, who had served in the POUM militia, and also to find out what had happened to other ILP/POUM volunteers on leave in Barcelona – including Orwell, just out of hospital after being shot in the throat by a Nationalist sniper. On the run for two days, Orwell had been so angered by a poster cartoon 'representing the POUM as a figure slipping off a mask marked with the hammer and sickle to reveal a maniacal face marked with the swastika' that, though by no means uncritical of the party, he had scrawled 'Long Live the POUM' on walls as he slipped from one hiding-place to another.

At Port Bou just on the Spanish side of the Pyrenees, Brockway was delighted to find this seaside town plastered with pro-POUM posters put up by the CNT; and at the CNT office he talked to fugitive POUM sympathizers, among them Willy Brandt, at that time a correspondent for Norwegian newspapers. In Valencia Brockway interviewed Largo Caballero, but found him a physical and mental wreck, 'a living corpse'. He met Nin's wife 'hiding in a workman's house' and was assured by government officials that Nin was alive and would be brought to Valencia for public trial within a few days.

Brockway revealed that arrested foreign volunteers such as Georges Kapp, the Belgian commander of the POUM unit in which Orwell served, had been put under intense pressure to sign a confession that the POUM was in contact with the fascists and that John McNair, the ILP representative in Barcelona, was an agent of British Intelligence. Yet while Brockway (who had himself been imprisoned – as a conscientious objector – in World War I) was gathering this evidence and Orwell was having difficulty finding a publisher for his version of events, a literary circus organized by Pablo Neruda was lending intellectual prestige to the government. In July 1937 delegates to an International Writers' Congress attended by Hemingway, Stephen Spender, Julien Benda, André Chamson, Ilya Ehrenburg, Ludwig Renn and André Malraux, were driven in Rolls-Royces from Valencia to Madrid and on to Barcelona, proclaiming their admiration for the Republican defence of democracy.

It was, says Spender, a moving and at times an intensely embarrassing experience. 'At Minglanilla, a little town near Madrid, we were given an excellent meal, almost a banquet, on trestle tables set out in the street. Children danced and sang to us in the square below. The wife of the poet Octavio Paz suddenly began to sob hysterically. A peasant woman took my arm and implored, "Sir, can you save us from the black birds?" By which she meant the aeroplanes which machine-gunned the villagers when they were working in the fields. Then she invited Paz and me back to her home and wanted to give us some sausages. She seemed to think that we would go hungry, and that she identified her situation with ours was terribly upsetting and acted like a reproach. Years afterwards I asked Paz whether he remembered this, and he said yes, that it was one of the most vivid memories of his life.'

Behind the lines the revolutionary terror was supplanted by a counter-revolutionary GPU-SIM terror which filled the jails with suspects and shot some of them. The war settled to a dull, slogging pattern of set-piece Republican offensives – at Brunete, near Madrid (6–26 July 1937), at Belchite in northern Aragon (24 August to 15 September), and at Teruel in southern Aragon (14 December 1937 to 22 February 1938) – in which an initial breakthrough was contained and thrust back. Casualties were heavy on both sides: but the Republicans lost much valuable material which was hard, even impossible, to replace. Blazing heat and tormenting thirst on the barren Castilian plain made the Brunete a gruelling battle. The Republicans suffered worst because the air superiority that had been so vital in the defence of Madrid vanished as Messerschmitts and new-model Heinkels and Savoias outfought Soviet planes. Nationalist artillery was heavier and more effective and casualties among the International Brigades were so high that there were field mutinies. Yet the offensive, partly designed to ease pressure on the northern front, delayed the Nationalist advance there by only a few weeks.

The battle for Teruel, fought in snow blizzards and sub-zero temperatures, ended in recriminations between the Communist commanders Valentín Gonzáles (known as El Campesino), Líster and Modesto. El Campesino claimed that the Russian General Grigorovich had deliberately starved the Republican garrison of ammunition to ensure failure and thus to discredit the war minister Indalecio Prieto, and that Líster and Modesto, his Communist rivals, had left him and his men to die when they might have come to the rescue. Líster retorted that El Campesino was a coward. Timoteo Ruiz, who

served under all three commanders, comments that El Campesino was too reckless, Líster competent but inclined to feel that he was fighting the war single-handed. 'For him it was "my war." Every victory was due to him, every defeat someone else's fault. He would never admit that any of our successes were due to the ability of Modesto, probably the best of our Spanish military commanders but not so well-known as Líster because he didn't seek publicity.'

Colonel Escofet, who had returned from France to command a Catalan Popular Army brigade at Teruel, where he was badly wounded, found himself hampered by an atmosphere of sullen mistrust. 'The government had divided career officers into three categories – loyal, indifferent, and fascist. I – would you believe it? – was classified as "indifferent". There was no discipline and you couldn't pull rank. I ordered an anarchist captain to attack a ridge. He refused, saying: "You just want to get us all killed."' So Escofet led the attack himself. 'The political commissars were a problem too. They wanted to curry favour with the men in order to indoctrinate them. For instance, a soldier would request leave to visit his pregnant wife in Barcelona. I would say no because we were fighting a war. Then the commissar would authorize the leave. Many career officers lived in constant fear of being murdered by their own troops.'

Josep Costa, a CNT union leader, enlisting in a mixed brigade which included remnants of the original Durruti column, found an atmosphere of

OPPOSITE ABOVE
August 1937. Republican troops occupy Quinto, northern Aragon, after a temporarily successful offensive.

OPPOSITE BELOW
August 1937. Republican Maxim gunners in action during the battle for Belchite, northern Aragon.

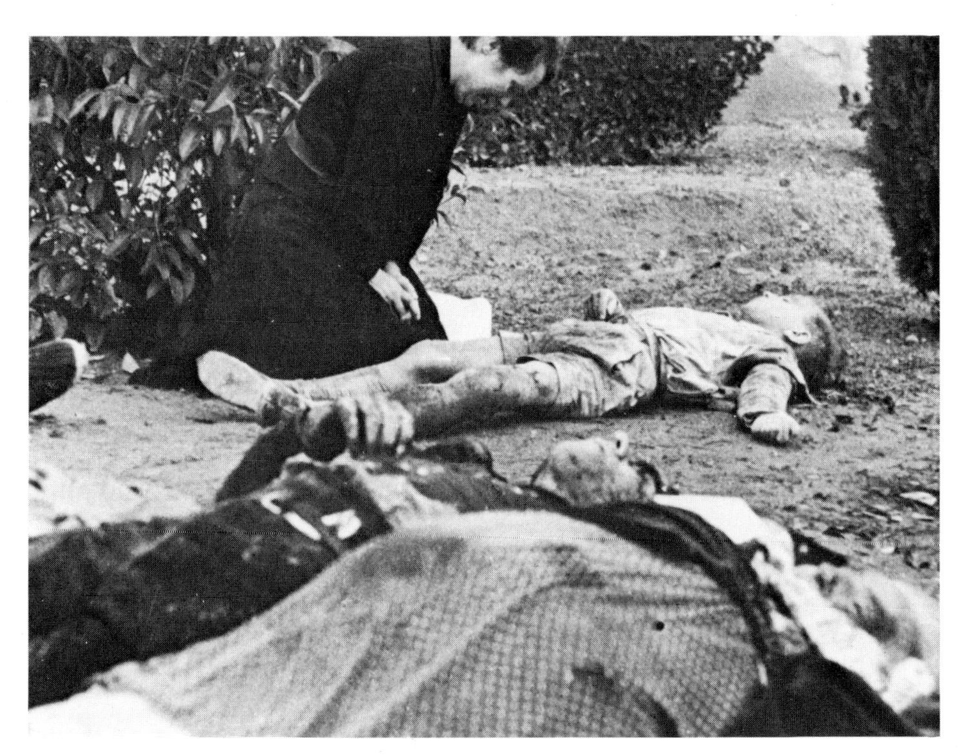

November 1937. A mother mourns her dead son, among other victims of the Nationalist bombing of Lérida.

almost total demoralization – 'extraordinarily pessimistic. The men were like lambs going to the slaughter. There was no longer an army, no longer anything. All the dynamic had been destroyed by the treachery of the Communist party in the May events. We went through the motions of fighting because there was an enemy in front of us. The trouble was that we had an enemy behind us too. I saw a comrade lying dead with a wound in the back of the neck that couldn't have been inflicted by the Nationalists. We were constantly urged to join the Communist party. If you didn't you were in trouble. Some men deserted to escape the bullying.'

The pyrrhic pursuit of unity and the political infighting which surrounded it was startlingly illustrated by the Belchite campaign, aimed as much at demolishing the Council of Aragon, that anarchist state-within-the-state, as at achieving any significant result against the Nationalists. According to Líster, the Aragon purge was initiated by Prieto in the hope that it might force an end to the war. 'Prieto ordered me to go to Aragon to dissolve the Council and shoot all the anarchists I had to. He wanted to cripple our military potential and thought that the best way would be to arrange a new civil war between anarchists and communists . . . Prieto calculated that the anarchists would move two divisions from the front and that I would have a fight on my hands.'

Whatever Prieto's secret hopes may have been, the invasion of Aragon was

December 1937. War Minister Indalecio Prieto watches preparations for the Republican offensive at Teruel, southern Aragon.

preceded by an anti-CNT press barrage by the communists. *Carabineros* began confiscating lorries loaded with farm produce, while the UGT set up a rival Council at Barbastro and appealed for government recognition. Publication of the decree dissolving the CNT Council was delayed until 11 August, when the harvest was in, and immediately afterwards Líster led the 11th Division into Aragon 'on manoeuvres'. 'We paraded our tanks through Caspe,' he says; 'they had never seen tanks there before, and on receipt of coded orders from Prieto we began arresting Council members.' There was no opposition. Joaquín Ascaso escaped but the others came quietly. 'Aragon was the easiest victory I ever had. The anarchists didn't resist because they were scared. So that's how it was done, and it needed to be done. That Council was a tyranny. We found hundreds of corpses the anarchists had shot. But all those stories about me dissolving the Council by force and shooting people are lies.'

Timoteo Ruiz believes that 'there was a rebellion of the Aragonese themselves against forced collectivization'; and certainly under the protection of the 11th Division 'private' peasants carried out their own decollectivization. Perhaps a third of the collectives were broken up, but in the interests of production some were restored.

Ruiz makes an interesting comparison between collectivization, or cooperativism, in his home province of Toledo where the UGT and the communists directed operations, and the more dogmatic approach in Aragon. 'Labourers and smallholders both joined the cooperatives voluntarily because of the obvious advantages. In my village near Toledo there was a great improvement. Everybody was paid a daily wage and each family was given a pig or a lamb from time to time. The peasants had never been so well off.' There is no reason to dispute his contention that many Aragonese peasant farmers – the equivalent of the kulaks who in the USSR were being so mercilessly liquidated – welcomed Líster's troops as liberators: just as, seven months later, they welcomed liberation by the victorious Nationalists.

Juan Manuel Molina, who saw CNT power in Barcelona crumble when the leaders hesitated to use it, now, as a member of the Aragon-Catalonia defence committee, endured a similar humiliation. The CNT divisions, with their tinny home-made tanks and out-of-date weaponry, were no match for Líster's troops; and they were stretched thin from the Ebro to the Pyrenees with no reserves. To pull them out of the line when news came of the 11th Division's 'manoeuvres' would, he says, have been to risk a Nationalist breakthrough. Some commanders were willing to run that risk in order to fight the trespassers, but Molina was sent to Valencia to interview Negrín before a final decision was made.

'He was as talkative as ever, cracking jokes, saying: "Shit, it seems that I'm surrounded with secrets." I told him that our divisions were covering the entire front without reserves. Negrín said he had heard that they were completely demoralized and that men were deserting to the enemy or going back to Barcelona, to which I replied: "A Prime Minister should be able to

January 1938. Capture of the bullring at Teruel by the Republicans. Fighting in sub-zero temperatures, Nationalists recaptured the city in February.

distinguish between true information and information designed to cause trouble. I am here to inform you that my comrades at the front are waiting for my decision as to whether to open fire on Líster's troops – which could spell the end of the war, of your government, and of the Republic." Negrín promised to visit Aragon next day to see for himself, but he did not go.' Nor did the CNT's national committee, called together when Molina returned to the front, seem any keener on action than they had been during the May Days. The threat of retaliation probably played some part in modifying Líster's repression. Executions were few and the arrested members of the Council of Aragon were released. 'But,' says Molina, 'that was the end of the CNT's influence, the end of its leadership.'

The Belchite offensive which followed was at least partly motivated by a desire to justify the occupation of Líster's area of conquest with 'sound' Republican troops and to keep the anarchist divisions busy fighting the official enemy. Four months later, in November 1937, the last flickers of

Catalan independence were snuffed out when Negrín decided to settle the question of authority by installing the central government in Barcelona.

The move was made without consulting the Generalitat and with a brusqueness which was almost as insulting as Líster's invasion of Aragon. Negrín avoided personal contact with Companys. Catalans complained that the government's only decisive actions were those aimed at humbling Catalonia. General Pozas' Army of the East was seen as an army of occupation, whilst the dismissal or dispersal of Catalan police had opened the way not only to another army of occupation – that of 'foreign' *asaltos* and Republican (civil) guards – but to the activities of the hated SIM. With the help of the GPU, Negrín's government could now, like Franco, fairly claim to be defending Spain against the menace of 'bolshevism'.

'I often thought the war was lost,' says Lorenzo Iñigo, 'but I was certain of it when the government moved to Barcelona. Morale was bound to suffer when they retreated like that, with their backs to the wall of the Pyrenees.' Tarradellas confirms this impression. Once more, as when the Anti-Fascist Militias Committee had virtually ruled the city, a system of dual control left the Generalitat powerless. 'With Negrín in Barcelona and the Communist party in full control, our autonomy disappeared. Morale disintegrated and I saw the end near before the Ebro battle began.'

Droves of refugees had doubled the population and food was scarce. 'Those poor women with so many children and babies were queueing up for bread,' says Teresa Pamies, 'and we climbed up lamp-posts and told them that we would win the war . . . that they would have the possibility to live a joyous life . . . It wasn't just demagogy, because we actually felt it and believed it. But these good ladies looked at us in such a way . . . as if to say that we were scamps, if not thoughtless as well.' Nationalist air bombardments reached a peak on 16–18 March 1938 when seventeen raids by Heinkels and Savoias using delayed-fuse and anti-personnel bombs caused about 2,500 casualties (1,300 killed). As with earlier raids, the Italians based in Majorca acted independently without consulting Franco.

Mussolini expressed delight that Italians should be 'horrifying the world instead of charming it with a guitar'; and Teresa Pamies admits that 'if the fascists were trying to demoralize the population they were succeeding. We had practically to live in the shelters.' Pons Prades, on leave from training as a machine-gunner, reckoned that the mid-March bombing was so severe that 'half the people fled to the hills and woods around the city. I was assigned to a casualty post and whenever there was a raid, about every three hours, we went out to collect people who weren't seriously wounded. Sometimes we were still picking them up in the Plaza del Pino by the cathedral when we were caught by the next raid and had to start all over again.'

In May 1937 Orwell had noted the startling contrast between sleek and well-armed police in the rear and ragged, ill-equipped CNT and POUM militiamen in the line. In his novel *The Affair of Comrade Tulayev* Victor Serge, an ex-anarchist and lifelong revolutionary, summarized the new reign of

General Miaja (left), commander of the Republican forces in Madrid, with Valentín González ('El Campesino'), a notoriously reckless anarchist-turned-communist commander.

terror, the civil-war-within-the-civil-war of the professional heresy-hunters directed by Soviet experts. 'You think you can take us in with your claptrap about winning the war first,' says an anarchist militant to one such expert. 'You'd be damn well taken in if we won it! I'm perfectly willing to get my head smashed in – but to lose the revolution, the war, and my own skin at the same time is a little too much. And that's just what we're doing with all this skulduggery . . . 20,000 men behind the lines guarding 10,000 anti-fascist revolutionaries, the best of the lot, in jails.'

As the military and economic crisis deepened, the SIM, which reportedly had 6,000 agents in Madrid alone, was one of the few growth industries in Barcelona. The search for 'fascist' spies and 'defeatists' could pull almost anyone into its net, notably anarchists and POUMists. The Negrín government exercised little control over its activities, the Generalitat's attempts to intervene were seldom successful. Summary trials before special tribunals and special prisons equipped with torture chambers completed this 'parallel system of justice' for enemies of the people.

Many anarchists wished, like Josep Costa, that the chance had been taken in May 1937 'to clean out the communist plotters and their petit-bourgeois lackeys. The war would have ended sooner, I suppose with Franco's victory, but it would have saved us from having to wait two wretched years for the same result.' But Pere Ardiaca, the PSUC leader, comments that most citizens welcomed the ending of anarchist gang-terrorism and that the system of 'parallel police' and 'parallel justice' – necessary to restore law and order – was approved by at least some anarchists. 'We were in favour of a Catalan government which would govern; and acting from inside this government we helped it to set up the police force. On its management committee were not only communists, who were in the minority, but anarchists too and even a trusted associate of President Companys, Artemio Ayguadé, who was in charge of the Council for International Affairs.'

At the end of March 1938, after the failure of the Republican offensive at Teruel, General Yagüe swept through Aragon. The Republican forces, including the International Brigades, were demoralized. Anarchist units were starved of ammunition, their leaders sometimes arrested on suspicion of treachery. Field executions did nothing to stop the rot as Nationalist planes bombed and strafed almost at will; and there was at least one anarchist reprisal when Francisco Sabaté, who later became a celebrated guerrilla fighter, shot a communist officer and a political commissar when ordered to defend an exposed position. Barcelona seemed to be at Franco's mercy. But he opted for an advance to the Mediterranean coast. By mid-April 1938 Republican Spain was cut in two and Serrano Suñer announced in a speech, yet again, that the end of the war was in sight.

CHAPTER SIX

DEATH OF THE REPUBLIC

THERE were moments between March and the end of September 1938 when the war seemed likely to end in a compromise peace, a partition similar to that which later was to divide Germany or Korea. In mid-March, as the Nazis occupied Austria and the Czech crisis loomed, Negrín persuaded the French premier Léon Blum to reopen the frontier at Cerbère for the passage of war material, including heavy artillery and new Soviet fighter planes. The openly defeatist Indalecio Prieto, who had conceived the Teruel offensive primarily as a means of strengthening the government's hand in peace negotiations, was replaced as war minister by Negrín, who had much the same objective but pursued it more vigorously. There were clear signs that Soviet aid would taper off: but to balance that, Hitler was considering the withdrawal of the Condor Legion ('our soldiers cannot learn any more'), especially the pilots – who, he thought, might be better employed as instructors to the Austrian air force.

Encouraged by Yagüe's praise of the Republican army and criticism of the Axis forces, Negrín launched a peace offensive. As a statement of war aims his Thirteen Points were in marked contrast to Franco's reactionary decrees and insistence on unconditional surrender. They envisaged a plebiscite on the form of a new republic; respect for regional liberties and for individual freedom of conscience; agrarian reform to create a substantial land-owning peasant democracy; the exclusion of foreign military and economic penetration; a political amnesty; cooperation with the League of Nations; and generous treatment for foreign-financed businesses whose owners had not been actively pro-Nationalist. The UGT and the CNT approved this declaration of intent, though the FAI denounced it as a betrayal of the revolution. But it failed to persuade the Western democracies to abandon their 'neutrality'.

Non-intervention, which was simply a facet of the appeasement policy that gained momentum under the direction of Neville Chamberlain, remained proof against bribes or insults. Not even Largo Caballero's offer, made in February 1937, to hand over the Moroccan protectorate to France and Britain (thus ending the recruitment of Moorish mercenaries) had tempted their governments to square up to Hitler and Mussolini. In June 1937 Germany

OPPOSITE *Madrid, 27 March 1939. After nearly three years of clandestinity, Nationalist supporters celebrate the victory of Franco.*

and Italy had pulled out of the Non-Intervention Committee's naval patrol after Republican planes bombed Italian and German warships in the harbours of Palma de Majorca and Ibiza; and the Portuguese had forced the withdrawal of British frontier observers. Three months later a piratical Italian campaign which in a matter of weeks had sunk or damaged thirty supply ships, eight of them British-owned, was cut short by an Anglo-French threat to attack any unidentified submarine. But the campaign had succeeded in almost closing the sea route for Soviet aid.

The Non-Intervention Committee had nothing to say about the bombing of British-registered supply ships in Spanish waters, often in Republican-held harbours. Between April and June 1938 eleven were sunk or damaged, 21 seamen (and several of the Committee's observers) being killed. These attacks continued until February 1939. Lloyd George suggested reprisal bombings of Italian air bases in Majorca. Winston Churchill wanted Franco to be told that 'if there is any more of this, we shall arrest one of your ships on the open sea.' But, while requesting compensation from Burgos for damage done to British blockade-runners, the Chamberlain government urged Daladier, the new French premier, to close the frontier (which he did in June 1938) and concluded a pact with Italy whereby, in return for recognition of Italian rule in Ethiopia, Mussolini agreed to 'respect' the status quo in the Mediterranean and, in due course, to withdraw some of his 'volunteers' from Spain.

Since early 1937, by which time thousands of Moors and Italians had entered Spain, the Non-Intervention Committee had called for a ban on non-Spanish recruits, all of whom were classified as volunteers, though only the International Brigaders (or most of them) truly qualified as such. Franco stipulated that an equal number of 'volunteers' should be subtracted from each side, an arrangement which favoured the Nationalists in the ratio of about 4:1. The USSR countered by insisting that all foreign volunteers should be withdrawn. The futile argument continued, though Lord Halifax, the British Foreign Secretary, was ready with his formula for shelving awkward questions. Britain, he hinted, might consider drafting 'an appeal to the contending sides to stop the war. Such an appeal would, of course, be based on grounds of humanity, Christianity, and so forth . . . It would not be likely to succeed, but it would strengthen the moral position of His Majesty's Government.'

For Chamberlain and Halifax, continuing Soviet intervention was evidence of Stalin's determination to make mischief for his own ends; and indeed war-weariness and the growth of a 'peace party', led by Azaña, Prieto and Julián Besteiro, a much-respected moderate socialist, reinforced Negrín's dependence on the communists as the only Spaniards with an unqualified will to continue the war.

The failure of his peace proposals left him with little option but to continue military resistance in the somewhat macabre hope that, as the European crisis intensified, the Republic would be welcomed as an ally in an anti-fascist world war which, with any luck, would break out before Franco had time to

Enrique Líster, Moscow-trained organizer of the communist Fifth Regiment.

complete his conquest of Spain. The result of these calculations was the Ebro offensive, in which the higher commands were almost monopolized by communists, from Modesto – commander-in-chief of the Army of the Ebro – and Líster downwards. This saga, lasting from late July to mid-November 1938, cost perhaps 100,000 casualties in total, with 15,000 Republican and 10,000 Nationalist dead. But the Munich Pact of 30 September assured Hitler and Mussolini that there would be no Anglo-French objections to any plans they had for Spain, and at the same time finally convinced Stalin that the Anglo-French alliance for which he had been working was not to be. Soviet aid was cut as Stalin prepared to appease Hitler in the interests of a non-aggression pact, however temporary. If time had to be bought, the abandonment of the pretence of defending Spanish democracy was a smallish price to pay.

In summer 1938, as the Ebro offensive was prepared, such considerations were far from the minds of the combat troops. Morale in the army was high,

25 July 1938. Crossing the Ebro for the last great Republican offensive.

especially in the International Brigades. There had been a new and substantial consignment of Soviet arms. Negrín's leadership seemed firm and inspiring. As for purges in the USSR, Bill Bailey, an American communist in the Lincoln Battalion, was aware only that he and other Brigaders had been selected as shock troops in the greatest anti-fascist battle of the war. 'If we did hear of the purges, we were always told that the person who had been killed was evil. At the time we didn't see through that, and we had more important things to think about, like the fascists we were fighting.'

Kurt Goldstein, who had come from Palestine to join the Brigades, had seen action at Jarama, Brunete, Belchite and Teruel, where he was badly wounded. So he too missed the Ebro offensive, having been sent as political commissar to a hospital at Santa Coloma de Farnés in Catalonia. There he fought the good fight according to his convictions and opportunities, helping to set up a kindergarten and canteen for refugee children.

The crossing of the river Ebro was to be made at several points about seventy miles inland from the Nationalist salient on the Mediterranean coast. Its objectives were to draw off some of the forces that were threatening Valencia and, if possible, to restore land communication between Catalonia and the Republican central zone. The long weeks of preparation were tedious, but, says Bailey, 'all the rehearsing paid off. When the time for action came and we were crossing that river to put them bastards on the run, I tell you

Bill Bailey (centre) and other American International Brigaders who fought in the battle of the Ebro.

truthfully it was like sitting on cloud nine. We had no fear of death, no fear of nothing, as those boats slid out from the rushes along the bank.'

Frank Deegan, the docker from Liverpool, had been involved in the rearguard action that had delayed the Nationalist drive to the Mediterranean in March-April 1938. 'Talk about an ill-equipped army! Often we had only thin canvas shoes and when they wore out we wrapped rags around our feet. Our standard gear was an open-necked shirt and khaki trousers. We wore bandoliers of bullets like Mexican bandits in films, with a further supply of ammunition in our pockets and hand-grenades tied to our belts.' Sometimes there was little or nothing to eat for several days; and cigarettes were hard to come by. 'We tried everything to get a smoke – wheat, leaves of all descriptions. The best were sun-dried potato-leaves – almost like real tobacco.' Since Spaniards were now being mixed into the Brigades, Corporal Deegan had to learn enough Spanish to understand and give orders. Then his battalion was posted to the Ebro.

'On the night before the crossing we had a good sing-song: "Hitler and Franco your future looks black/Workers' battalions are driving you back/Sons of the masses forever we be/Forward ye toilers to victory . . . " The crack divisions led by such as Líster and El Campesino went over first in small boats and quickly advanced about 18 miles on a wide front. The enemy was taken by surprise. What a change! This was great stuff. We were in the third wave, crossing the pontoon bridges after the Canadians.' Hill 481, a key point protecting Gandesa occupied by Moors, was the main target. Willy Burger, who had been in action with the Thaelmann Battalion since November 1936 – in Madrid, then in the battles of Jarama, Guadalajara, Brunete, Belchite and Teruel – was a company commander at the Ebro, but was hospitalized early in the fighting after being wounded during a tactical retreat.

By 2 August the Republican advance had been halted by overwhelming superiority in artillery and aircraft. The heaviest fighting on the barren, rocky hills around Gandesa, assaulted day and night by the 15th International Brigade, was a frightful ordeal in the pitiless glare of an Aragon summer. Bill Bailey watched the British Battalion storming Hill 481. 'Those guys trying to climb that hill with no cover. The fascists at the top throwing grenades and the British – some of them – stumbling back. An hour later the same thing, three or four times. It was crazy. I guess that's why the fascists called it the hill of death.' Hill 666, which the Americans were attacking, was also a tough assignment. 'The most vicious of all the spots I'd been in. Most other places you could dig in and hope for the best, but you couldn't dig in to that god-forsaken hill. The best you could do was to pile a rock on a rock and you lay out in the blazing sun and frizzled. No water and flies buzzing around you and the stench of dead, bloating bodies. Clobbered with shells from five in the morning to late at night and sometimes all night too. Bombed from the air and rock splinters flying. Sweating and puffing to carry cans of ammunition up. The Spaniards we relieved crossed themselves as they came down and said "Oh boy, *malo, muy malo*" (very bad). The whole hillside was on fire.

Everything was burned up, nothing but charred black stubble. It was horrible. We couldn't help asking ourselves: Is this goddam piece of real estate worth fighting for?'

After two weeks on Hill 481, Frank Deegan worked as a stretcher-bearer around Hill 666, carrying some of his best friends in the battalion, dead, dying or badly wounded. 'The heat was terrific. We dug down until we reached mud, which we squeezed in our shirts to wring out a few drops of liquid to moisten our parched throats. Two or three weeks of this kind of action was a long time, especially when you were under continual heavy barrages with little means of replying. In a way it seemed inevitable all along that we would lose because we were fighting international capitalism. It was something like El Salvador now. They are fighting America.'

Juan Crespo, the disillusioned young Nationalist officer, was shot in the belly soon after the battle began; he remembers the Ebro as the climatic opposite of Teruel, where there had been almost as many casualties from frostbite as from enemy action. During a nine-hour, twenty-mile night march, eight Moors collapsed and died of dehydration. 'One man asked me to shoot him in the head to put him out of his misery. Bearing in mind that Moroccans are used to dry heat, you can imagine what that furnace was like.' In October, not wanting to be parted from his unit, he left hospital with the stitches still in his wound, returned to the Ebro front, and was shot in the leg.

Timoteo Ruiz, promoted a lieutenant on Modesto's staff, remembers how the Brunete-Belchite-Teruel pattern was repeated. 'We didn't have enough reserve troops. As soon as our advance was halted, anyone could see at once that we would be defeated. The enemy had a crushing advantage in weapons, in planes, in artillery, in everything. In such dreadful conditions I don't know how our troops resisted for so long with all the bombing and shelling.' Líster, who led the assault on Gandesa, thinks that failure was at least partly due to an ingrained defensive mentality, a lack of confidence. 'After the third day it was a battle of attrition. What happened was that the centre-south zone betrayed us. Those in command were preparing a coup against Negrín. They kept the air force in the Levante around Valencia in the first crucial days. For four months our finest soldiers bled to death on the Ebro while they in Valencia, which had been saved by our exertions, didn't lift a finger to help.'

The war had lasted longer than had seemed possible in July 1936, and the Republican war effort had been astonishingly resilient. What, apart from increasing Nationalist superiority in food resources and in every aspect of foreign aid, were the reasons for its ultimate failure? General Diez Alegría recalls that in the early stages of the decisive Ebro battle Nationalist casualties were so great that 'in the rearguard it was thought that we might be losing the war,' and considers that only a switch from the frontal attacks favoured by Franco to more flexible tactics tilted the balance. 'All of us had a great respect for the rank-and-file Republican troops. They were, after all, Spaniards. But there was not the same respect for the officers. Those who were professionals were seen as rebels, traitors, and those who were not as little more than bandits.

'Vicente Rojo, the Republican chief of staff, whom I had known before the war when he was a captain and I a lieutenant, was their best brain. Many of the operations he planned – Teruel, the Ebro – were excellently conceived. Brunete, too, was well-planned, but it failed for the same reason that the Republican army often failed, for lack of sound junior officers. There were moments when advancing troops were so surprised by the ease of the operation that they stood around waiting for orders. Then, too, the Republicans made a great mistake at the beginning of the war. They branded career officers as enemies, and not being sure of their loyalty began to isolate and harass them; so that those who stayed with them did not have much enthusiasm. In this way they deprived themselves of the possibility of having a number of good officers.'

Enrique Líster, on the other hand, considers that the main problem was the lack of faith in the Popular Army shown by the professionals and by some Republican politicians. 'Only a few professional soldiers came to understand the nature of our war and to trust in our army. The vast majority, especially those in the high command, continued to see us as the rabble militias of the early days. Some were sincerely loyal and gave of their best. More were on our side simply because the war found them in the Republican zone. Their thoughts were with the enemy, and they had to be relieved of their commands because they hadn't grasped the first thing about the kind of army we had or the kind of war we were fighting – a national revolutionary war, an anti-fascist war.

'In Azaña we had a president of the Republic, and in Prieto a war minister, who were defeatist from the start. They wanted us to lose so that the war would end. Why? Because in my view they were more scared of a revolutionary outcome than of a reactionary one. The new Republic wouldn't have been like that of 1931. It would have been a popular democratic republic tending towards socialism. The people weren't going to back down, they had the weapons. Very likely there would have been internal struggles, a whole series of problems, but it wouldn't have been possible to go back.'

To the argument that the war was lost because the Communist insistence on centralized control, uniformity, and a revolutionary go-slow made it anything but a revolutionary war and contributed to defeat by demoralization, he replies that 'in the Republican zone we set up the first really popular democratic regime, before any such experiment had been attempted elsewhere. There were faults, a lot of them, and many mistakes were made through impatience and extremism, but I maintain that the revolution was carried out. Didn't the peasants get the land? Didn't the workers take over the factories? Weren't the universities opened to the children of workers? Wasn't the Church separated from the State? Wasn't a Popular Army created in which most of those in command were workers, peasants, students or intellectuals? If that's not a revolution, then I don't know what is.'

Federica Montseny, the anarchist intellectual who in November 1936 had become Spain's first female government minister and had appealed for an end to internecine strife in Barcelona in May 1937, takes a different view. 'The Communists said that we had to win the war first and then bother about the revolution. They never understood that people fought not to defend the bourgeois status quo of the 1931 Republic but to defeat fascism and to defend the revolution. Winning the war and preserving the revolutionary gains had to go in parallel. But the Communists destroyed those gains, or wanted to destroy them, as Líster did with the peasant collectives in Aragon: and this weakened morale and the fighting spirit at the front and in the rear.

'We might have lost the war anyway, but we might have lost it in better circumstances. I am one of those who believe that from the beginning of 1938, when negotiations began aimed at a Nazi-Soviet pact, the Russians and the Spanish Communists too did everything possible to ensure that the war would

Barcelona, 16–18 March 1938. 1,300 people were killed and 2,000 injured in day-and-night-bombing by Italian planes based in Majorca.

finally be lost by the people. There were various actions that might have been taken to prolong resistance and link it up with what became our great hope, the approaching world war, which would have necessitated help for the Republic from the Western democracies.

'I've always thought that the day the people began to be militarized, the day the spontaneous character of popular warfare was destroyed, on that day the war began to be lost. If we had developed guerrilla combat, which in Vietnam succeeded in defeating powerful American forces, Franco would not have triumphed. But the Communists wanted to fight a war of regular armies, and in such a war we were worse off. We didn't have any great military leaders, nor did we have enough arms, and what's more our fighters were by temperament *guerrilleros* and therefore, logically enough, bad soldiers.'

General Líster admits that more might have been done to develop guerrilla warfare – 'guerrilla' being a Spanish word and the Spaniards having been famous for guerrilla warfare since the time of the Roman invasion. 'The Communist party was pro-guerrilla, but we did not do as much as we should, and could, have done in this direction. To avoid confrontations with non-Communist members of the government, we neglected to organize a real guerrilla movement. In some places there was spontaneous organization, as in Galicia and in several other regions where the insurgents were victorious in the first few days and people formed guerrilla bands in the hills and mountains. Some of these bands actually sent delegates to the government asking for advice, leadership and arms but did not receive sufficient attention. The combination of regular armies with large-scale partisan forces was not tried out until the Second World War. Vietnam is a misleading example because there the people only perfected guerrilla techniques after thirty or forty years of struggle. But I think that we Spaniards could have done it with our experience in this kind of fighting, notably in the war of independence against the French. Later, in the 1940s and 1950s, we organized guerrilla operations under much more difficult conditions . . . '

By mid-August 1938, as the do-or-die Ebro offensive stalled and it seemed that the crack Republican army might be surrounded and annihilated with its back to the river, Negrín had a political fight on his hands – with the peace movement which, led by Azaña, proposed to form a government headed by Julián Besteiro. He countered immediately by decreeing the nationalization of Catalan war industries under Communist direction and scaring Azaña with a show of force when Republican planes flew low over Barcelona.

The surge of optimism followed by morale-sapping disappointment which characterized the opening stages of the Ebro battle was paralleled by the development of the Czech (Sudeten) crisis in September. In Nationalist Spain the fact that the Republic had been able to mount a major offensive at all, let alone to achieve an initial success, had caused alarm and renewed murmurs against Franco's leadership. Even Chamberlain seemed to be shocked by Hitler's latest demands. The Royal Navy was mobilized, European war seemed inevitable, Franco hastened to declare Spain's neutrality in that event, German and Italian aid temporarily dwindled, and the dogged resistance on the Ebro and at Valencia seemed about to become more than a last, bloody stand.

Mussolini was resigned to a mediated settlement of the Spanish conflict. Flying to Switzerland, Negrín opened secret negotiations with the Nationalist diplomat, the Duke of Alba. All these hopes were dashed when, in Munich at the end of September, Chamberlain and Daladier agreed that the Sudetenland should be transferred to Germany, while 'guaranteeing' the remaining frontiers of Czechoslovakia. Not surprisingly, when Chamberlain suggested that the same technique of 'mediation' might be applied to Spain, with the four Munich powers drafting a settlement while both sides in the 'dispute' ceased fire, neither Franco nor Negrín was enthusiastic.

As part of his own appeasement of Hitler, Stalin agreed that the International Brigades should be withdrawn. Their days of glory and propaganda value were over. Most of the first volunteers had been killed or had left Spain. By September 1938 around 60 per cent of the Brigaders were Spaniards, conscripts from disciplinary battalions and army jails as often as volunteers. So the proposed repatriation of all foreign Republican volunteers, supervised by a commission appointed by the League of Nations, represented, numerically, no great loss.

They last went into action on 22 September. The British Battalion of the 15th International Brigade again suffered heavy casualties (in the final

Barcelona, 15 November 1938. Manuel Azaña (left), president of the Republic, and Dr Juan Negrín, prime minister, at a farewell parade of the International Brigades.

reckoning, of about 2,000 British volunteers 500 were killed and 1,200 wounded). Frank Deegan was among them. 'During September we had hardly any rest, we were being rushed here, there and everywhere. The strain was tremendous. One evening, the 22nd, our battalion was ordered back up the line. We were marching in the early hours of the 23rd when I was approached by Alan Williams, a Welsh lad attached to the telephone unit. He said that Premier Negrín had declared in a speech that the IBs were to be withdrawn. This should have taken effect on the 22nd but the enemy had broken through and we were to fill the breach for twenty-four hours until Spanish reinforcements arrived. I thought to myself, this is going to be a long day.'

Lying in a slit trench on a hillside under a heavy barrage, Frank Deegan kept his head down. 'Suddenly everything went quiet. I peered over the top and saw enemy soldiers about twenty yards away. My legs seemed rooted to the ground and I went on firing. Then the only other man left in the trench, a Scots lad called Dunlop, said: "Come on Frank, let's go!" We jumped out and ran down the other side of the hill. The enemy lobbed grenades at us. Some exploded close to me. I fell and when I got up I was covered with blood. Luckily I could still run. I met some Spanish troops moving up. One of their medical orderlies used up all the bandages in his rucksack dressing my wounds, they were that numerous. I remember him saying "*muy valiente*" (very brave). Later I was taken to a caravan and strapped to a table. A

Communist leaders La Pasionaria (left), José Diaz, and Margarita Nelken at a farewell parade of the International Brigades.

Young women bid farewell to the International Brigades.

surgeon removed the shrapnel from my wounds without anaesthetic. The pain was unbearable. I was cursing everyone in choice Spanish. Looking up I saw a girl and a boy about 12 years old standing on the caravan steps looking in and laughing their heads off. I'm afraid I passed out.'

In hospital at Mataró near Barcelona Deegan had to face another ordeal: a visit of inspection by the League of Nations supervisory commission. 'They looked ridiculous in their spick-and-span uniforms loaded with decorations,' he writes in his autobiography. 'There was an Indian Army colonel, a typical Blimp with a large moustache and a whisky face; a very upper-class Royal Navy captain; a couple of French and Persian army officers; and three Americans in civilian clothes. They seemed to regard the Brigades as funny peculiar for having come to fight in Spain. I bet they looked on the Germans and Italians on the other side as heroes. The Americans clearly thought we were daft. Their political knowledge was nil. We politely informed them that capitalism might suit people who are well off, but it didn't fulfil the needs of the impoverished working class.'

Bill Bailey was in Barcelona, waiting for orders to rejoin the Brigade after being discharged from hospital, when he heard the news of the disbandment. 'It was a shock. In a sense I was happy to be going home, and I thought that if we were being withdrawn it would mean that the Germans and Italians would have to go too. But they stayed on to do the job for Franco.' He took part in the farewell parade in Barcelona on 15 November. In her speech La Pasionaria explained that 'political reasons, the welfare of that same cause for which you offered your blood, are sending you back, some of you to your own countries, others to forced exile. You can go proudly . . . You are legend, the heroic example of democratic solidarity . . . We shall not forget you, and when the olive tree of peace puts forth its leaves again, mingled with the laurels of the Republic's victory – come back!'

'Everyone who was able to walk was in the parade,' says Bailey, 'and the street was lined with people, throwing flowers, running out to hug and kiss us, tears in their eyes. It was sad to leave all these wonderful Spaniards at Franco's mercy. The last words spoken to us were that we should continue the anti-fascist struggle wherever we might be. And we did that to the best of our ability.'

Less than half the 10,000 Brigaders actually left Spain. Some had taken Spanish nationality. Willy Burger and Kurt Goldstein were among the many political exiles – German, Czech, Hungarian, Yugoslav – who stayed behind, to be caught up in the last desperate scramble of the war in Catalonia.

In autumn 1938 Hemingway declared himself disgusted by 'the carnival of treachery and rottenness on both sides'. 17-year-old Pons Prades might well have shared that sentiment. On leave in Barcelona from the Ebro front early in September, he and several friends decided 'to visit some wounded comrades in a hospital some distance away. We had to hire a car to get there and forged a military permit for that purpose, the hospital being in the zone of the Army of the East. Assault guards stopped us at a road-block and discovered the forgery.' They also found some 'White Aid' (fifth column) leaflets in the car. Pons Prades was in deep trouble, especially when it emerged that he had belonged to a CNT union and had fought in Pueblo Seco during the May 1937 events. After questioning, he was taken to a prison in the former convent of San Elias. 'As well as libertarian and POUM militants, there were about sixty Falangists or Nationalist sympathizers. They were treated with great respect by the prison director, who obviously wanted to keep in with the winning side . . . During air raids they would go into the patio and cheer the fascist planes as they flew over . . . Most of them seemed to be idealistic youngsters who believed in their cause and ran the risk of being executed – some had been sentenced to thirty years in jail.'

Later Pons Prades was blindfolded and driven at night to a SIM *checa* in Calle Muntaner. He was asked for the names of those who had organized the defence of Pueblo Seco, why he had joined the army, why he and other soldiers had insisted on burying and marking the grave of a boy who had been shot as a fascist spy, how he came to be distributing fascist propaganda. 'I was there for about three weeks. Why they bothered with such small fry I don't know. I suppose they had nothing better to do and said: "Let's have that boy in San Elias sent here." . . . The worst session was when I was forced to sit in a kind of dentist's chair. It could be made to go up and down, backwards and forwards, and to swing around. My hands were tied and as the chair swung around they

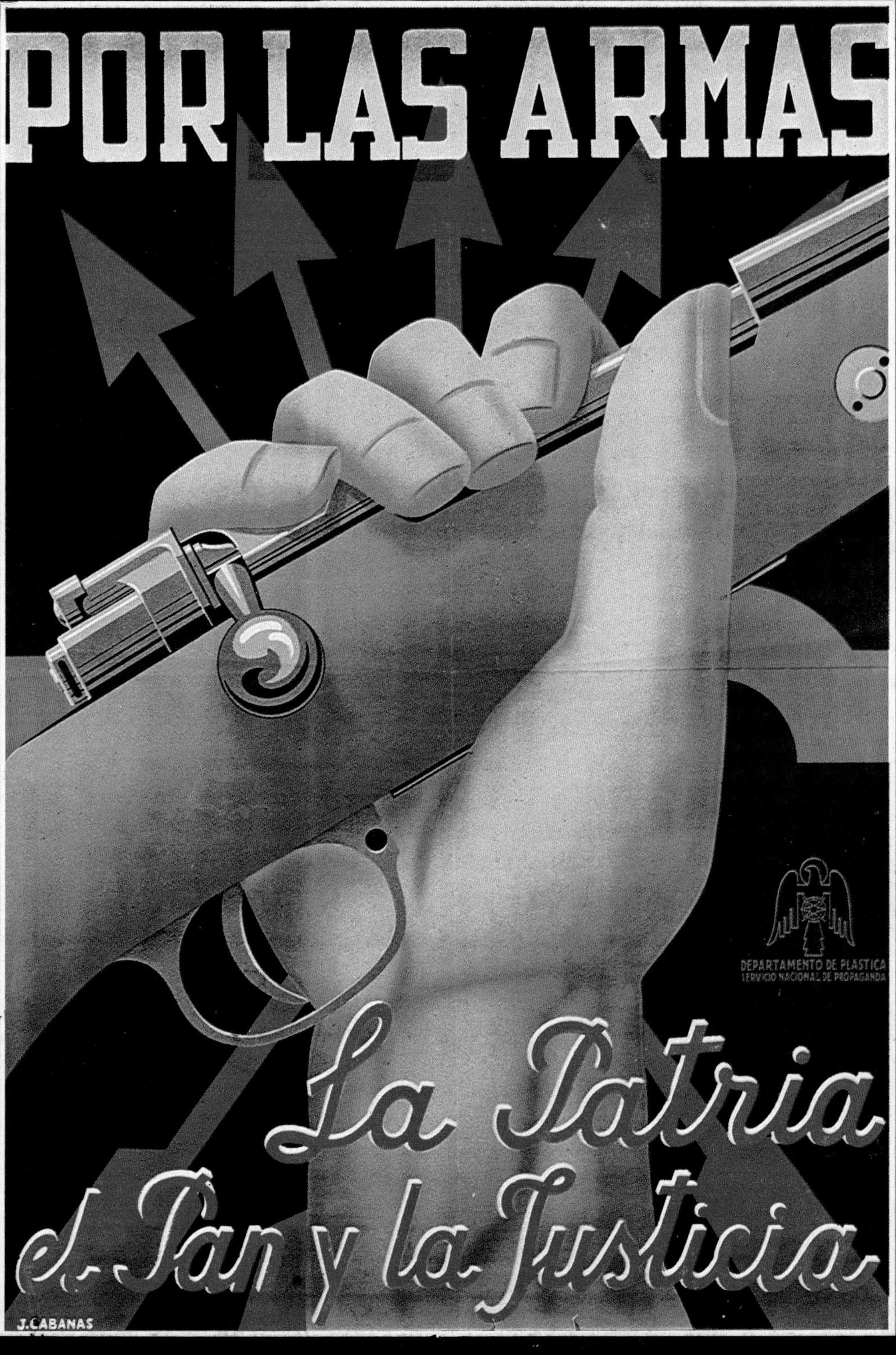

'Fight for the fatherland, bread and justice': a Nationalist poster incorporating the red arrows of the Falange.

Nationalist posters glorify 'those who shed their blood for Spain and its leader Franco' and proclaim 'Up with Spain!' above the fascist salute.

would slap me or hit me with a belt on the face, the arms, the legs . . . I was unconscious and bleeding, but when I came to I heard the poor man in the next cell – an International Brigader, British or Canadian I think – keep crying out for water.'

Taken back to San Elias, Pons Prades was released thanks to the efforts of 'an old anarchist who had been up to all sorts of tricks in his time – forgery, smuggling. He bribed the guards and phoned my mother, who contacted an influential union leader.' In October, shortly after the release of Pons Prades and sixteen months after their arrest, six POUM leaders, including Enric Adroer and Julián Gorkin, who had been held in a special prison, were finally brought to trial. The public prosecutor who, says Gorkin, was 'a GPU agent or someone who had sold out to the GPU,' demanded the death sentence for all of them as fascist spies and traitors; and Negrín was deluged with communist-inspired telegrams, often from units at the fronts, demanding that they should be executed. But though the POUM and its youth branch were officially outlawed, the eight-day trial was a lively affair and something of a victory for the defendants.

The defence lawyer, Benito Pabón – who received so many threats that he fled to the Philippines to escape communist vengeance – was able and well-briefed. There were no communists on the panel of judges. An international campaign of protest at the murder of Andrés Nin and the persecution of the POUM, and the presence of a number of well-known observers, including Willy Brandt (who made an effective speech for the defence), turned the occasion into a belated triumph for liberal goodwill. Nin himself figured in the trial. 'As we believed that he was the essential element, the element that had disappeared,' says Adroer, 'we thought he should be present. So we left one chair empty and put a huge picture of Nin on it. The prosecutor, whom I addressed as Señor Vishinsky – you know that Vishinsky was the prosecutor in the Moscow Trials – was made to look so clumsy and stupid that people in the public gallery were laughing and shouting quips.'

Jordi Arquer, one of the accused, caused further amusement by his insistence on speaking Catalan. Republican ministers and ex-ministers, led by Largo Caballero, testified in favour of the POUM. A representative of Trotsky stoutly denied that the POUM was Trotskyist. Two of the accused were acquitted. The rest, though cleared of the charges of treason and espionage, received sentences of from eleven to fifteen years for their part in the May events and other activities 'prejudicial to the war effort'.

In August 1938 19-year-old Teresa Pamies travelled to the USA as a member of the Republican delegation to a World Youth Congress for Peace at Vassar College. With others, she toured the southern States and got a great welcome from the Protestants, though Catholics were hostile, even picketing meetings. Local newspapers called her 'The Spanish War Girl' and she spoke at pro-Republican rallies in St Louis, Kansas City, Baltimore, Philadelphia,

Atlanta and Washington DC to raise money for a children's relief fund. 'I had learnt a few key sentences in English and kept repeating them. I remember those hundreds of black hands and white hands pressing mine and saying "Spain, Spain, Spain" like an incantation . . . I also remember a reception given by Mrs Eleanor Roosevelt. We all sat around on the floor. She was very charming and seemed sincerely concerned about the bombing of defenceless towns and the plight of our children. Margarita Robles, one of my companions, asked her why the government couldn't lift the embargo on arms for the Republic. There was a long silence. Then "I'm not a member of our government," said Mrs Roosevelt, smiling as though she expected a round of applause. Nobody applauded.'

In October Teresa returned to Spain, stopping briefly in London and Paris. After the bright lights of those cities she was saddened by the gloom of Barcelona, a town in complete darkness, the people shabby and hungry, 'an enormous desolation already from Figueras onwards. It was excruciating and I felt a deep pity and an almost physical love for the country which, beneath it all, was mine. That vision of Barcelona is one of the profoundest memories I have of the war. It seemed to me that the rest of our lives should be dedicated to seeing that this should never happen again.'

There was famine throughout Republican Spain. Much of the food had to be purchased abroad and supply ships were constantly bombed. On leave in Barcelona in June 1938 Frank Deegan found that 'there was no food in the shops. Even the wine was ersatz. We went into a large hotel for a meal. There was only one course, a plate of rice cooked with a few vegetables and a sprinkling of meat which was probably the usual stuff, horse or mule. I noticed some very well dressed civilians with small paper parcels which, when opened, revealed their bread rations – about a quarter of a pound.'

Two months later Bill Bailey and his friend Joe Bianca, also on leave, arrived in Barcelona with a packet of 'odds and ends scrounged from other Brigaders – a loaf of bread, some cans of sardines', and 'managed to find a couple of women who were hungry. We had a really good time.' But they were struck by the air raid damage. 'In the harbour there was a British ship keeled over with a big hole in the side. Oranges, oil and wheat were bobbing around in the water, and the city was full of starving people. Seven days a week the planes from Majorca, having reached a high altitude, would cut their engines and glide in over the city. Even if supply ships weren't hit, the incessant raids delayed unloading, sometimes for weeks.' As a gesture of defiance Joe Bianca gave a hurdy-gurdy man 20 pesetas 'to play nothing but the Internationale. And the guy just ground out that tune over and over until everybody up and down the street was sick as hell of it.'

Raw materials were scarce and industry dependent on long-disused generators since the hydro-electric plants were in Nationalist hands. Short-working and lack of lighting contributed to the city's misery and squalor, as did the presence of a million refugees, more than half of them children. Scurvy, scabies and pellagra were common, deaths from malnutrition rose alarmingly. In one highly effective propaganda raid Nationalist planes scattered bread instead of bombs.

In Madrid the city was still the front, as it had been since autumn 1936. The aim of the regular Nationalist artillery bombardment was so predictable that the Gran Vía was rechristened Shell Avenue. In the winter of 1938–39 half a million people survived on a daily ration of two ounces of lentils, beans or rice with an infrequent allowance of salt cod or sugar. Alvaro Delgado, pushing a handcart as a delivery boy for his father's clothes shop, noticed that 'only the communists seemed to have much faith left. I suppose they were hoping for a European war to start or for a more powerful Soviet intervention.'

Most people were obsessed by the need to keep warm and to fill their bellies. 'I remembered the breakfasts of the past, the smell of toast and coffee, the butter spread thick. I belong to a generation which stopped really eating in 1936 and went hungry for ten years. In winter we suffered badly from chilblains, and lack of vitamins produced a plague of boils – on the neck, in the armpits.' For those with money there was a flourishing black market. Otherwise families looked forward to extra rations brought back by soldiers on leave. The right-wing relatives of Delgado's mother, one of them a Falangist who, like some other right-wingers, had got a job with the SIM, helped out. 'They seemed to have plenty of food. Their generosity was patronizing, but we just had to humble ourselves to their arrogance.'

The black market was a profitable sideline for embassy officials, who sometimes sold half the rations intended for refugee 'employees'. By 1938 most of the 15,000 people who had originally sought haven in the embassies had been allowed to leave Spain. Little credit was given to the Republican government for a tolerance which had no counterpart in the Nationalist zone: indeed the 'sufferings' of the refugees were quoted as evidence of the viciousness of the Red Terror. But for the 3,000 or so remaining inmates of those diplomatic prisons, mostly those with least influence or money, life was far from pleasant. 'In the morning,' says Miret Magdalena, 'we had a cup of sugarless malt, at mid-day and in the evening a bowl of hot water with a few grains of rice and pepper and a wafer-thin slice of bread.' Several inmates were persuaded by phoney refugees to try and escape through a sewer which became known as 'the tunnel of death' – because the victims were machine-gunned from behind as they were about to reach the Nationalist lines.

For both cities the day of reckoning was near; but for Barcelona, as the Nationalist counter-offensive on the Ebro, launched on 30 October, swept forward with ominous speed, it was nearer. In mid-November, as the first snow of winter fell, the Republican army retreated across the river. On 23 December, fortified by the knowledge that, in return for fresh mining concessions in Morocco and an agreement to pay the expenses of the Condor Legion, substantial German aid was in the pipeline, Franco set in motion the final, crushing offensive in Catalonia. Only the comparatively well-disciplined, though inadequately armed, units led by Líster and two other communists, Galán and Tagüeña, put up any serious fight. Hunger, weariness, and resentment at Negrín's 'dictatorship' had broken the Catalan will to resist. On 10 January 1939, says Tarradellas, 'a group of councillors assembled to discuss what now seemed inevitable – our escape to France. On 21 January the Generalitat held its last meeting. Companys, the other councillors, and I left for the frontier next day. Negrín demanded that the treasury be handed over to the central government. But as Finance Councillor I took some of the money into exile to be used in relief work.'

More refugees streamed into Barcelona, halting only briefly before starting the 100-mile trudge to the frontier. Soon they were joined by Barcelonans and deserters from the melting fronts as the enemy closed in from the south and the west. Exhortations to make the city a 'second Madrid' and the river Llobregat a 'second Manzanares' fell on deaf ears, particularly as they were made by communists. On 16 January Teresa Pamies broadcast an appeal for mass citizen resistance. 'But I couldn't conceal the gravity of the situation. I'll never forget the wounded limping or crawling out of hospital, begging a ride to the border.' In the PSUC's Karl Marx barracks Timoteo Ruiz, sent to recruit a defence company, could muster only older men who had been exempted from military service because of their industrial skills and had no stomach for combat. ' "Oh, just so long as it finishes," they said, and I realized that there was no hope of establishing a new front.' Remobilized with other stateless International Brigaders, Willy Burger and Kurt Goldstein took part

Barcelona, 29 January 1939. General Yagüe and Nationalist troops at an open-air service of thanksgiving for the capture of the city.

in an action which delayed the Nationalist advance at Granollers for a few days.

With other correspondents, Willie Forrest, now reporting for the London *News Chronicle*, watched the Nationalist advance from the summit of Mount Tibidabo behind Barcelona. 'We had a magnificent grandstand view of the battlefields. The city, choked with refugees, was being bombed by the Italians. It was wintry cold. What a contrast to those summer days of August 1936 when I'd seen the streets filled with laughing, cheering crowds of anarchists and communists who piled into flower-decked buses on their way to the Aragon front! In the early hours of 25 January when I was in the press room sending my last dispatch of the night, I heard that the Nationalists were about to cross the river Llobregat and that it was a matter of urgency for us to get out. In the hotel foyer the night porter was having a nap: but, rudely awakened by our hasty entrance, he jumped to his feet and gave the fascist salute. No doubt a rehearsal for the next night.'

On 26 January Teresa Pamies and other young communists were still trying to rouse a spirit of resistance. 'It was absurd, but we had to do something and so we started to build a barricade with the paving stones around the tramlines in the Plaza de Bonanova. Then we saw fascist troops – they were Italians – descending the slope of Mount Tibidabo, their bayonets gleaming in bright sunlight. Suddenly I couldn't think of dying like a brave revolutionary. When a JSU car came by we dropped our shovels and jumped

Women and children greet the conquering Nationalist army in Barcelona.

in. Everyone was running away. The streets were littered with paper, torn party cards, shredded archives, ripped posters. I went to collect my mother but she refused to leave. "You go, girl. If they catch you . . ." she said. I picked up my little brother Paul and we kissed our mother goodbye. We never saw her again.'

Nearly 500,000 troops and civilians were heading north. In Gerona the confusion was bewildering. 'It was as though people were just beginning to realize that the war was really lost,' Teresa Pamies recalls. 'Outside the cathedral young soldiers who had lost contact with their units wept with misery and frustration. I recognized one of them and tried to give him heart. He looked at me bitterly: "You politicians are to blame for this." I reasoned that we are all politicians, but he persisted: "You are to blame because you are always bickering. Anarchists and Communists, Negrinistas, Prietistas, Caballeristas . . . "'

The preamble to the decree rescinding Catalan autonomy, signed by Franco in April 1938, proclaimed his intention 'to restore to those provinces the honour of being governed on an equal footing with their sister provinces in the rest of Spain.' Soon after General Yagüe's Army of Morocco and General Gambara's Italian troops entered Barcelona, a Law of Political Responsibilities coldly outlined the shape and scope of the repression to come: 'All those persons who from 1 October 1934 to 18 July 1936 helped to create or to aggravate the subversion suffered by Spain; and all those who, from the second above-mentioned date, opposed the National Movement actively or passively, shall be considered answerable for their political activities . . . '

For five days the Moors went on a looting spree and Barcelona's surviving Falangists were allowed a fiesta of *paseos*, killing their quarries with impunity before military tribunals regularized the slaughter. Reprisals were accompanied by a drastic cultural purge. The Catalan 'dialect' was to be replaced by Castilian, 'the language of empire'; Marxist, anarchist and Catalan nationalist books and periodicals were destroyed or suppressed; Catalan forenames, the use of Catalan in church services, even the *sardana* (the national dance), were forbidden; industry was decollectivized, new currency coined, revolutionary posters and slogans removed, the inscriptions on the tombs of Durruti, Ascaso and other libertarian heroes erased.

With the agreement of Fernández Cuesta, the Falangist propaganda chief, Dionisio Ridruejo had worked out a plan for reconciling anarcho-syndicalists to the Falangist brand of syndicalism, wooing rather than terrorizing the Catalan bourgeoisie, and preserving Catalan culture. But General Alvarez Arenas, the new military governor, would have none of this kind of missionary zeal. Repentance, not reconciliation, was the watchword.

With Nationalist troops hard on its heels and Nationalist planes bombing the roads, the huge exodus continued in drenching rain and icy snow. Many were on the move for a second time, having long ago fled from Andalusia, Extremadura, Asturias or the Basque country. At Figueras on 1 February, in the castle which had been a transit centre for International Brigaders en route

Refugees at the French border town of Le Perthus. About half a million Spaniards fled to France after the collapse of resistance in Catalonia.

to Albacete, the rump of the Cortes gathered gloomily for the last meeting to be held on Spanish soil. The venue had been kept secret for fear of Nationalist bombing, says Willie Forrest, who with other pressmen was taken by car to 'a huge courtyard, then escorted to a staircase leading down to an enormous whitewashed vault lit by naked electric bulbs. There was an attempt at ceremony – gilt chairs, some carpets, a table with a red cloth. Only about sixty deputies were present. Some had died natural deaths, others had been shot on both sides, and of course the surviving right-wingers were with Franco. Negrín started reading from a prepared text, but when, after a while, he threw this aside and spoke impromptu, pacing up and down, some fire came into his voice as he blamed France and Britain for failing the Republic – which was, in effect, fighting their battle against fascism.'

But the main purpose of his speech was to propose that the thirteen points for a negotiated peace should be reduced to three: the evacuation of all foreign elements, the right of the Spanish people to choose their own form of government, no reprisals. All the deputies supported the proposal; but since Franco still demanded unconditional surrender, this was an empty gesture.

Threading through the tangle of people, cars, carts and army lorries,

ABOVE *Spanish refugees escape to France after the collapse of resistance in Catalonia.*

RIGHT *Clutching a few possessions, this old woman epitomizes the tragedy of the refugees.*

Forrest crossed into France next day. 'Half a mile from the frontier I saw a crippled woman lying in a ditch gazing blankly at her hands, which were too weak any longer to grasp the crutches beside her. She seemed to me a symbol of the fate of the Republic, which had for so long, and so often in vain, appealed to France for help.'

Appalled by the approach of the starving, desperate horde of refugees, the French government at first refused entry to them, proposing a neutral zone on Spanish territory where the problem could be dealt with by an international relief commission. When Franco rejected the proposal the French agreed to open the frontier to civilians and wounded soldiers. But as retreat became rout there was no way of turning back the Republican troops except by force: so they too were admitted on condition that they surrendered their weapons. By 12 February, when Navarrese and Italian troops had virtually sealed the frontier, more than 200,000 men of the Republican army had joined the 10,000 wounded and 230,000 civilians (mostly women and children) who had crossed the border since 28 January.

Colonel Escofet, as commander of the Catalan Presidential Guard, escorted four presidents – Azaña, Companys, José Antonio Aguirre (of the Basque Republic), and Martínez Barrio (president of the Cortes) – to the frontier, and then followed with a contingent of Catalan para-military police. But he was angered when the French police tried to turn him back. 'I told their commander – just look, I've got a thousand men here, all with machine-guns. You think you can stop me? You may pass, he said, and that was that. But I began to suspect that beneath the uniform of a gendarme lay the soul of a Hitler.' Timoteo Ruiz, who for nearly two weeks had been fighting a rearguard action, was embittered almost beyond endurance when he saw 'trainloads of military equipment – cannons, machine-guns, ammunition – which had been halted by the French government when we so badly needed it. I wept with grief.' Kurt Goldstein and Willy Burger were among the last across at Port Bou. They had to give up their only remaining freedom, their guns.

Juan Molina, most recently political commissar to the Eastern Army Corps, 'felt ashamed of having asked our men to accept Negrín's win-the-war line, knuckling under to militarization and communist leadership. Their morale had been sapped. We marched across the frontier in perfect formation, for what that was worth. I offered to fight in Madrid, but got no reply.'

'They were very cold, those days of our exodus,' says Teresa Pamies. 'The legions of the defeated slowly wound their way into the Pyrenees, mothers trying to keep their children warm and fed, men not caring any more. At the border post the gendarmes pushed us around. Men in white coats asked us if we had VD or any other infections. They even asked us if we were virgins. My friend Nina, who spoke French, burst into tears as she translated this.'

In a transit centre at Le Boulou refugees were sorted out for dispatch to various internment camps. Among the civilians, families were separated, men going to one place, women and children to another. The soldiers were penned,

February 1939. A Senegalese soldier stands guard over refugee Republican troops at an improvised camp near Perpignan in France.

like prisoners of war, in seven stretches of sand dune surrounded by barbed wire, the main areas being those at Argelès, St Cyprien and Barcarès.

Colonel Escofet found himself 'in a corner of the beach behind rusty wire guarded by Senegalese troops. But what else could have been done under the circumstances? We could hardly expect comfort and if the fascists had caught us they would have killed us all.' Enric Adroer considered himself comparatively fortunate to be suffering such indignities, since he, Gorkin and the other POUM leaders imprisoned in Barcelona since their trial had nearly been left there at the mercy of Nationalist justice. 'This worried us because we weren't entirely convinced that Franco would believe the communist story that we had been allies of his.' Political assassinations were not uncommon during the flight to France and the POUMistas, though escorted by prison guards, had had moments of anxiety when, in Agullana, they found themselves uncomfortably close to Líster's headquarters and the temporary premises of the Soviet embassy.

Ideological feuds flourished in exile. The internment pens were ideal places for the summary settlement of old scores. At Argelès, for instance, a hated SIM officer was buried alive. Contempt for the French was a common bond; otherwise every Spaniard had his own idea of who was most to blame for the catastrophe. Ideological battles distracted the mind and kept the adrenalin flowing. Adroer was determined that the communists should not impose the kind of dictatorship they exercised in some camps. 'I volunteered to serve as head of our block and we placed CNT and POUM people as representatives

March 1939. Spanish refugees delousing in a French concentration camp at Bram.

in other blocks. The communists were furious. They behaved as disgustingly as ever, cheering the news of German victories after the Nazi-Soviet pact had been made and Stalin became Hitler's ally. When we were shipped out to Mexico some communists threatened to throw me overboard, but I was well protected.'

On 27 February 1939 France and Britain recognized the Nationalist government and President Azaña resigned. In Toulouse the exiled politicians had argued heatedly about whether or not to end the war. Azaña, Companys, Aguirre and Martínez Barrio insisted that further resistance was futile. Negrín, Alvarez del Vayo and the communists favoured resistance at least until the several hundred thousand Republican troops in the central zone were guaranteed against reprisals.

Timoteo Ruiz 'cherished the hope of returning to fight in Madrid. If the central zone could hold out a little longer, until war broke out in the rest of Europe, the Western democracies would have to help the Republic. When some of us volunteered to work in the mines near Perpignan I escaped, but was captured and jailed.' Líster was convinced that the war in Spain could have been kept going 'for another six or seven months. The Republican zone still covered almost a third of Spain, from Madrid to Valencia and south to Almería. There were still four undefeated armies of about half a million men. At least it would have been possible to retreat gradually, destroying communications. As for loss of life, it would not have approached the 200,000 deaths in the repression that followed surrender.' In the hope of organizing

About 50,000 Spaniards eventually went to Mexico. Others fought in the French Resistance during World War II.

resistance Negrín and Líster flew to the central zone early on 10 February.

It was an impossible undertaking. Without a government since the fall of Barcelona, troubled by rumours and a sense of drift since the collapse of the Ebro offensive, the Republican zone resembled a magnified version of the French internment camps. The one element of unity in a defeatist Popular Front of anarchists, moderate socialists, Left Republicans and fair-weather-communist career officers, including General Miaja, was suspicion, even hatred, of the failed communist saviours and of Negrín – whose increasing dependence on his communist entourage deepened these suspicions and helped to precipitate a confrontation in Madrid not unlike that of the May events in Barcelona. Only this time, in a series of skirmishes known as the 'Semana Comunista' (6–12 March 1939) which took place under the guns of Nationalist besiegers and ended a mere two weeks before the city fell to Franco, the communists were defeated: a come-uppance that still, more than forty years on, gives aged anarchist militants like Juan Molina a certain grim pleasure to recall.

Closely questioned by representatives of the CNT, the FAI and the Libertarian Youth in Valencia, the tired, harassed Negrín explained that he had come back to finish the war and to try to save as many people as possible. Though some anarchists, including Eduardo de Guzmán, hoped to gain support for thoroughgoing scorched-earth resistance, official CNT policy was exactly that which Negrín had summarized. The question was – could he be trusted to put it into effect?

In Madrid on 12 February Negrín met Colonel Segismundo Casado, an efficient, hard-working career officer who commanded the Army of the Centre. Convinced that Negrín's reputation as a Comintern mouthpiece was largely responsible for Franco's refusal to discuss surrender terms, he had since late 1938 been in touch with Nationalist agents in Madrid and in Burgos. Widely accepted as the leader of a 'National Defence Council' which was ready to take over the responsibility of government, Casado was eagerly backed by the strongly anti-communist anarchist general, Cipriano Mera. He told Negrín that conditions in Madrid were such that the war had to be ended quickly. This was no exaggeration. A Quaker Commission had recently concluded that the city was in a state of near-starvation with no heating, no hot water, and a dangerous lack of medical supplies. Casado also reported that he had only forty aircraft, little in the way of artillery, and few automatic weapons, whereas the Nationalists had 600 aircraft, unlimited artillery, and plenty of tanks. Many of his troops, he said, had no shoes and no overcoats. According to Casado, Negrín accepted his offer to help with peace negotiations, even promising to remove communists from his government should they prove obstructive.

But when Negrín chose to set up headquarters in a country villa near the small town of Elda, twenty miles from the port of Alicante and very close to the communist headquarters at Elche (now dominated by the able and energetic Comintern supremo Palmiro Togliatti), his intentions seemed only too obvious to his opponents: to save himself and his communist cronies and leave the rest to their fate while urging heroic resistance. Willie Forrest, who had flown back to Madrid, shivered in his room at the Ritz Hotel. 'There was no heating – and no food. People were starving. I had to go to a sort of soup kitchen twice a day for a bowl of watery gruel and a bit of hard bread no bigger than a match-box.' La Pasionaria asked him to 'tell the British people that in spite of everything we shall fight on. Brave words, but it was an open secret that Casado was negotiating for a surrender.' Forrest got the impression that Negrín stayed away from Madrid out of consideration for its inhabitants: 'Whenever he was there the fifth column got word to the Nationalists and shelling was intensified.' Socrates Gómez, a municipal councillor in Madrid and a close friend of Julián Besteiro, comments that whatever the explanation for the premier's absenteeism, the result was demoralizing. 'Negrín could not be found or contacted. Ministers went to my father, the civil governor, for information. The National Council of Defence, supported by all unions and parties except the communists, tried to fill this vacuum.'

Cipriano Mera suggested kidnapping Negrín and forcing him to open peace negotiations. Communists in Madrid planned to arrest Casado and take control of the city. On 3 March news came of the appointment of communists to a series of important commands, notably in Alicante, Valencia and Cartagena. The first open challenge to the communist coup, probably designed to stiffen resistance rather than – as was suspected – to facilitate the flight of Negrinistas, had a disastrous effect. In the naval base of Cartagena the new communist commandant was forced to resign. A communist column was sent to quell the rising, and at the same time ended an attempt by local Falangists to seize the town. But in the confusion – it had been threatened with bombardment by shore batteries and alarmed by the sudden appearance of Nationalist warships – the Republican fleet, consisting of three cruisers, eight destroyers and many smaller craft, fled and was interned by the French at Bizerta. A terrible loss, not least because the only hope for a major evacuation of Republican refugees had now vanished.

In Valencia the military governor refused to give way to General Líster, and the Army of the East prepared to oust the communist trespassers by force. On 5 March the National Council, under the presidency of Colonel Casado but with CNT, UGT and Left Republican members, came out into the open. In a broadcast appeal it sought approval for its pocket *pronunciamiento*. 'People of anti-fascist Spain! As revolutionaries, as proletarians, we cannot tolerate any longer the imprudence and recklessness of Dr Negrín's government . . . We who oppose the policy of resistance give our assurance that not one of those who ought to stay in Spain shall leave until all who wish to leave have done so.' This assurance was purely rhetorical. On 6 March Negrín, Líster, Modesto, Alvarez del Vayo and most of the communist political leaders and Comintern advisers left the country. Forced to acknowledge that the only combativeness they had aroused was directed against them, and that they were likely to be arrested – and perhaps handed over to Franco – the recently all-powerful Negrinistas had nothing left to save but their lives.

Willie Forrest was present when Negrín admitted defeat. 'There were rumours that Negrín was living it up in those last days with crates of champagne and a bevy of chorus girls. But for the record I can state that we only drank coffee and Spanish plonk and that there was no sign of chorus girls in the villa. During an interview on 4 March Negrín said that he realized the situation was desperate and had decided to reduce his three conditions to just one – no reprisals. Next day there was a cabinet meeting. I and a Belgian woman journalist were invited to dinner and during the meal news reached us of the Casado coup. While speaking to Casado on the phone, Negrín relayed to us the gist of the conversation. "They've rebelled." "Against whom?" we asked. "Against me." Negrín verbally dismissed Casado from his post, but the game was up. There were two planes waiting on the airfield at Los Llanos for this eventuality, and there was little time to spare.' As Líster guarded the airport with a commando of eighty picked men, troops were on their way from Alicante to arrest Negrín and his entourage.

Ignorant of these events, communist-led army units in and around Madrid moved to close the approaches to the city and seized the central districts, including most of the governmental offices. Casado's troops, led by Mera, were driven into the suburbs. But the communist commanders, Manuel Tagueña and Luis Barceló, waiting for orders from Togliatti, who, accepting the inevitability of Republican defeat, had stayed behind to arrange for the communist movement to go underground, paused and lost momentum. As

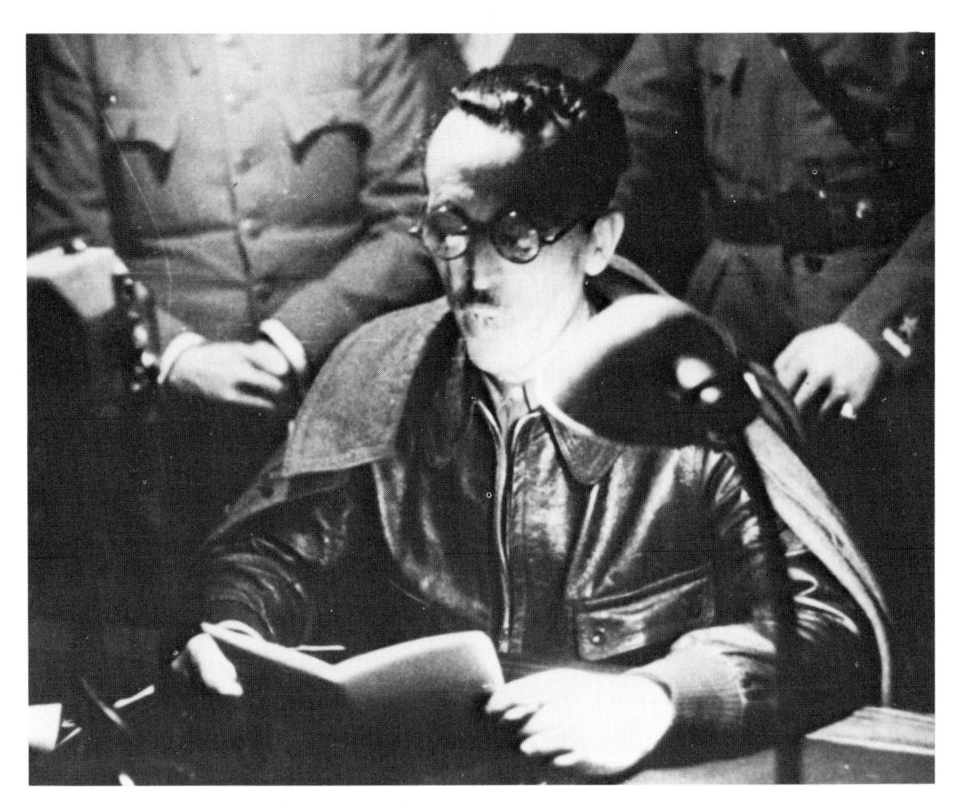

Madrid, midnight 5/6 March 1939. Colonel Casado announces that a National Council of Defence has risen against Negrín's communist-dominated government.

the Nationalists began cautiously to advance from the Casa de Campo and Mera's troops fought their way in from the suburbs, the 'rebels' (who claimed to be defending the legitimate government of Negrín) were surrounded. On 12 March the 'Communist Week' ended with a cease-fire and a few executions. There had been perhaps 1,000 casualties.

Most *madrileños* were apathetic spectators of this last fratricidal surfacing of always barely submerged tensions. For Alvaro Delgado, now attending an art school, it added a romantic thrill to his adolescent love affair with a fellow student – 'very blonde, very spiritual, she lived in the communist zone and I was in the Casado sector. It was possible to cross the lines to visit her – hostilities didn't usually begin until the evening. We were so used to seeing corpses around that a few more made little difference. Once when we were strolling along discussing a translation of Goethe's poems, a shell whistled overhead. We threw ourselves on the pavement, but a passer-by had his head smashed. We ran over to see if we could help. Part of the brain had been spattered against a tree trunk and was still faintly pulsating. Nothing to be done, so we left the scene and resumed our verse-reading.'

There was a curious flicker of resistance, or pride, when, as Nationalist planes dropped 'sacks of fine, white bread wrapped in leaflets calling for surrender,' police and party patrols tried to enforce an order which made the eating of this fascist gift a punishable offence. 'So to help them resist temptation people made up the idea that the bread was poisoned. In the art school, though, we were lucky. A sack fell through a skylight into a patio and we had a secret feast.'

The Defence Council's negotiations with Burgos achieved nothing but time for a number of army, union and Party leaders to follow Negrín's example by fleeing the country. Franco refused to make any concessions. German troops marched into Prague on 15 March and the belated Anglo-French guarantee to Poland on 31 March opened a prospect which a united Republican government might have been able to exploit. Years later, when they met in London, Negrín told Willie Forrest that if only resistance had been prolonged for a few weeks 'a similar guarantee would have been given to Republican Spain.' Perhaps, but this was just one more of the 'ifs' with which the course of the civil war is littered. On 26 March, as the Nationalist armies began to advance on all fronts, Republican commanders were ordered to raise the white flag and send hostages. Besteiro, who unlike other members of the Defence Council stayed in Madrid, broadcast a message urging soldiers and civilians to advance – but only to greet the Nationalists as brothers.

Régulo Martínez had just returned from yet another abortive peace mission – to France, where he interviewed his old, but now politically impotent, idol Azaña. In Martínez's view, 'Casado and Besteiro were honourable men who realized that all that could be done at that stage was to avoid more bloodshed . . . But the last day before the enemy entered Madrid was heart-breaking. I remember seeing a car full of Falangists shouting "Franco! Franco!" The car stopped and one of the men got out and approached me. "Don Régulo, please go home and stay there," he whispered . . . I didn't recognize him but he was obviously one of ours who had dressed up as a Falangist to save his skin. I wept as I walked home.'

To Miret Magdalena, still hiding in the Paraguayan embassy, the street fighting of the *Semana Comunista* had seemed to indicate that liberation was at hand. 'Then we feared that the communists would break in and kill us. On 26 March I was woken by cries of *Viva España!* We walked out and felt the sun on our faces for the first time in nearly two years. The Nationalist troops were still outside the city but we drove around in a lorry shouting and rejoicing.'

On 27 March Alvaro Delgado saw Republican soldiers piling their weapons in the plazas. Some were forced to give the fascist salute. '*Han pasado!* [they have passed]', yelled the crowds as lorries filled with Nationalist troops began to parade through the streets. 'In the Puerta del Sol the sort of people who had stayed home during the celebrations of April 1931 and February 1936 were laughing, embracing, and crying "Long Live Spain!" My mother was in tears, fearing what might happen to the left-wingers of the family, including me as I belonged to the Socialist Youth. A communist uncle arrived to take refuge in our house.'

Régulo Martínez was soon arrested. 'At police headquarters a Carlist started punching me and calling me an assassin. Despite the intervention of a priest whose life I had saved – I got him a job as an interpreter with the

International Brigades – I was sentenced to death . . . I sat in a crowded cell waiting for my name to be called out. It was strange. Non-combatants went to their death quite calmly. Veteran soldiers shook like leaves. "During a battle you forget about the bullets," one of them explained, "but when you know you're certainly going to be shot it's unbearable." . . . The warders were sadistic. Martínez is a very common name, so they would make a long pause before reading the second surname [in this case Sanchez] leaving me and others in suspense.' One visiting day he heard the fascist ideologue Giménez Caballero tell the children: 'Don't cry. We have to kill your fathers because they are Reds. But you have us, the fathers of the New Spain, to look after you.' Régulo Martínez was offered his freedom if he would sign a document admitting that he had been politically misguided and wanted to become a priest again. 'I replied that if I did so I would have to commit suicide because I couldn't live with myself.'

There was virtually no resistance to the occupation of Madrid. One of the very few casualties was an elderly anarchist writer, Mauro Bajatierra, who shot it out with the police when they came to arrest him. But an ominous presence in the victory parade was that of two hundred officers of the Juridical Corps, accompanying lorry-loads of documentation of alleged Republican crimes. On 1 April, by which time the Republican troops in Extremadura, Andalusia and the Levante had surrendered, Franco curtly announced that 'having captured and disarmed the Red Army, Nationalist troops today took

Barajas airport, Madrid. Franco reviews a farewell parade of the Condor Legion and Italian air squadrons.

their last objectives. The war is finished.' The USA recognized his regime, the Non-Intervention Committee expired, and, listening to Franco's broadcast in a pension in Montpellier, Tarradellas felt 'rage and impotence. Franco called us Reds and murderers. We at the Generalitat had helped 160,000 people to escape during the war. But Franco wasn't forgiving a single enemy.'

OPPOSITE *Madrid, 19 May 1939. Franco takes the salute at a victory parade.*

Between 29 and 31 March around 50,000 'enemies' gathered in the ports of Valencia, Alicante, Gandía, Cartagena and Almería, waiting – in vain, thanks to the desertion of the Republican fleet – to be evacuated. Frightened by the numbers involved, the few ships which did show at Alicante, where 15,000 people trembled for their lives, sheered off. The only vessel that came right in to the harbour proved to be a Nationalist cruiser. A battalion of Spanish troops disembarked to take over control of the town from the Italian Littorio Division, led by the more mercifully-inclined General Gastone Gambara. 'They called on us to surrender, but many refused,' says Eduardo de Guzmán. 'Then they fired a few bursts and it was a question of either jumping into the sea or doing as we were told.' Women and children had been sent away to take their chance, and the men who remained spent the night debating whether to commit suicide as several hundred people already had done. 'Some argued that suicide was the most effective protest we could

BELOW *In Milan, Italian 'volunteers' returning from Spain are given a hero's welcome.*

make against fascism at that point. Others said we must continue the struggle.'

Some Spaniards, remembering the internecine hatreds that had flourished in Republican Spain, felt that though Franco's repression would be savage, a Popular Front victory might have presaged a second and even bloodier civil war.

Sometimes the victors taunted prisoners with the lack of unity which had contributed to their defeat. When, after six weeks in a concentration camp at Albatera, near Alicante, Guzmán was taken to Madrid, the police found amusement in trying to fan smouldering hatreds. 'A hundred of us were rounded up by the military police. Seventy were sent to various jails. Of the thirty left in the police station, five were beaten to death, two committed suicide. I was beaten and interrogated for fifty days and they tried to make me fight with the editor of *Mundo Obrero* because he was a communist and I was an anarchist.'

Returning to her convent in Velázquez Street, Cristina de Arteaga discovered that 'it had been taken over by the Líster Brigade and used as a *checa*, so you can imagine in what state it was left. We were told that all the paintings and ornaments in the church had been burnt in a bonfire in the middle of the garden. In a corner where the rubbish used to be we could see the place where executions were carried out . . . the marks of the bullets on the wall. The church was full of ruts, very deep ones, so it was a sorry sight. As soon as we could, we sold that convent and established a new one.'

The thrice-wounded Juan Crespo, always independently-minded, was horrified that only Nationalist ex-servicemen qualified for disability pensions. In Madrid for a final medical check to determine his grade in the Disabled Corps, and with expectations of a comfortable income for life, he encountered a one-legged boot-black in a café. 'This man had been a sergeant in the Republican forces and lost his leg in October 1936 when a Russian tank – one of the first to be used – was hit by a mortar shell in the fighting around Madrid. He told me: "For the rest of the war I got disability pay, but now – in the name of peace, bread and justice according to the slogans on the walls – I'm forced to try and earn a living like this. Tomorrow you'll be a disabled officer and I'll still be a fucking cripple!"' Crespo's reaction was to forgo his privileges and to propose, at a meeting of war-wounded delegates, that 'enemy' soldiers should be allowed to join the organization. 'One man came up to me and said: "If I didn't know your war record I would have you shot." But I felt that I had to protest. If the regime was going to excommunicate half of Spain for having fought on the other side, how would we ever heal our wounds?'

For the other Spain justice was rough, bread (in the terrible famine of 1940–42) infrequent, peace purgatorial. In Asturias the miners endured a second humiliation to rival that of 1934. 'Forced labour, working barefoot for shifts of twelve hours without earning a peseta, that was our contribution to rebuilding the state,' says Manuel Montequín. 'There was a 9 p.m. curfew, so

I went from house to work, from work to house, and for eight years I had to report to the barracks every day.' When the Germans invaded France, the Ozamiz children returned to Spain after an absence of nearly three years, and were kept for a while in a convent of disapproving nuns in Bilbao. 'They treated us like miniature monsters, the children of Reds. When our parents arrived, the nuns pushed us out and clang! slammed the door behind us as if we were mangy animals.' For some time Javier, the little boy, clung to his elder sister Koni, regarding her as his mother. Luckily the father, who had sworn that 'so long as I have my ten fingers we won't starve,' was not arrested and managed gradually to build up a repair business in a disused garage. But the bewildered children, who had been taught socialist songs in France, now had to learn the Falangist anthem, *Cara al Sol* (Face to the Sun): 'For Spain is awakening/Spain – united! Spain – great!/Spain – free! Spain – arise!'

Sometimes personal intervention saved a life, as in the case of Régulo Martínez, reprieved as a result of the persistent pleas of the priest whose life he had saved; or blood loyalty proved stronger than ideological division, as in the case of Alvaro Delgado's family, where the 'fascists' contrived to protect the 'Reds' against reprisals. But, visiting Spain in July 1939 when the repression was past its peak but still hectic, the Italian foreign minister Count Ciano noted 'trials going on every day at a speed which I would call almost summary,' and estimated that there were 'in Madrid alone 250 shootings a day, in Barcelona 150, in Seville 80.' Of the family of Socrates Gómez, his father was executed while he, his mother, and his two brothers received thirty-year jail sentences.

'My trial was the same as all the trials at that time,' says Gómez. 'The accused had about a minute to defend himself and his lawyer not much longer. They easily got through 40 or 50 hearings in about an hour. Perhaps thirty would be condemned to death, ten to thirty years' imprisonment, and the rest would get say ten years.' In Córdoba Francisco Poyatos was sickened by the malice and corruption of the postwar repression. For instance, a peasant was shot for refusing to sell his mule to the chief of the civil guards in his village. A woman who was about to lose a law-suit with her two nephews denounced them as Reds and they were executed. A widow was having trouble evicting her tenants and a friendly judge expedited the matter by having them all shot. Meantime army officers and Falangist officials who ran the black market were making fortunes.

The anarchist newspaper editor Eduardo de Guzmán spent eighteen months in death row before being reprieved. 'Every night I expected to be led out and shot. When the list was read and I was not on it I felt a fierce, selfish joy and a sudden craving for food, though I was ashamed of such reactions when my comrades were going to their deaths. The poet Miguel Hernández, who was tried with me, was also reprieved but, like Julián Besteiro, died of hunger and neglect.' Prisoner solidarity could be touchingly sacrificial. 'I survived partly because other prisoners gave those who had been sentenced to death part of their meagre rations so that at least they would not have to die on quite such an empty stomach.'

Of those Republican leaders who had escaped to France, Luis Companys, ex-President of Catalonia, was handed over by the Gestapo and shot in October 1940; Azaña died in a hotel in Montauban at about the same time; Largo Caballero died in Paris in 1946 after four years in a German concentration camp. When the Germans invaded France Timoteo Ruiz was forced to work on coastal fortifications at Brest, but escaped to join the Maquis in Bordeaux. 'The Spaniards,' he says, 'were the backbone of the Resistance in southern France,' and after the liberation much of south-west France was temporarily ruled by Resistance Committees in which Spaniards predominated. Spanish consulates were seized, Toulouse Radio used for Republican propaganda: but an invasion across the Pyrenees in October 1944 failed for lack of support. Subsequently, says Ruiz, 'the Party sent small guerrilla groups to various parts of Spain . . . With nine other comrades I set out for Valencia, sleeping by day, walking by night . . . We had several brushes with civil guards and only four of us reached our destination . . . Later, in Madrid, I worked underground as propaganda commissar for the regional committee until I was captured and sentenced to 25 years' imprisonment.'

Ex-International Brigaders were objects of suspicion in their own countries. Back in Liverpool, Frank Deegan was paid £1 5s. a week by the Spanish Aid Committee until he qualified for unemployment benefit of 17 shillings a week. 'I received a summons signed by His Majesty's Under-Secretary of State for Foreign Affairs requesting me to pay the sum of three pounds fourteen shillings, the cost of my fare home from Spain. Then I was graded unfit for service in the armed forces. I wasn't particularly worried. This was a capitalist war and I had no real desire to fight for the rich who would be trying to prevent their counterparts in Germany from grabbing some of their properties.' For a time he worked as a navvy digging trenches.

On arrival in New York the FBI confiscated the passports of returning Brigaders. Many volunteered to fight Hitler but as alleged security risks these proven anti-fascists were not allowed to go abroad until the closing stages of World War II. The Lincoln Battalion's veterans' organization was declared a subversive group in 1946 and throughout the McCarthy era of the 1950s any connection with the Spanish Republican cause was regarded as politically undesirable (as indeed it was in the USSR, where many Russian 'Spaniards' were liquidated).

Josep Costa ('we were thrown away like garbage: when I think of it I am filled with grief and rage') and about 150 International Brigaders were interned in a camp at Le Vernet, together with nearly 2,000 other 'Reds' arrested by the French police. In *Scum of the Earth* Arthur Koestler describes the scene. 'This was the end of the Comintern's crusade . . . the leper barracks at Le Vernet. Half of the human ruins there were from Germany and Austria . . . A cigarette end in the gutter was a reality while political ideas had lost all

British International Brigaders, released from prisoner-of-war camps, on their way home.

meaning.' Yet 'sectarian hatred between Stalinists, Trotskyists and Reformists still existed – whispered memories of political controversies which had been settled by a bullet in the back on the battlefields of Spain.'

Such experiences – veterans of political and racial persecution reckoned that food and conditions were worse than they had known at Dachau or Oranienburg, the Gardes Mobiles almost as bad as the SS – seemed to justify Stalin's claim that reactionary France, not Hitler, was the real enemy; and the Soviet jackal operations in East Poland and Finland were hailed as victories for the revolution. Willy Burger, cultural commissar at Le Vernet, where there was a theatre company and groups for musicians and writers, managed to do some printing by pricking cigarette papers with a needle – and in 1941 made a book of poems and drawings for Stalin's birthday. After three years at Le Vernet, Kurt Goldstein, who with many other internees was handed over to the Gestapo, somehow survived three years in Auschwitz, where almost as many people were liquidated in a couple of weeks as had been executed or assassinated in the two-and-three-quarter years of the Spanish civil war.

In *The Spanish Cockpit*, one of the first and still among the best analytical accounts of the earlier stages of the civil war, Franz Borkenau firmly classified Franco's regime as 'simply a reactionary military dictatorship such as Spain has seen in dozens . . . a phenomenon profoundly different from the supposedly parallel movements of its German and Italian allies, which arose on the basis of deep-rooted mass sentiments.' In 1941 Hitler toyed with the notion of fomenting another civil war to topple the Franco-Serrano Suñer 'regime of parsons' and said that he would not be surprised to see the real Falangists join with the Reds to get rid of 'the clerico-monarchical muck'. Some old-shirt Falangists did actually debate assassinating the Caudillo, and Narciso Perales tried unsuccessfully to organize a clandestine *Falange Autentica* to keep alive the spirit of revolutionary fascism.

When at Stalingrad the tide of battle began to turn against Hitler, Franco prepared for a gradual shift away from his Axis orientation by dropping the Minister of the Interior, Serrano Suñer. But condemnation of his dictatorship by the United Nations and an attempted boycott of Spanish goods had the effect of rallying nationalist (with a small 'n') sentiment behind Franco; and

Madrid, 1940. Franco, in the uniform of the restyled Falange – Carlist red beret, Falangist blue shirt – at a mass rally.

the changing priorities of the Cold War, a sensationally expanding tourist trade (by 1973 the annual figure for foreign visitors was estimated at 34.6 million – one for every Spaniard), and substantial investments by foreign industrialists and businessmen enabled the regime not only to survive but to push forward the bourgeois revolution which the communists had struggled to enforce during the civil war.

For this reason alone, thinks Felix Moreno de la Cova, the Andalusian landowner and agricultural expert who had fought in a Nationalist column around Cordoba in the summer of 1936, 'Franco is, after Philip II, the most important figure in Spanish history. I don't say that there are no economic problems left, but for the most part they are the problems of all Europe. Before Franco you couldn't buy a bicycle in Spain. Now Spain is one of Europe's leading car manufacturers. What's more, people whose father never owned a car today have as good a car as I do, maybe a better one – yet my father had two Cadillacs and a Dodge. There's a good system of social security and there's been plenty of social levelling. The root of the problem was a huge surplus of rural population, and the tremendous growth of industry has provided alternative employment on a much larger scale.' However, Spain had suffered twenty years of repression, poverty and near-famine before the economic 'miracle' occurred.

The day Franco died (20 November 1975) Timoteo Ruiz was in jail again. 'I was one of those arrested in the famous Operación Lucero [Operation Morning Star] when Franco was dying. I was in the court cells when two orderlies told me the news. I asked: "Is there anything to drink?" "Only Coca-Cola," they said. "Well, bring me a Coca-Cola to drink to Franco's death."' Ruiz denies that he harbours a desire for vengeance. 'Even before the Party resolved on a policy of reconciliation in 1956 I had realized that the two Spains could only be brought closer together along democratic lines, so that people could express their political views without fighting to death over them. In 1977 I came to my village to speak of the need for reconciliation, and a lot of right-wingers turned out to hear me.'

Teresa Pamies, exiled in Mexico, Prague and Paris from 1939 to 1975, particularly remembers talking to rebel students during the May 1968 rising in Paris. With slogans such as 'No to all parliamentary solutions!' and 'There is only one reason for being a revolutionary – because it's the best way to live', the atmosphere vividly reminded her of Barcelona at the height of its revolutionary turmoil. 'It frightened me a little because things had not turned out so well for us and I had become sceptical. But it was good that these young people could still dream.'

Josep Tarradellas, who had signed the decree of 1932 convoking the Generalitat, lived to sign the 1980 decree for elections to the restored Catalan Parliament. Enrique Líster, who fought in the USSR, Poland and Yugoslavia during World War II and went to France to help organize the guerrilla movement in Spain (quite lively until well into the 1950s), later formed his own hardline Communist party in protest at the Eurocommunist line of the

PCE under the leadership of Santiago Carrillo. He claims that he was 'always an anti-militarist' and only took to soldiering from necessity; considers that Stalin did his best for the Republican cause under very difficult circumstances; and explains that the purge terror in the USSR would not have happened unless Stalin's mind had been 'poisoned by spies from Germany and other countries'. Pere Ardiaca, now leader of the pro-Soviet wing of the PSUC, also refuses to condemn Stalin. 'I believed in him during the civil war and I still do, only now I see his bad side as well as his good side.'

Juan Manuel Molina and Lola Iturbe, anarchists for sixty years, regret that Franco's long rule broke the link between generations. 'We haven't been able to educate the young people. Yet we believe that if the world is to be saved from catastrophe it must be with ideas very like ours – anti-militarism and a passion for social justice.' Francisco Poyatos reckons that 'the democracy we have may make many mistakes. The Spanish people have been shackled so long that we can't walk confidently all at once. But we must be allowed to stumble on. There must be no more shackling, no more dictatorship, no more war. That's how I see it.'

Giovanni Pesce, active in the Italian Resistance during World War II, remembers his time with the Garibaldi Battalion as a marvellous political and military training, and points out that ex-International Brigaders were prominent in resistance movements throughout Europe. General Mantelli, the former ace pilot, rates his year in Spain as the most interesting of his life and is proud to have been one of the pioneers in 'the struggle against the great enemy of the western world – communism'.

Florentino and Agapito, the peasant farmers in Castrogeriz, near Burgos, who welcomed the Franco regime as ending the tyranny of the union in their village, regret the passing of the Caudillo. 'We were better off under him. But in the end how little the war solved. We still have to pay taxes for this, that and the other . . . Ideals? What did we know of ideals? There used to be a lot of religious feeling, but there's less now because the priests themselves are destroying it . . . We never did understand politics and we still don't. But one thing's for sure – whatever happens to the rest of us, the politicians have got it made. We shit on their mothers.'

Other peasants look back on the civil war as a golden age. Not long ago Pons Prades spoke to an old man in Jaén, Andalusia. 'I asked him about a nearby village where there had been a mixed CNT-UGT collective which worked well. "Ah yes," he said, "life in that village had never been so good and probably never will be again. It was the first time that we, the wretched labourers, realized that we were worth something in this world." Then, after a long pause: "The pity is that for this to happen there had to be a war and we had to kill each other."'

FURTHER READING

BACKGROUND TO THE WAR: Franz Borkenau, *The Spanish Cockpit* (Faber & Faber, 1937); Gerald Brenan, *The Spanish Labyrinth* (Cambridge University Press, 1943); Raymond Carr, *Spain 1808–1939* (Oxford University Press, 1966); E. J. Hobsbawm, *Primitive Rebels* (Manchester University Press, 1959) and *Bandits* (Weidenfeld & Nicolson, 1969), for chapter 8, 'The Expropriators', on Francisco Sabaté and other Spanish anarchist 'ideological gunmen'; Salvador de Madariaga, *Spain: A Modern History* (Jonathan Cape, 1961); Paul Preston, *The Coming of the Spanish Civil War* (Macmillan, 1978); A. J. P. Taylor, *The Origins of the Second World War* (Hamish Hamilton, 1961); Gwyn A. Williams, *Goya and the Impossible Revolution* (Allen Lane, 1978), for illuminating parallels between guerrilla resistance to Napoleonic occupation and the bourgeois revolution (1808–14) and similar attitudes during the 1936–39 civil war; George Woodcock, *Anarchism* (Pelican, 1963), in general and especially chapter 12 on anarchism in Spain.

GENERAL COVERAGES: Antony Beevor, *The Spanish Civil War* (Orbis Publishing, 1982); Raymond Carr, *The Republic and the Civil War in Spain* (Macmillan, 1971); Ronald Fraser, *Blood of Spain: The Experience of Civil War 1936–1939* (Allen Lane, 1979, Penguin, 1981); Gabriel Jackson, *A Concise History of the Spanish Civil War* (Thames & Hudson, 1974, paperback edition 1980); Frank Jellinek, *The Civil War in Spain* (Gollancz, Left Book Club, 1938); Hugh Thomas, *The Spanish Civil War* (3rd edition, Hamish Hamilton/ Penguin, 1977).

MEMOIRS, EYE-WITNESS ACCOUNTS, BIOGRAPHIES: Again, Franz Borkenau, cited above; Segismundo Casado, *The Last Days of Madrid* (Peter Davies, 1939); Count Galeazzo Ciano, *Diaries, 1937–38 and 1939–43* (Methuen, 1952, 1947); Claud Cockburn, *Crossing the Line* (MacGibbon & Kee, 1958), and as 'Frank Pitcairn' reporting for the *Daily Worker* – *Reporter in Spain* (Lawrence & Wishart, 1936, with introduction by Ralph Bates); Brian Crozier, *Franco: a Biographical History* (Eyre & Spottiswoode, 1967); Ilya Ehrenburg, *The Eve of War*, volume IV of *Men, Years, Life* (McGibbon & Kee, 1966); Ian Gibson, *The Death of Lorca* (W. H. Allen, 1973); Arthur Koestler, *Spanish Testament* (Gollancz, 1937), *Scum of the Earth* (Jonathan Cape, 1941), *The Yogi and the*

Commissar (Cape, 1945) for the chapter 'Scum of the Earth' on Le Vernet, *The Invisible Writing* (Hamish Hamilton, 1956); Laurie Lee, *As I Walked Out One Midsummer Morning* (André Deutsch, 1969), for impressions of Andalusia in early stages of civil war; George Orwell, *Homage to Catalonia* (Secker & Warburg, 1938, also Penguin, together with his 1943 essay *Looking Back on the Spanish War*, and *An Age Like This*, vol. 1 of *Collected Essays etc* (Secker & Warburg 1968, now in Penguin) for 1937 essay *Spilling the Spanish Beans*; C. E. Lucas Phillips, *The Spanish Pimpernel* (Companion Book Club, 1960), the exciting cloak-and-dagger story of Captain E. C. Lance, DSO, who smuggled many right-wingers out of Spain via Alicante; Victor Serge, *Memoirs of a Revolutionary 1901–1941* (Oxford University Press, 1963); Ramón Sender, *The War in Spain: A Personal Narrative* (Faber & Faber, 1937); J. W. D. Trythall, *Franco: a biography* (Hart-Davis, 1970).

INTERNATIONAL BRIGADES, SOVIET AND LEFT-PROGRESSIVE ATTITUDES: Ronald Blythe, *The Age of Illusion* (Hamish Hamilton, 1963), for chapter 12, 'The Crucible of Grief'; Vincent Brome, *The International Brigades* (Heinemann, 1965); Gabriel and Daniel Cohn-Bendit, *Obsolete Communism: the Left-Wing Alternative* (André Deutsch, 1968), for interesting parallels between the scorn for official, anti-revolutionary communism of the rebel French students of 1968 and that of Spanish anarchists and POUMistas in 1936–37; Robert Conquest, *The Great Terror: Stalin's Purges of the Thirties* (Macmillan, 1968), for their repercussions in Spain; Valentine Cunningham (ed.), *Spanish Civil War Verse* (Penguin, 1980), a selection, including John Cornford's letters to Margot Heinemann, with a long, useful introduction; Isaac Deutscher, *Stalin: A Political Biography* (Oxford University Press, 1949); Valentín Gonzáles (El Campesino), *Listen, Comrades* (Heinemann, 1952); Dolores Ibarruri (La Pasionaria), *They Shall Not Pass* (Lawrence & Wishart, 1967); Malcolm Muggeridge, *The Thirties* (Hamish Hamilton, 1940); Esmond Romilly, *Boadilla* (Macdonald, 1971, with introduction by Hugh Thomas); Stephen Spender, *World Within World* (Hamish Hamilton, 1953); Julian Symons, *The Thirties: A Dream Revolved* (Cresset Press, 1960), for chapter 12.

PRESS/PROPAGANDA TREATMENT OF THE SPANISH CIVIL WAR: Phillip Knightley, *The First Casualty* (André Deutsch, 1976); again, George Orwell, *Homage to Catalonia*, cited above; Herbert Southworth, *Guernica! Guernica!* (University of California Press, 1977); again, Julian Symons, cited above, chapter 12; William White (ed.), *Bylines: Selected articles and despatches by Ernest Hemingway*, for chapter 3 on his reporting of the civil war in Spain.

NOVELS: Ernest Hemingway, *For Whom the Bell Tolls* (Jonathan Cape, 1941, Granada paperback, 1981); Victor Serge, *The Case of Comrade Tulayev* (Penguin, 1968) and *Birth of Our Power* (Gollancz, 1968); Ramón Sender, *Earmarked for Hell* (Wishart, 1934), a grippingly dramatic account of the Spanish army in Morocco and the military disaster at Annual in 1921, and

Seven Red Sundays (Faber & Faber, 1936), an imaginative presentation of the Spanish anarchist mentality and its clash with communist 'realism'; André Malraux, *Days of Hope* (Routledge, 1938); Henry de Montherlant, *Chaos and Night* (Penguin, 1966), a black comedy of the boredom and militant fantasies of a Spanish anarchist exiled in Paris; Norman Lewis, *The Day of the Fox* (Cape, 1957), a memorable evocation of post-civil-war feuds and tensions in a Catalan fishing village; Maria Isobel Rodriguez, *The Olive Groves of Alhora* (W. H. Allen paperback, 1979), a light-hearted variation on the same theme, with a communist 'hero' of the civil war returning to his village after the death of Franco.

INDEX